Trauma

D1563653

In recent years a number of high profile disasters have heightened public awareness of trauma. This book offers a comprehensive guide to all aspects of trauma counselling, covering:

- Trauma assessment
- Resourcing the trauma client
- Trauma aftercare
- Working with trauma in private practice
- Trauma and the therapist
- A brief history of trauma

This practical and effective guide to trauma counselling will be invaluable to counsellors, GPs, social workers, human resource managers, emergency response organisations and all those involved in treating trauma victims using counselling skills.

Thom Spiers is Head of Counselling at London Underground Occupational Health, Marylebone, London.

This book is dedicated to the memory
of Karen, Jaffa and my Dad

Trauma

A practitioner's guide to counselling

Edited by Thom Spiers

First published 2001 by Brunner-Routledge
27 Church Road, Hove, East Sussex, BN3 2FA

Simultaneously published in the USA and Canada
by Taylor & Francis Inc
29 West 35th Street, New York, NY 10001

Brunner-Routledge is an imprint of the Taylor & Francis Group

Typeset in Times by Mayhew Typesetting, Rhayader, Powys
Printed and bound in the UK by Biddles Ltd, Guildford and King's Lynn
Cover design by Liz Bussell

British Library Cataloguing in Publication Data
A catalogue record for this book is available from the British Library

Library of Congress Cataloging-in-Publication Data

Trauma : a practitioner's guide to counselling / edited by Thom Spiers.
     p. cm.
   Includes bibligraphical references and index.
   ISBN 0-415-18694-3 – ISBN 0-415-18695-1 (pbk)
     1. Post-traumatic stress disorder–Treatment. 2. Crisis
intervention (Mental health services) 3. Mental health counseling.
4. Psychic trauma—Treatment. I. Spiers, Thom.

   RC552.P67 T733 2001
   616.85'21—dc21
                                                              2001037525

ISBN 0-415-18694-3 (hbk)
ISBN 0-415-18695-1 (pbk)

Contents

Illustrations

Acknowledgements

Extract from *The Faithful Gardener* by Clarissa Pinkola Estes, published by Rider. Used by permission of The Random House Group Ltd.

Reprinted with the permission of Scribner, a division of Simon & Schuster, Inc., from *The Collected Works of W.B. Yeats, Vol. 1: The Poems, Revised*, edited by Richard J. Finneran. Copyright © 1933 by Macmillan Publishing Company, copyright renewed © 1961 by Bertha Georgie Yeats.

Contributors' Acknowledgements

Hattie Berger – I wish to acknowledge Ulrike Encke whose generosity of feedback and insights have been shaping my work over the last few years as well as this chapter. I would like to thank my clients, whose spirits and individuality maintain my interest and growth in this field, and the team I work with at London Underground, who remain a great source of support, challenge and good humour. Last, but by no means least, thank you Kieran.

Francesca Diebschlag – I would like to acknowledge and thank: Emerald-Jane Turner, Prue Rankin-Smith and Anna Harrowell, my trainers and supervisors in the Hakomi Method of Body-Centred Psychotherapy; Pat Ogden, Christina Dickinson and Kekuni Minton, my trainers in Hakomi Integrative Somatics; and the many teachers of Chinese medicine with whom I have studied over the past 17 years, particularly Peter Firebrace, Claude Larre, and Elizabeth.

Alison Dunn – My gratitude goes to all the clients who have shared their traumatic experiences and reactions with me – I have learned so much from our collaborations. My thanks go also to Thom Spiers, Hattie Berger and all my colleagues for their support. Thanks also to my family, Jim, Steven, Laura and Michael for their support and tolerance – to Laura especially for the teas, coffees, and penny sweets!

Guy Harrington – I wish to thank Thom Spiers for encouraging me to continue with this book project and to acknowledge that I completed it.

Carrie Jess – I wish to thank my clients and patients who have so often over the years moved and inspired me with their courage and personal journeys. To my students who have challenged me, loved me, laughed and cried with me; I learned so much too! To Margaret Ramage mentor, supervisor and guide – your ongoing faith in my personal and professional self will remain with me always. To Amy for her love, kind words and patience and the many proofreadings of my work, and finally to Angela Louise whose journey inspired me to write this chapter.

Thom Spiers – I would like to thank Guy Harrington, with whom I began this project, for his help, support and friendship. I would like to express my gratitude to all my teachers, two of which include Carrie Jess and Emerald-Jane who have contributed to this book. I would especially like to thank Ulrike Encke for her guidance of my work, and my clients who have allowed me to learn so much about myself. My thanks to the staff of the Hakomi Somatics Institute who continue to broaden my understanding of trauma and my team at London Underground for their endurance. And of course, last but not least, a special thank you for Thomas.

Emerald-Jane Turner – I would like to express deep appreciation and gratitude to Maura and Franklin Sills who continue to inspire me. Thanks also to Dr Angwyn St Just for all her kindness and support and her wonderful mind. To those at the Hakomi Somatics Institute and my clients for allowing me to share their work. Thanks to my son Jordan for his many hours of American football which gave me the space to undertake this project.

Jeremy Woodcock – I wish to thank my colleagues at the Medical Foundation, Alex Sklan and Asefa Qayyum for their most generous insights into the richness of their religious traditions, of which my rendering is but a poor reflection. To Mary Campbell-Johnston and Fr. Damian Howard S.J. for their perceptive criticism of the emerging text. To Fr. A.M.A. Samy S.J., Gen-Un-Ken, priest and roshi for his Teisho at De Tiltenberg, November 2000. To Jeanette Campbell Johnston and Fr. Bill Broderick, mentors, companions and guides on a personal spiritual journey. To Dr Cecilia Goodenough – time with Celia was of inestimable value and lives on in so many of my daily encounters. Finally, for the courage, resourcefulness and human generosity of my patients at the Medical Foundation who have so moved me with a passion to write.

Introduction

Thom Spiers

I must confess that I seldom if ever read the introduction to a book. I am so eager to get started that I flick straight through to the main body of the text and plunge right in. This is a good analogy for what can happen in some forms of trauma counselling. There is often a temptation to rush to the core of the traumatic event in order to retell the story in detail and rework the past. This is often encouraged by our counsellor training, which espouses the need to explore the core need or event shrouded in our everyday conscious experience. It is the shared experience of all the contributors to this book that such a rushing in cannot only create 'resistance' but also runs the risk of overwhelming the client once again.

So what is presented in these pages is a gentle approach to trauma counselling, one that works on the principle that the person you are and the person you work with, are far more important than any technique you might use. What naturally grows out of this attitude is that the client's needs begin to set the tempo of the counselling and the counsellor supports the client's recovery by helping maintain a pace at which the client remains empowered. The contributors to this book have sought through innovative practice to address the many areas of human experience impacted by traumatic events. What this book seeks to do is to move away from a cognitive or verbal practice alone and provide insight into how traumatic responses may be worked with in mind, body and soul.

Whilst writing this introduction, I had a dream. I dreamt of a man and woman trapped in an underground cavern which was rapidly filling with water. They were clearly in peril and there was a pervading sense that something terrible had happened. The man and woman were back to back, skittishly edging around one another in a bizarre shadow dance. The man was out-manoeuvring her, ensuring that she did not see him. Only the man's voice could be heard. It was calm and reassuring but stressed that it was imperative that the woman should not turn around, conveying a sense that she would become hysterical if she knew exactly how desperate their situation was. Almost at once, as if from a watching place, I became aware that the man had been decapitated and that he was holding his head out of the water by the hair. This was the 'something else' terrible that had happened which he was desperately trying to prevent her from seeing. The content of this dream is not unusual given the context of my work and experience but rare in its occurrence. However, it conceptualised well what has become my understanding of trauma to date.

Traumatic responses are created by life-threatening events either to self or others (the man and woman trapped in the flooding cave). The response often involves some degree of fragmentation of thoughts (the calmly speaking male) and feelings (the female). The dance of denial taking place between the male and female elements of the self, represents to me the precarious management of feelings which is often indicative of how clients cope with their situation. The separation of cognition from bodily sensation (represented by the decapitated head) is also symptomatic of some traumatised clients. Dissociation – the ability to observe the traumatic experience and even talk about it in great depth without any apparent reaction (the watching position) – is also characteristic of the traumatic response. Beyond this there is the dreamer dreaming the dream. This is the transpersonal, higher or spiritual self that transcends the existential crises induced by trauma, bringing integration and understanding to life-threatening experience.

Therefore if we begin to speak and write about trauma we must begin to address how we can encourage these elements to relate to each other once again in a way that is safe and restorative. This is what contributors have written about here: how in their experience safety, reconnection with and integration of traumatic events may be achieved. It is not about a particular model or technique and how to use it but about what practitioners have come to know to be true through their practice. There may be no absolute truth but if 'truth is found in life' then there is truth to be found here, for all of what is written about is the real-life experience of the counsellors and therapists who daily work with those who have been traumatised. It is also a record of the lives of clients (although disguised) who kindly agreed to allow their stories to be shared with others.

The book opens with a statement of its humanistic bias. It is a response to my experience of specialist trauma skills training that raised for me two important questions. How do these techniques fit with what I've already learned in my counsellor training? And how do I use these trauma treatment methods in a way that does not further injure my clients? I have come to understand that it is the trusting relationship between counsellor and client that makes the re-experiencing of traumatic events bearable. Chapter 1 endeavours not only to argue this case but also illustrates how this works in practice. It answers the first question by outlining the various streams of psychotherapy and shows how each tells a story of the impact of trauma. It is designed to help each counsellor locate themselves in their chosen theory base whilst beginning to develop a common language with which to understand the thinking of other schools of psychotherapy. The second question is answered by elevating the relationship-building skills of therapy to a central place in this work.

Chapter 2 introduces assessment of traumatic reactions in terms of the DSM-IV definitions of acute stress reaction and post-traumatic stress disorder. The definitions, although quite rigid, have been helpful particularly at London Underground, where tensions between sickness absence, staff care and service delivery have been part of the wider organisational context within which some of the work in this book has been undertaken and developed. The definitions separate life-threatening events from everyday suffering and set out and distinguish between intrusion, arousal and avoidance symptoms. Using Daniel Weiss's comprehensive work on the impact of event scale, reactions to life-threatening events are explained and normalised. For those working in an organisational setting this may be a credible way of expounding the validity and success of your work. The chapter ends by looking at how assessment can be used to determine not only traumatic reactions but also an individual's suitability to exposure-based treatments.

Chapter 3, 'Resourcing the trauma client' by Francesca Diebschlag and Emerald-Jane Turner, was perhaps the most difficult chapter to place. Although resourcing can stand in its own right, it is also the foundations of much of what is written elsewhere in the book. It is the broad container within which all the other chapters, including assessment and the integrated model, are held. Trauma is by its very nature overwhelming. There is a tendency in post-traumatic states, whether short- or long-term, to dwell on, one might even say to rush towards, the most distressing aspects of the experience. This invites dissociation and retraumatisation. Resources are like the pegs that hold down the guy ropes of the psyche. The number and strength of the pegs determine our ability to hold our ground in the storms that assail us in life and which are revisited in therapy. Resources are what keep us from being blown away. Emerald-Jane and Francesca draw from a therapeutic method called 'Hakomi' which is based on Buddhist and Taoist principles of mindfulness, non-violence, unity and body-mind-spirit holism. Resourcing, however, is not specific to 'Hakomi' but can be used to underpin and support any method of psychotherapeutic work. Indeed, work with persons who are traumatised will be successful only to the extent that the client's resources can be reinstated or built anew. Chapter 3 shows how resourcing the traumatised client is possible and how lost, missing and unavailable resources can be restored to clients.

Chapter 4 by Alison Dunn is based on years of collective experience. Having worked with various methodologies including defusing and debriefing, Alison believed that there was a lack of integration of these methods into a general counselling framework. She discusses the recent disillusionment and questions raised about the efficacy of debriefing, and her suggested model is in part a response to this critique: not a replacement but a broadening out of the methodology. The four-stage model she describes was originally conceptualised as a four-session model aimed at working with people immediately following traumatic incidents and up to the point of post-traumatic stress disorder (PTSD) diagnosis. Individual process however tends to defy any rigid parameters we might put around it. So this is better understood as a four-stage model, since, depending on their response, people can remain at a particular stage for several sessions or progress through them quickly. Throughout the chapter a range of techniques are mentioned including Traumatic Incident Reduction and Eye Movement Desensitisation and Reprocessing. It was not within the scope of this book to explain and discuss these fully. There are a number of books written about these methods and the idea is to encourage practitioners to train in and use these. What the chapter provides is a method of integrating these techniques into general counselling practice.

What may surprise some readers is the emphasis given to the body in this book. However, traumatic reactions are essentially psycho-physiological, that is, they affect both the psyche and the body. Recovery has as much to do with biology as it has to do with finding meaning. Attempting to work with trauma without consideration of the body may in fact be detrimental to some clients' recovery. As counsellors we may work with the body differently, variously or not at all, and Carrie Jess in Chapter 5 helps give some insight and direction into the important role the body plays in traumatic reactions. Carrie shows how the body can be taken into consideration from different therapeutic perspectives. The chapter is interesting not only because of this but because it is written from the perspective of a body-centred practitioner who works in private practice and who is outside the 'specialist trauma world'. It shows how the therapist draws upon his or her own general theoretical knowledge and uses this to inform his practice and develop a treatment strategy. Whilst of interest to other body-centred practitioners this chapter is of particular use to those who have no specific training in trauma work. It shows how the therapist might draw on his or her own theoretical background to construct a way of working with a client who presents in private practice following a traumatic experience. It encourages others to reflect and consider more actively their own theoretical background, assumptions and practice along with specialist PTSD work discussed elsewhere in the book.

Many survivors emerge from traumatic events with a sense of existential change, which for some only really makes sense within a religious or spiritual framework. Jeremy Woodcock's chapter, 'Trauma and spirituality', maps out why this happens and how the therapist can work with those experiences. It begins by offering a psychological understanding of how a sense of connection to the transcendent can emerge out of trauma. It then summarises the beliefs and practice about trauma, suffering and change from the standpoint of several religious traditions. The chapter goes on to consider how, despite the innate pressures of working with trauma, the therapist can maintain his or her capacity for effective practice, making good use of his or her current experience and working across the boundaries of spiritual and cultural difference. Those unfamiliar with religious and spiritual ideas are guided through a fascinating but complex territory. To ease understanding some quite complex ideas are presented in a factual way, although the deeper issues are also indicated. It is hoped that those who wish to continue reading will follow up the references in the text, which provide a rich bibliographical resource.

Hattie Berger's chapter, 'Trauma and the therapist', considers a much-neglected area: the impact on the counsellor of working with trauma. It takes an honest look at the hopes and fears present in the counsellor as he or she approaches working with those in distress, what draws us here and how we can utilise our own wounds to enrich and improve the effectiveness of our work – and in so doing perhaps heal ourselves. It specifically considers the unique ways in which traumatic reactions resonate in the bodies and minds of practitioners and encourages us to be more considerate toward ourselves as a model to our clients. Specifically Hattie describes how trauma related countertransference may reveal itself, the forms it takes and how it can be utilised. Beyond this she places emphasis on the social and organisational context within which trauma counselling takes place, showing how unsupportive systems create an emotional cost to those who work within them. In contrast she highlights how compassionate systems can be developed which resource the practitioner, enabling him or her to meet the considerable demands of trauma counselling. In particular she looks at the components of secondary traumatisation and compassion fatigue and how these can be identified and minimised and at times even used to increase the effectiveness of the counselling relationship. Part of this chapter will also be particularly useful to both beginning counsellors and those new to trauma work. Hattie looks at difficulties which may arise in their work and gives direction as to how they might develop support systems for themselves.

The final chapter written with Guy Harrington may seem oddly placed. However, the history of trauma only really makes sense once the dynamics of the traumatic reaction are fully understood. It shows how knowledge gained can be quickly forgotten in a way that reflects the oscillation which occurs between arousal and denial in the traumatic response. It also asserts that the degree to which society is receptive to individual vulnerability depends upon the political climate at a particular time. It therefore challenges the counsellor to become a custodian of knowledge who preserves this receptivity even in the face of social disapproval. For a further history of trauma, Chapter 1 of Judith Herman's *Trauma and Recovery* (1992) is essential reading.

I trust that this introduction encourages you to study further what is written and hope that you will enjoy and benefit from what you read.

Chapter 1

An integrated treatment model

Thom Spiers

At the heart of this book lies a desire to treat people first and foremost as human beings. This may seem an unusual place to begin, as the assumption may be that this position is taken for granted by most counsellors. However, increasingly the work of counselling is pressed to follow a pre-determined course. Commercial and social pressures encourage counsellors to produce a result measured by our ability to rid people of symptoms or to facilitate change. Little value is now given to what may be profitable or transformational in the unfolding of a person's adversity or the counsellor's ability to stay close to the client during this process. The ability to quantify how and why distress sometimes disappears is invaluable and undoubtedly the desire to alleviate distress is a worthy one. But the ability to work with those in distress simply on the basis of their humanity and not because of an anticipated outcome infuses counselling with a palpably different quality.

If we worked simply from a place of symptom removal we would have to concede that at times we could not achieve our goal. As Victor Frankl (1959: 156) says, with some conditions such as schizophrenia our work might be considered pointless. Perhaps from a political perspective we might even begin to question the value of having such people around in society at all, since they cannot be 'put right'. However, as Frankl gently explains, we work to heal the hurts in others and ourselves in the belief that whilst people may lose their functionality they can never lose their humanity. It is this attitude which is so important as we work with trau-matised people. Trauma counselling in particular is awash with techniques which seek to prevent, reduce, manage and cure the symptoms of trauma. The current emphasis on these procedures is so great that the client can easily become an object that is dealt with rather than a person who is met with. The need to refocus on the person cannot be emphasised enough (Johansen and Kurtz 1991: 62).

Working with people who have been traumatised is a work of integrity. It is essentially about restoring wholeness to individuals whose trusting relationship with the world has been betrayed by nature or circumstance. Rebuilding trust can only take place when the counsellor and the client build a strong-enough alliance to enable the client to move from reticence to boldness in the exploration of his[1] traumatic experience. This includes perhaps an examination of those actions and reactions he finds unacceptable in himself.

This chapter is an exploration of trauma as an issue, and some of the ways to work with it. It draws on the accumulated wisdom of many schools of counselling and is a synthesis of ideas, methods and techniques that have illuminated work with those who have been traumatised. This however is only part of the story. Explaining the way this work is accomplished does not illustrate how it unfolds in a relationship. To capture this it is important to set this integrated model amidst broader principles of how we relate to each other as people. This is why we begin with the humanistic influence on our work.

The humanistic contribution

The way of working presented here rests in the humanistic tradition. So, primarily, it is concerned with what people are actually experiencing in response to traumatic situations and how they are coping with this, rather than enquiring 'why' they are feeling this way. Whilst there is some consideration of predisposition and vulnerability to trauma it is more concerned with those who have had a reaction, what form this takes, the purpose this response serves, and most of all how best the person in distress can be helped.

The humanistic tradition emphasises our relationship to the world in which we live. It recognises that human survival whilst instinctual, is not inevitable, and depends on relating to what is sometimes a hostile environment. Thus what is understood as problematic or symptomatic can be understood as a 'creative adjustment' to an often antagonistic world. Post-traumatic reactions are therefore seen as self-supporting, and evidence of humanity not pathology. This then prompts consideration of diagnosis from a humanistic perspective. Although this model draws on a helpful psychiatric description of post-traumatic symptoms, it seeks to emphasise the unique experience of each individual. People's reactions to trauma may contain common elements but their recovery will depend on the development of a treatment which meets their singular needs. From a standpoint which sees post-traumatic reactions as usual, this model runs contrary to some orthodox psychiatric views that would assert judgementally that such reactions are a 'decompensation' a jargon term, meaning 'failure to

---

1 Throughout Chapters 1 and 2 the client is referred to as male. However, the material is intended to refer to both sexes.

generate effective psychological coping mechanisms in response to stress, resulting in personality disturbance' (*New Oxford Dictionary*, 1998).

Humanistically, post-traumatic reactions are seen as part of a process towards health and recovery. Even where these symptoms appear to persist beyond their usefulness they are understood to be self-supporting strategies. The symptoms themselves serve a healthy function but are problematic in that they are an habitual and ongoing response to new, non-threatening situations.

From a humanistic perspective each person is seen to make his or her own bargain with life. Trauma forces people to cut a new deal for themselves and this involves choice and responsibility. Decisions about the individual meaning and personal relevance of an experience are therefore central in trauma recovery.

This model derives from humanistic practice a desire to create a more egalitarian therapeutic relationship. Trauma impacts significantly on a person's sense of power and control over the world and so restoring a connection with his personal authority is an essential part of recovery. This restoration is accomplished in the way the counselling relationship is conducted and flows naturally from the philosophy, which guides it.

This helping model rests on the belief that when counselling takes place there are simply two people meeting, one called counsellor and the other client. These names are helpful for both. For the client they provide assurance that they are in the presence of a compassionate witness to their experience who has expertise in working with those in distress. For the counsellor they are a reminder of professional obligations to the client who is in his or her care. The time spent meeting is thus designed to honour the client's need for safety and for the counsellor to remain open to learning from this particular client. Out of this relationship will come healing. The techniques discussed in this book, although powerful, are only useful in the context of a relationship in which trust allows people to abandon self-protection and re-experience their psychological pain in safety.

The task of counselling in humanistic terms is conceived of as a process of reintegration where people have become aware of a fundamental split in their self-concept (Spinelli 1994: 13). This notion of fractured self-concept plays an important part in trauma counselling (particularly where people believe they should have been able to deal with experiences more competently or should feel differently about their experience). This returns us to our starting point: treating people in their entirety as human beings. Trauma counselling is therefore about the client achieving the self-acceptance that comes out of a validating and congruent relationship and not only about removal of symptoms through treatments applied by the counsellor.

Although humanistic philosophy determines how this model is practised it does not claim a unique understanding of trauma. It is merely one indispensable contribution to our understanding of trauma treatment. The model suggested here is a combination of the insights proffered by several systems of psychotherapy. Most counsellors will find some common ground with the theoretical construction offered. At the very least they may find processes they know well called by different names; at best they will enrich their understanding of trauma work through the deeper insight provided by considering the valuable perspectives held by various schools of thought.

The psychoanalytic contribution

Love him or hate him, Sigmund Freud is the grandfather theoretician of counselling and psychotherapy. Indeed love and loathing pursued Freud throughout his life, and the understanding of humankind he bequeathed is perhaps a testament to this. Freud's journey of understanding led him to encounter women in great distress. He discovered through hypnosis that often the source of their disturbance was early traumatic experience often related to childhood sexual abuse (Herman 1992: 13). These women had 'erased' the experience from their conscious mind so that ordinarily these memories were inaccessible to them.

From this knowledge Freud hypothesised that the mind had a three-part structure. A conscious part made up of thoughts and feelings of which we are currently aware, a preconscious part containing thoughts, feelings and memories we can easily recall, and an unconscious part containing experiences too painful to recall (Hall 1979: 54). From his work with 'hysteric' patients Freud postulated that premature exposure to sexual experience had overwhelmed their conscious mind resulting somehow in an active covering over of the experience which was then 'forgotten'. This process he named repression. Significantly Freud saw that the unconscious remained an active influence in everyday life. The memory of these experiences was buried in the unconscious but buried, as it were, still very much alive. As Freud and his peers pursued the aetiology of hysteria, those afflicted found that in telling the story of their abuse and having their agony recognised their psychological torment ended (Freud 1964: 173).

Over many years, as his thinking became increasingly focused on intra-psychic conflict, Freud abandoned the reality of sexual abuse in people's experience, replacing it with a notion of fantasised incestuous relationships (Herman 1992: 14). He added to the contents of the unconscious, unsavoury instincts and destructive impulses that, along with traumatic experiences (because of their menacing potential), had to be repressed. Whilst the reasons for this shift in emphasis were regrettable and in some cases had grievous consequences for those abused, the healing effect of the investigative relationship born of Freud's work was powerful. From this developed the talking cures widely practised nowadays.

From this brief synopsis of Freud's work we can review the valuable contributions he made to our understanding of trauma. Firstly though, we have to turn the psychoanalytic process on its head. Comprehending adult suffering by fathoming the depths of the unconscious to uncover those crises, real or imagined, which organise current behaviour is the stock in trade of most developmental-based psychotherapies. However, in trauma counselling, by studying blows to the adult psyche we can perhaps gain insight into how the patterns of survival which are called neurosis or pathology actually form in childhood (Lifton 1993: 12).

Dissociation and mechanisms of defence

Psychoanalysis has given us an understanding of the human mind's capacity to disintegrate in the face of great danger. Our ability to separate from experience is a final life-preserving mechanism when our usual responses to danger, fight or flight, are to no avail. With our defences in disarray, confounded by the magnitude of what we are facing, dissociation works to diminish the intensity of what we are experiencing (Sainsbury 1986: 60). There is a momentary breach in the continuity of the self as the stricken individual contracts away from the trauma. The experience is left, incomprehensible, unfelt, numbed out, forgotten and, crucially, disintegrated! Here it may remain, out of awareness yet exerting a limiting influence on potential, perhaps waiting like a behemoth to be reawakened by subsequent traumatic incidents.

Unfortunately dissociation, although a sophisticated defensive procedure, is undiscriminating. Once applied it blunts the individual's whole emotional acuity. The psychoanalytic school puts forward this conceptual view to explain those symptoms of trauma which include reduction of emotional response, detachment from others, etc. (See Chapter 2 for a fuller description of this.)

Psychoanalysis furnishes us with rich insights into how the psyche defends itself against inner and outer conflicts. It can be argued that the many mechanisms of defence so discretely named by Freudians are in fact elaborations on a theme, with dissociation and repression at their core. They are essentially about 'feeling and not feeling' in relation to a traumatic event (Jacobs 1988: 81).

The clearest example of this is denial. Denial put simply is the individual's refusal to accept an 'unwelcome or unpleasant reality' (Sandler 1985: 333). It is a way of repudiating the thoughts, feelings or sensations that would be overpowering if a person were to accept the actual enormity of a situation. So just as someone may deny the meaning of their loss following the death of a loved one, in the wake of traumatic incidents individuals may protect themselves by denying the importance or significance of the experience. They may report that they are unaffected: 'I don't feel anything' or 'You just have to get back on the horse/bike/front of the train', or whatever. Of course this may well be the person's genuine feeling but equally it may be a self-protective reaction, a conscious suppression or unconscious repression of responses. Denial usually occurs to prevent expression of specific feelings such as sadness, anger or guilt, which if admitted create a conflict in the person's perception of who he is ('self-concept'). It is therefore important that the counsellor holds an awareness of which feelings are not present when meeting with a client and to gently acknowledge these. Although the client may not be amenable to counselling at this point, embracing the potential of what could be present conveys a message to the unconscious that many reactions are possible and per-missible. The client may then return at a later date if the self-help of denial becomes weary or is fractured by another trauma, safe in the knowledge that he is accepted no matter what the symptom is.

In the past, social and cultural pressures have supported the use of denial. Nowadays, whilst people may be more prepared to talk about the impact of events, they remain unwilling to speak about not managing this impact.

Danny was a bus driver. He came to counselling after a tourist had stepped out in front of his bus and was badly injured. Danny explained that there was nothing wrong with him and that his manager just wanted him 'to get checked out'. The counsellor noted that Danny's initial conversation was quite flat. He asked if Danny had any thoughts or feelings about the incident. 'No!' he replied sharply. 'It's not my fault these bloody tourists are always walking out, it's his own stupid fault he got hit, nothing to do with me.' His counsellor responded, 'So not even a little bit angry or . . .' Danny interrupted, 'No, I'm fine honest, thanks!'

The way in which psychoanalytic theory has developed, moving ostensibly away from external trauma and into exploration of conflicts which emerge within the self, has enabled us to acquire knowledge of the complexity of the human mind and its versatility in finding a range of ways in which dissociation can be expressed.

It is thus crucial that the trauma counsellor gains familiarity with mech-anisms of defence including, splitting, projection, fixation and regression, since these are naturally present in all life-threatening experiences. It is important for the counsellor to know if and when the client has perhaps introjected elements of the traumatic experience or notice when the client's feelings about the traumatic event are displaced into other settings. This reflection provides valuable information about the nature of the indi-vidual's reaction and guidance as to which interventions may be helpful.

The therapeutic relationship

Psychoanalysis as it was formulated recognised something significant about the relationship between counsellor and client. Motivated to understand the erotic and dependent feelings his patients developed whilst being treated, Freud's work led to the emergence of the concept of transference. In the classic sense this came to refer to the perceptions and expectations that the client brought to the counselling relationship (Khan 1991: 25). Depending on their previous experience of relationships in particular familial relationships, patients would approach the therapy relationship with hopeful anticipation or desperate apprehension and much in between. Past experience, good and bad, was literally transferred to the present. Similarly, although initially considered to be the counsellor's reaction to the client's 'material' it was later acknowledged in the concept of countertransference that counsellors too came with their own history and possessed their own hopes and fears about relationships. So now a broader view of transference and countertransference refers to all feelings experienced in the counsellor-client relationship.

The benefit of such an understanding of relationships is immeasurable. Take for example a traumatised person who comes with a generalised expectation of being blamed. This is likely to influence his involvement in the counselling process, perhaps experiencing the counsellor's request to retell details of the incident as inquisitorial, searching for their culpability rather than a supportive exploration of their experience.

David was a senior police officer involved in a public incident in which many people were injured. As he recounted his experience he did so methodically and in minute detail. Occasionally he would stop speaking and look directly at the counsellor. The counsellor found himself saying, 'and then what happened' while continuing to record verbatim what David was saying. Gradually the counsellor became aware of tightness in his shoulders, a feeling he experienced when he felt under pressure to get things right. He wondered what this was about in relation to this session. As he allowed himself to sense this he became aware of how the session was proceeding more like an incident inquiry than a counselling session. He decided to share this with David. 'You know I'm beginning to feel like I'm policing you in the way I'm asking these questions. It's more like an inquiry. Is that how it feels to you?' David disagreed, he knew the counsellor was there to help him. However, he was worried that the inquiry would blame him for the incident.

The trauma counsellor must therefore be aware of the impact of transference and countertransference and be able to work with these phenomena in the counselling relationship. Chapter 7 on the therapeutic relationship explores this aspect of trauma counselling more fully.

A protective shield

The psychoanalytic notion of a protective shield, which operates to preserve the self from a devastating encounter with death, is also useful in understanding the intrusive imagery which often accompanies post-traumatic reactions (Lifton 1993: 15). This 'traumatic memory' is unique in that the recollection is usually of the entire incident, preserved in unchanged form. Although often described this way it is not a memory in the accepted sense. It is in fact characterised by 'immediacy', in other words it doesn't fit neatly into a person's history but continues to be present and, unlike usual memories, is not recalled but arises unbidden from the shadows. Significantly these traumatic memories are often characterised by an absence of feelings, words and sensations so that in attempting to describe them the person either cannot articulate their experience, feels numb or is more in contact with arousal feelings. The traumatised person may therefore be able to recall his experience in great detail but has a severed connection with it. In a sense the person may 'believe experience is one's own but not experience it as one's own' (Spinelli 1994: 157).

Loss and trauma

The earliest work of psychoanalysis was related to loss. Breuer's work with Anna O., which led to the development of initial theories about how adult trauma can lead to the development of neurotic symptoms, was essentially grief counselling (Murray Parkes 1972: 15). Anna's father was terminally ill and this precipitated in her a strong grief reaction including quite significant physical symptoms. What Breuer's work with Anna O. showed most clearly was the interplay between trauma and loss. By definition trauma involves threat to life and very often in traumatic situations someone may die. The death of a loved one in traumatic circumstances can come with such suddenness and ferocity that nothing can mediate the intensity of the loss. There is no preparation for, or anticipation of, death.

However, it is not just loss of another which leads to bereavement following a trauma. Often it can be what is felt to have been lost. The person may have lost a sense of who he or she was: 'the protective mother' or 'strong man', he or she may grieve over lost plans or potential or what could have been done differently at the time of the incident. What is clear is that there is a pattern to human grief which can include shock, disorganisation, denial, depression, guilt, anxiety, aggression, resolution and acceptance and reintegration (Worden 1983: 20). Awareness of this process of grieving and how it may interweave with trauma work is imperative for the trauma counsellor. As with death in more usual circumstances a person's grieving will not necessarily follow a linear pathway but may zigzag back and forth through various stages. Staying with the grief may be difficult for both counsellor and client. This can be compounded by the pressure to help created by traumatic incidents. The counsellor may pick up unconsciously on the client's blocked 'fight or flight' responses and may feel compelled to act when all that is necessary and indeed possible is stillness and tender presence. Attentiveness to the emergence of grief and the scrupulous presentation of experiences with clients in supervision will enable this careful blend of trauma and grief counselling to unravel.

The cognitive-behavioural contribution

Psychology, another science of the mind, arose at the same time as Freud's psychoanalytic work. Cognitive behavioural therapy (CBT) was born of a marriage between the early behavioural and later cognitive schools of psychology. Seeing how thoughts and feelings are connected is central to understanding CBT.

Behaviourists were primarily concerned with behaviour and, unlike Freud, did not seek any unconscious meaning in peoples' actions. Based on the work of Pavlov, Skinner and others who undertook extensive and at times gruesome experiments with animals and people, behaviourists developed a notion that human behaviour was founded on the law of effect. Most simply put this suggested that any behaviour which had pleasant effect would probably be repeated (Hayes 1994: 849). Through their research the behaviourists discovered that by applying stimuli in a particular way many behaviours which were previously considered to be innate could in fact be modified or at times apparently eradicated, and that new behaviours could be learnt.

The work of Volkova (Hayes 1994: 849) with Russian children in the 1950s illustrates this. The children were given a spoonful of jam each time the word 'good' was said. It was discovered that when they later heard the word in the absence of jam they still salivated. Interestingly though, this response generalised so that it was found that they also salivated when they heard sentences which they interpreted as having 'good' meanings.

In other words, more than just affecting behaviour, this work suggested that the children understood the 'good' sentences and their possible implications (i.e. I might get some jam on hearing this) showing a possible link between cognition and behaviour. Flowing from this, more recent behavioural research has focused on how a 'prediction' or what we expect to happen is based on some form of mental representation which shapes our responses (Hayes 1994: 850). In a post-war social context which demanded we understand more about problem-solving and decision-making aspects of our behaviour, psychologists began to explore cognition. They began to focus increasingly on which mitigating factors affected our individual ability to learn. Thus they became increasingly concerned with perception. People's perceptions were understood to determine their actions in the world and in turn their experience of it.

Transferred into the therapeutic setting these ideas saw mental ill health in terms of a cycle of poor perception creating negative experience and consequently disturbed behaviour. The cognitive psychologists proposed that perception of life events was made up of expectations about others and ourselves and particularly about confidence in our ability to produce the results we desired (Joseph et al. 1997: 71). Thus this view stressed the importance of self-efficacy in determining how we understand our lives. Similarly our appraisal of events as positive or negative appeared to affect the level of anxiety experienced and this was in part shaped by attribution: what we believe causes things to happen. Internal and external locus of control is an essential part of attribution determining whether we see events as a result of our own efforts, skills and abilities or whether these lie beyond our control, determined by greater processes than we can control ourselves. Finally, perception is constructed from beliefs about how the world operates.

The cognitive behavioural therapists drew on this idea that we hold schemata or internal representations of others, the world and ourselves based on our experiences. As we have new experiences we do not discard these plans but actively organise new information to fit our existing map. We tend to use the most familiar and simplest form of deciphering the world, making assumptions based on what we already know. These schemata, they asserted, are revealed in the flow of automatic thoughts a person has. These inform the therapist about how the individual makes sense of his world. In CBT the most important consideration is how these automatic thoughts block, in an unhelpful way, new here-and-now information on living. Psychological disturbance is seen as the result of people's tendency to assimilate experience by extending their existing schemata (maps for life). Thus if their maps for living are either limited or negative, new experience will be squeezed into this unhappy structure. There is a strong normalising bias in CBT which understands all mental distress to have a basis in negative cognitions with each condition having its own schemata. Conversely mental health rests firmly on realistic perceptions. Consequently, the task of the therapist is to enter into a 'disputational dialogue' with the client in order to contend irrational beliefs and encourage the development of new ways of thinking. Additionally, experiential evidence from trying out new behaviours is also encouraged to widen the range of possible responses to any experience.

Trauma and CBT

As we can see from a CBT perspective the main psychological task is to integrate new experiences into existing schemata. When an experience is fully comprehended a cognitive completion occurs which allows the experience to be 'sealed over' so that it is assessed, coded and stored along with other similar useful information about life (Joseph 1997: 73). The symptoms of PTSD are said to occur when the existing schemata cannot cope with the new experience so that this integration is prevented or does not occur. Traumatic recollections of the incident are thus replayed to enable this 'cognitive completion' to occur, which in turn stimulates arousal. To prevent emotional overload a system of filtration develops whereby intrusion and avoidance interact to regulate the information available for processing and the accompanying arousal to allow for the gradual creation of new schemata (Joseph 1997: 75).

Knowing this enhances trauma counselling in that it emphasises the importance of the individual developing his own understanding of what has happened to him. For some, the connection to who they understood themselves to be and how the universe operates is shattered by the trauma (sometimes simply because of how they themselves or others acted at the time of the incident). They may then feel they are no longer the same person as their reactions do not fit with their self-concept or worldview. CBT suggests that restoring the client's connection to himself may be achieved in part by challenging the rationale in his point of view, thereby helping him to accommodate the experience within a new, wider framework of self-understanding.

Integration of experience may involve changing the person's whole meaning. This may not be problematic if he is able to identify the trauma as the cause of change and use it as an explanatory bridge with the past. An example might be someone who describes a nervous breakdown as a breakthrough stating, 'I recognise my life was a mess before, things had to change.'

In this way CBT increases our understanding of trauma treatment by drawing attention to the importance of individual perception in post-traumatic responses. In relation to trauma it is suggested (Hodgkinson and Stewart 1991: 21) that there is a greater sensitivity or vulnerability to the development of PTSD as a result of the individual's belief system. This may be true in some cases however it is certainly untrue in many. Often people with a robust sense of self-efficacy can in fact develop PTSD. Indeed, as already suggested, the nature of trauma is such that given a particular constellation of unfortunate circumstances anyone can develop PTSD (Appel and Beebe 1920: 1470).

It is useful also to consider the possibility that some people may develop negative thinking as a consequence of their traumatic experience, perhaps as a result of their schemata being obliterated by the ferocity of the trauma. Where once they held trust in the world as a reasonably safe place they come to believe their trust has been in vain and that there is nothing sure or certain in the world any longer. Here cognitive therapeutic techniques can assist by addressing distortions in perception, assisting clients in rebuilding an understanding of the world, themselves and other people.

> Bob was a minicab driver who had worked in the East End of London most of his adult life. He was known for his charm and ability to avert conflict when customers became troublesome. He was astute and always aware of whom the potential troublemakers might be. One day he spoke to an overexcited customer outside the cab office in his usual polite but firm way. He was then viciously attacked. Bob described how prior to this he had been fearless. He had generally ended his evening duty by taking his dog for a walk at 3 a.m. and had often sat in the local park at this time. Now he could not bring himself to face the world out there, it was too frightening.

Hodgkinson and Stewart (1991: 25ff.) cite three principle clusters of views which underpin the traumatised person's perceptions:

I am invulnerable versus I am vulnerable.
The world is a safe place versus the world is a dangerous place.
I am a good person versus I am a bad person.

The occurrence of traumatic events brings forth the negative end of these spectra, creating difficulties in adjustment. The task of the CBT therapist is to move the person back to the positive or more rational view of himself and the world. It is best if these ideas are embraced in a fluid way, considering these cognitive extremes as polarities rather than alternatives. Healthy and safe living appears to depend upon a person's ability to move flexibly between these extremes. It may be more helpful to see these as the outermost points on the arc of a pendulum with the axis being psychological equilibrium. As we face each new life situation it may be necessary for us to make creative adjustment toward one polarity or another in order to achieve emotional balance.

As an example, if we are driving gently along the motorway we may believe ourselves to be invulnerable. This will be reflected in calmness and unconsciously competent driving skills. If we decide to overtake the car in front by moving into fast-moving traffic we are likely to make a shift of awareness toward our vulnerability shown by a slight rise in anxiety which is reduced by greater consciousness of our driving. When a traumatic response develops it is not that either vulnerability or invulnerability is healthier but that the traumatised person has in effect become frozen into one polarity – I am vulnerable – restricting their ability to creatively adjust and thus losing their zest for life.

Together these three cognitive clusters reflect concisely the contributions of CBT to the understanding of trauma and its treatment. In the first instance, 'I am vulnerable' versus 'I am invulnerable' suggests that, based on prior learning, people develop schema which allow them to live from a place where they can assert that, 'If I am reasonably cautious nothing dreadful will happen.' Following a traumatic event a person's belief in safety can be so shaken that neither he nor the world seem secure. Helping reconstruct a view of the person's identity in a way that accommodates this new experience therefore in part brings about recovery from trauma.

In the second cluster, 'the world is safe' versus 'the world is dangerous', the loss of a sense of safety indicates the magnitude of the blow delivered by traumatic experience. In this sense, however, the person is seen to lose their knowledge of the world as predictable. Behaviourists placed great emphasis on the importance of predictability in that it shapes both people's experience and their behaviour.

The third cluster, 'I am a good person' versus 'I am a bad person', expresses how, when the world becomes unpredictable it also becomes uncontrollable. When this occurs self-efficacy or the ability to control one's own life is destroyed. The result is diminished self-esteem. The person may then judge himself or herself to be bad.

As an effective response to all three clusters, trauma counselling must above all emphasise safety and provide structures that help explain what has occurred so that predictability and stability returns to the client's life.

Exposure-based therapies

All exposure-based therapies are an offshoot of cognitive behavioural thinking. They have their roots in the work of Watson and Rayner (Hayes 1994: 305) whose infamous experiments with nine-month-old 'little Albert' taught the child to fear a white rat by startling him with a loud noise each time he played with it. His association of the rat with the noise and his own startle response caused Albert to develop a rat phobia. This phobia generalised so that Albert became afraid not only of rats but other furry white objects. For Watson and Rayner this was understood within a straightforward stimulus-response model whereby Albert, through unpleasant association, developed anxiety and avoidance responses to the rat.

In relation to trauma some behaviourists suggest that post-traumatic reactions are straightforward anxiety and avoidance responses to situations or events with which the person associates unpleasant experience. The wider symptoms of avoidance, like Albert's generalised phobia, are the result of the negative connections made by the person internally. The social learning perspective, which basically says that we learn by experience, adds a further dimension. Stress responses are seen as the result of incomplete processing of the event. In other words the person only takes in partial or imperfect learning from an experience. The person is therefore left with faulty learning about the incident, causing distress. This deficient viewpoint becomes the format for future behaviour and therefore, although the person's behaviour appears disturbed, it is a logical consequence of what they 'know' to be true based on their experience.

Working from this premise, that phobic or avoidance reactions could be learned, behaviourists asserted that, by implication, they could also be unlearned. From this theoretical model two key treatment practices have developed which are systematic desensitisation and implosive therapy.

Systematic desensitisation works by first teaching people to relax. The feared object or situation is then gradually introduced. The person is aroused and gently encouraged to stay with their anxiety and relax. As they become desensitised to this frail form, stronger versions of the anxiety trigger are introduced in slow progression until the associations with anxiety are broken.

Implosive therapy rests on the notion that fear and anxiety demand a level of physical and emotional energy that cannot be sustained indefinitely. Avoidance is therefore seen as an energy-saving mechanism. Implosive therapy encourages prolonged exposure to the fear stimulus resulting in the exhaustion of anxious responses. When this occurs, the mind-body is said to 'habituate' or become accustomed to the stimulus until it no longer induces arousal.

Exposure-based therapies provide a significant contribution to trauma counselling. However, it is not just familiarity with the traumatic experience or the replacement of negative association with relaxation that leads to recovery. It is also that the technique allows for the measured emergence of the traumatic experience in its entirety allowing new information to be available to the client and thus enabling new learning to take place.

Even remembering fully the traumatic incident may not be what facilitates recovery, although for some this can at times bring great relief. What is crucial appears to be the gentle melting of dissociation enabling the individual to process emotionally and cognitively that which by the necessity of survival they were unable to do at the time of the incident. That this occurs in the presence of a supportive ally against whom the reasonableness of actions can be tested is vitally important.

Many of the exposure-based methods of treatment are easily and quickly learnt, promoting a seemingly magical recovery. This can bring to work with the traumatised a sense of mystery and exclusivity. However the artless use of rapid techniques can give the feel of demolition rather than the graceful spinning of spiders' webs it needs to be. There is much benefit in knowing a range of treatment techniques for trauma but the usefulness of this knowledge comes from being able to discern with whom, when and how these can be effectively used.

Emphasising being in relationship with people as they are and following their lead may seem a simple, almost naïve suggestion but again at the risk of being repetitive it is probably the most important and often forgotten element of trauma counselling. Whilst the trauma counsellor needs to be grand enough to believe he can be of help to those who are traumatised, he must be cautious about being grandiose, believing in some way that he is doing the healing.

The key concept in understanding mental ill health from a cognitive behavioural perspective is perception. It is suggested that it is not events themselves but what people make of them that causes disturbance (Scott and Stradling 1992: 19).

What sense people make of their experience is shaped by what they have learned about the world. From this learning each person develops an outline of who he is, what others are like and how the world works. It follows logically that if people's perception of events can be changed then so too can their experience of them. One way of doing this is to re-expose people to the core experience in a way which enables them to change their perception.

For some the need is as straightforward as that: they want to understand what has happened to them, what they are feeling and to make sense of their part in the whole thing. However for others the tragedy of trauma touches something deeper, stirring questions of meaning about the purpose and nature of existence.

The existential contribution

Perhaps the best-known example of existential crisis is found in the story of Adam and Eve in the Garden of Eden (Cooper 1990: 240). Having eaten of the Tree of the Knowledge of Good and Evil they were catapulted into awareness of their nakedness and they hide from God. As God walks in the garden he asks an unusual question for someone omniscient (all-knowing) and omnipotent (all-powerful). He asks, 'Where are you?' This obviously does not mean, where are you hiding? Rather, where are you in relation to yourself, the world and others in it now that you have awareness? Having previously depended on God, Adam and Eve are suddenly aware that there are no rules about good and evil and that they themselves must make of their lives what they will, a frightening prospect for the innocent (Cooper 1990: 243). In a similar vein, trauma has the capacity to thrust people into a sudden awareness of their vulnerability. Just as Adam and Eve became aware of their nakedness, a traumatic brush with death can raise questions about good and evil. But most of all the experience poses the question: 'Where are you?', which is essentially a question of meaning.

Authenticity, alienation and nothingness

Adam and Eve's nakedness sweeps us to the heart of existentialism, for much of existential practice is about being seen for who one is, and living authentically. Existentialists work toward people being able to stand apart from the roles and guises they have assumed in order to become a 'somebody' in life. They often fear underneath not that they are fiendish but rather that they are not very much at all. Traumatic events often come with such ferocity that the personae or masks for living which people have developed are ripped away, so that those who generally present themselves as tough, contained, in control or active, are no longer able to do so. The traumatic events and their actions or responses to these are discordant with their created self-image. People are often confronted with a sense of their own nothingness and this is the anxiety with which the trauma counsellor, if permitted, must work.

Likewise people who have constructed their identity around societal or familial 'shoulds and oughts' may have never truly encountered themselves. When the threat of death comes close, it can peel away the carefully manufactured defences against the finite nature of existence erected since childhood. The veil of comfortable monotony is torn apart and 'Who am I?' becomes a constant challenge. The realisation that they have lost connection with who they are may give rise to a deep feeling of alienation so that everything seems disconnected and their essential aloneness in the world becomes painfully acute.

Iris came to counselling on the recommendation of a friend. A year earlier she had been involved in a car accident in which both she and her daughter were injured. Following this she had a few weeks of disturbed sleep and intrusive thoughts but this passed quite quickly. However, a deep anxiety arose in her about a life unlived. She had always been committed to routines, fearful of change, and had had the same job since she was in her early twenties. Everyone, including Iris herself, expected that she would work a few more years and then take early retirement to do more gardening and perhaps some part-time childcare. Suddenly that had all changed. For as long as she could remember she had wanted to visit India. She now booked a ticket to go. She also decided to plan toward stopping work within a year and moving to be near her sister in the United States. Her friend had suggested counselling. Iris had no post-traumatic symptoms and appeared well adjusted. She spoke with a quiet confidence about having decided after the accident that 'life was too short not to do what you wanted'.

The existentialists' concern with separation from the truth of what we are extends to a concern with a separation from the truth of how things are. Irvin Yalom (1980: 265) writes of therapeutic outcomes and records existential insights cited by clients as beneficial in the development of their personal responsibility and hence from an existential standpoint, the positive outcome of their therapy. These included recognising that life was sometimes unfair and unjust, that ultimately there is no escape from some of life's pain and certainly no escape from death, and that no matter how close people become to one another we must all still face life alone. Additionally, each person ultimately has responsibility for his own life no matter how much advice is obtainable from others and in facing the issues of life and death, trivia are insignificant. Often people have developed elaborate ways to buffer themselves against these existential truths. A traumatic experience may not afford them this luxury. Such experiences can also limit individual responsibility. Since it is through responsibility that we actively create and therefore make sense of our existence the loss of this freedom can make people feel their existence is meaningless.

One of the most commonly asked questions is: 'Why did it happen?' This is essentially a search for cause and effect. The question assumes that if something happens there must be a reason. The expression 'shit happens' captures the essence of the existential response. At times death, suffering and pain are simply a part of life and it is our response to them which gives them meaning. More specifically this first question is more often phrased as: 'Why did it happen to me?' This often relates to deep-seated socio-religious beliefs and can be an exploration of 'Am I good or bad?' There is often a desire to discover who or what is to blame. In reality there is often no one and nothing to blame. Thus when undertaking trauma counselling one of the most important existential questions to ask is 'What does this experience mean to you?', since finding meaning in the traumatic experience is what will aid recovery. Chapter 6 on transformational aspects of the traumatic experience explores this more fully.

The body-centred contribution

Body-centred psychotherapy has a long and distinguished history. Sadly it is often decried as fringe or new age and thus we lose the significant contributions of this well-established body of knowledge. It can be useful to remember that, historically, psychotherapy is peppered with concern for the body. Both the founding fathers of counselling and psychotherapy and many of the creators of the modern-day definition of post-traumatic stress disorder were bodily physicians. Indeed Freud's stages of development, oral, anal and genital, are for example rooted in physiological processes (Jacobs 1985: xiii). It is in this tradition that body-centred work rests, holding as a central tenet that all psychological states have their foundation in bodily processes (Caldwell 1997: 8).

It is important to remember when working with trauma that arousal, as well as being a principle cluster of symptoms in a traumatic reaction, is primarily a physiological phenomenon. Daniel Goleman (1996) shows how when faced with danger the visual image of the threat is communicated from the retina to the thalamus 'where it is translated into the language of the brain' (1996: 19). Information transmitted to the amygdala then activates the fight or flight response by sending neurochemical messages that release hormones which in turn activate the large muscles, increase blood flow, and sharpen sensory awareness, priming the body to respond to the emergency (1996: 21). Body-focused counsellors use knowledge of these physiological processes to conceptualise about trauma and design interventions to assist those in distress.

Energy and expression

All body-centred psychotherapies give attention to energy (Caldwell 1997: 8ff). Energy is the '*elan vital*', the very essence of life. This energy is the force that gives cells, muscles, bones and tissues their vivacity. Each person is thus understood to be an energy system within which aliveness flows. Body-centred counsellors work with clients noticing for example the expansion and contraction of energy as the individual experiences it. Familiarity with the movement of one's own energy is the equivalent in other therapeutic approaches to developing understanding of oneself in terms of thought processes, transference or emotions. For instance, when in conflict a client's sensing of how he energetically expands toward or recoils away from confrontation will allow a knowledge of how his energy flows and therefore, it is suggested, enable him to know himself more fully.

All experiences are said to create an energetic response. For example, a situation which evokes anger might result in a racing heart, pushing blood to the head and hands, tensing the muscles, and changing breathing in order to do battle. The energy build-up in the physical system may then lead to expression in an angry outburst such as striking out both physically and verbally, thereby discharging the energy. This cycle of activated and embodied energy seeking out and completing expression, which in turn leads to resolution and a return to homeostasis or rest, is a central aspect of body-centred thinking.

Body-orientated approaches are particularly concerned with distorted expression, whether this is habitual exaggerated discharge or suppressed expression (Caldwell 1997: 9). The ability to build and hold charge as well as the capacity to release energy is considered vital to psychological health. Drawing on this and an understanding of the physiological process of arousal, traumatic reactions are understood to be a failure in the process of energetic expression, preventing completion and leaving the system highly charged. This energy remains in the system, perpetuating the state of emergency beyond necessity. The symptoms of trauma – hyper-vigilance, irritability, intrusive imagery and so forth – are seen as a result of an inability to properly discharge the surplus energy created to effect escape from danger.

Levine (1997: 26) suggests that this is illustrated by the disparity of symptomatic responses evidenced in children following the Chowcilla kidnapping. Those who actively worked to escape and fled their underground prison were seen to be less symptomatic than those who were unable to do so. In other words those who discharged their energy in escaping had fewer post-traumatic symptoms. Using this information the body-centred therapies seek to reinstate and effect completion of self-protective actions not possible at the time of the traumatic incident, thus allowing surplus energy to discharge.

Movement and dissociation

The body-orientated therapies say life is expressed through movement, whether this is heartbeat, digestive juices or walking. Where movement has become frozen or stilled life flow is said to be interrupted. Restoring movement is the work of counselling. Newer body perspectives on movement and trauma look to our status as animals, understanding dissociation as frozen movement that protects us from detection when in danger (Caldwell 1997: 11).

Pat Ogden, originator of Hakomi Integrative Somatics, has developed a comprehensive body-mind theory that places dissociation at its heart. Since dissociation is such a critical element of trauma her model brings valuable insight to working with dissociation. She advocates that quality of life is determined by an individual's ability to draw on and effectively use information from here-and-now experience. This information for living is gathered through the 'core organisers' which are inner body sensation (physical feeling or felt-sense), five sense perceptions (sight, smell, taste etc.), movement, cognition and affect, which together make up the interrelated and complex construct we call experience. When the core organisers 'work in concert' (Caldwell 1997: 162) as a responsive system, thoughts, feelings and sensations flowing together with movement and sensory information, we experience a sense of congruence. When they don't we experience fragmentation (Caldwell 1997: 164). During a traumatic experience we might dissociate from one or several of the core organisers. For example, sedating the physical pain or freezing movement or numbing out emotion. This dissociation allows for a gradual absorption of an overwhelming experience. When the traumatic incident is later recalled the elements of the experience will be reconstituted with similar movements, body sensations, and emotions, etc. It is when the process of integration stops or when remembering creates so much stimulation that the person is once again overwhelmed that therapeutic intervention is required. Body-centred methods work with the dissociation to slowly restore flexibility and movement.

For some 'the terms psyche and soul are interchangeable' (Hillman 1965: 47). It is only in modern times that soul has come to refer to the spiritual and romantic. Looking back into history we can see how our most ancient medicine sought to treat sickness of the soul. Peter Levine (1997: 58) uses a story from shamanistic medicine to describe the work of body-centred trauma counselling. In shamanism it is believed that when a person is overwhelmed by tragedy his soul will leave his body, a belief which is concordant with our present understanding of dissociation. This ancient description depicts graphically what many traumatised people attempt to express.

He may feel numbed to and detached from the things and people he once loved and enjoyed. With no clear way of aligning himself with his experience, he feels himself to be, and often appears, a 'lost soul'. In this folklore it is said that only the shaman has the ability to see that the soul has gone. The trauma counsellor must also develop the ability to recognise the signs and symptoms of trauma, allowing healing to begin. Once recognised, for healing to continue the shaman must create the conditions that will encourage the bewildered soul back to its rightful home. This is the essence of the therapeutic relationship where calmness, safety and care persuade the perplexed individual to return to his body-self. Finally, to effect the cure the shaman applies the rituals of calling back the soul, 'Come back to your country, your family, your friends . . . Come back to your mother, your father.'

Trauma counsellors also use techniques of returning clients to themselves and their loved ones, often reviewing the experience that initially drove them into flight. As is true of shamanism is also true of trauma counselling: although it is the shaman who calls, it is the soul which chooses to return. Chapter 5 of this volume is devoted to trauma and the body.

An integrated model

Figure 1.1 depicts what the treatment of trauma can look like. There is no hierarchy in the issues or methods presented in this diagram. Neither understanding, nor assessment, nor meaning can be espoused as the most

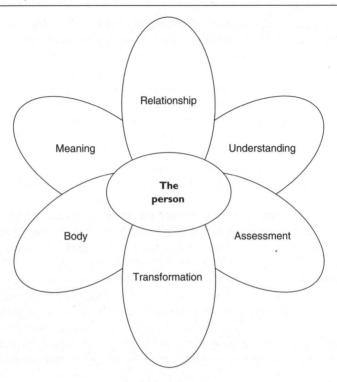

Figure 1.1   What trauma counselling looks like

important active ingredient in trauma treatment. It is what is useful for each individual that determines the effectiveness of each of these elements in a particular case. This is why the person is placed at the core of this model. This de-emphasis of method is less to do with a desire for integration, but more to emphasise the importance of not assuming that 'we know' what a client needs from trauma counselling. It is all too easy to get swept up in the dramatic impact of trauma and fail to recognise that trauma symptoms may not be the client's greatest concern.

Ciaran came for counselling following the sudden and traumatic death of his wife. Although he was deeply upset by her death and the manner in which she had died, and showing signs of PTSD, this was not the immediate focus of his concern in counselling. He was preoccupied with how he alone could care for his four children who were all under the age of twelve.

Trusting that the client knows what is best for him is a value easily lost in a field of counselling which emphasises psychological expertise and where the client's distress is in part about the loss of his understanding. When a person presents following a traumatic incident he may appear awash with anxiety and unsure of anything. In such a situation it is easy to respond to distress by 'knowing' what to do.

Indeed, ostensibly we *should* know what to do. However, even if we are sure we know what will be helpful we cannot be certain of it. Somehow we must leave enough space in our knowing to allow us to listen to what we are being asked to do. Only the individual himself can truly tell us what he needs.

To illustrate this point, a friend recently discovered that her cleaner was not only tidying up, but was in fact rearranging her furniture. She spoke to him, explaining that she liked things just the way they were and asked him not to make any more changes. Unfortunately he continued to move things around and so she had to let him go. Relating this to trauma counselling the story depicts the consequences of not allowing the client to lead the work we do. Like this cleaner we are hired by our clients to do a very specific job of work. As counsellors we are very well trained in how to move things around and may be quite skilful at doing so. Indeed, things may even appear to work better if we are allowed to rearrange them but, and this is especially true in trauma work, if this is not what the client wants, ultimately we will be sacked! Essentially trauma counselling, like all counselling, is the client's opportunity to address what he wishes to. Of course, if in our judgement the client appears to work against himself then we are obligated sensitively to point this out. However, if someone does not wish to address an issue or a trauma he will not do so. The client may even continue through the motions of counselling but once co-operation is lost the process is futile.

Iain came for counselling following an assault in which he experienced a hand injury. This experience reawakened memory of his time in the army, when his hand and arm were injured in combat. As he talked about the incident with his counsellor he explained that he was dealing with things by putting them to the back of his mind. As he was showing other signs of avoidance she encouraged him to talk to others as much as possible about the incident. She explained to him the use of imaginal exposure in treating trauma and prepared him for the next session when they would 'talk about' the incident. He arrived twenty minutes late for his next session and said he had had the worst

> sleepless night since the assault, however generally things were much better and he wanted to return to work. As there was not enough time to undertake exposure work the counsellor rearranged the session for later in the week. In the morning shortly before the counselling was due to take place, Iain phoned and left a message to say thank you, he was feeling much better, was back at work and had put things away for now.

The importance of listening to what the client needs is crucial, as the above example illustrates. Since the client may not only put a lid on the trauma itself but may also put in place another cover in relation to the counsellor, it may make it difficult to return to counselling if and when it is right for him.

How does it all fit together?

What is apparent is that the various approaches share a degree of commonality in their understanding of trauma, its impact and treatment. These similarities are identified here as seven shared characteristics.

All recognise the significance of trauma in affecting human character.
All acknowledge withdrawal from the experience as part of the individual response to trauma.
All identify the splitting of self in trauma.
All have a desire to bring people into the 'now'.
All of the models are relational.
All place the person central in some way.
All see reconnection as a key element in recovery.

All recognise the significance of trauma in affecting human character

Each method acknowledges that life-threatening experiences, whether real or perceived, can at times disrupt a person's sense of self, and that irrespective of how the 'self' is conceptualised this disruption produces symptoms.

All acknowledge withdrawal from the experience as part of the individual response to trauma

Each of the models recognises that a person will constrict away from traumatic experience protecting him from its overwhelming potential. Whether through the formation of a 'protective shield', the construction of a false self, or the blocking out of elements of the experience, a person will use some form of dissociation to buffer the physiological and psychological intensity of the trauma.

All identify the splitting of the 'self' in trauma

Each model agrees that trauma creates a breach in the order of the self. A traumatic experience may evoke such a strong response that the incident and the reaction to it become self-defining. The person may then describe his life and experience in relation to the trauma rather than as an ongoing flow of positive or challenging experiences. Trauma creates a point of departure in how a person has believed himself to be, and from the person's attempts to heal this rift, symptoms emerge.

All have a desire to bring people into the 'now'

All the models seek to bring people into the 'here and now' in relation to the traumatic experience. Some of them make this an explicit intention whilst others, such as the psychoanalytic tradition or cognitive behaviour therapy, hold to this implicitly, hoping to introduce here-and-now experience by purging present experience of the influences of past relationships or testing out negative thinking and incorrect beliefs against current reality.

All of the models are relational

All the models concur that effective treatment of trauma demands the creation of a trusting therapeutic relationship. Restoring reconnection with others is an important element in the process of recovery and this begins within the counselling relationship. In a calm way with little action and no demand, the counsellor first and foremost makes it safe to be in pain with no necessity to do anything but accept and acknowledge it. If this permissive atmosphere is modelled in the helping relationship, then perhaps the client can develop compassion toward himself. He can become the subject of his own kindness and form an alliance with himself within which a healthy self-reflection can develop. In this way the relationship develops a sense of safety which enables techniques such as disputational dialogue, Traumatic Incident Reduction or EMDR (Eye Movement Desensitisation and Reprocessing) to be used effectively.

All place the person central in some way

All of the models appreciate the importance of placing the person central in counselling, whether this is through a focus on individual perception, the development of personal meaning, the interpersonal dynamics of the relationship, the unique energy system or the individual transformation which results from the trauma.

All see reconnection as a key element in recovery

Each of the methods believes that reconnection is an important element in recovery. This reconnection may come in a number of different ways. It may involve rejoining with the bodily senses and emotions, reuniting with an understanding of oneself and one's experience, reconnecting with the meaning of life with others and through exposure methods with the actual event.

How it works in practice

Describing the components of working in this integrative way does not show how this work flows within sessions nor how it is felt in moment-by-moment contact with clients. Sue's story is used here to illustrate this unfolding. Her struggle reveals how staying close to the client's experience is more important than any template or technique suggested in this book. If every intervention had yielded successful results then it would not be true to life and might give the impression that trauma counselling is a flawless process. On the contrary, it demands that the counsellor knows a lot and yet develops an attitude of knowing nothing for sure. In this atmosphere healing can occur.

Sue referred herself to counselling following a vicious verbal assault at the busy city centre railway station where she worked. In the midst of helping one passenger with her children, another young male passenger's ticket jammed in the exit gate. Unable to offer him immediate assistance he angrily attacked her with severe verbal abuse. Despite her professionalism in attempting to calm the situation, her assailant continued his attack, pursuing her even as she retreated to the supposed safety of the staff room. Her manager responded by attempting to quell the passenger's anger but to little avail. Eventually Sue's fury broke and as she moved to strike out to protect herself she was restrained by another member of staff and the passenger left.

Tearful and fluctuating between upset and anger, Sue began the first session unsure of what could be done for her. She was stunned by her own reaction to this assault. 'People say and do all sorts of things to me and it doesn't ever bother me. I'm known as a strong person. This is just not me.' Clearly this assault had created a split in Sue's self-perception between the acceptable strong her and the unacceptable vulnerable her. This break was the main focus of her anxiety, hence my explaining to her the normality of the symptoms she was experiencing, although reassurance was to no avail. There was no relief because her focus was on understanding her reaction. It was evident to me that Sue's sense of herself had been altered creating a gap between how she saw herself and how she felt and she could not make sense of the incongruence. I made a mental note that Sue's underlying belief that she must always be strong was a possible indication of a long-standing emotional wound, it was certainly a self-defining belief into which her new behaviour did not fit. In the initial sessions Sue was adamant that she had had no previous traumatic experiences. The strength of her protest and the intensity of her reaction indicated to me that other issues might be present. Whilst I acknowledged these thoughts I was also aware of the possibility that they may have been my own self-protective minimisation of the real danger which Sue felt during the verbal assault.

With making sense of this experience at the top of Sue's agenda we began to address how she understood this particular incident. Although very aroused by her experience she modulated this by using displacement. She expressed her fury at how unsupportive her manager had been and then berated herself for being critical of a reasonably nice man. Whilst her criticism of him was to some extent valid, shifting the focus on to a peripheral character in the incident was also a way of protecting herself from being overwhelmed. It was more manageable for her to speak about her anger toward the manager than to speak about and contact her feelings around the central figure in the incident. Affirming her disappointment in her manager and simultaneously her liking for him allowed Sue to experience her ambivalence. At the time this was a natural counselling response and only later as our relationship developed did the importance of this become apparent. As Sue's life experience unfolded the absence of protection and her mixed feelings about this emerged as a central theme.

Sue's symptoms persisted and her question as to why she was reacting this way remained unresolved. The importance of understanding her experience suggested that she might benefit from using Traumatic Incident Reduction (TIR), a technique which is helpful in facilitating a cognitive shift in a person's view of an incident, helping them to integrate traumatic events. (TIR is described more fully in Chapter 4.) Having reviewed the incident with me several times it appeared to lose significance. However, when she returned a week later Sue reported little change in her symptoms.

We identified that the most painful memory of the experience was being called 'a fat slag'. We explored Sue's associations with this phrase, looking at her own body and self-image. Sue was an endomorphic body type, which meant genetically she had a thick bone structure with deep and rounded musculature. Initially when she came to the sessions she wore large, baggy clothes which exaggerated her size, making her appear overweight. As we examined her body image we examined alternative views of her size, including the reassurance that people might draw from seeing a physically strong woman supervising passengers on the railway. Again, whilst the impact of these interventions assisted Sue in developing her coping skills, her distress endured, and when she completed psychological assessment was found to have symptoms consistent with post-traumatic stress disorder (PTSD). Some of Sue's symptoms such as poor sleep had predated the incident and again I raised the issue of previous trauma. Again Sue remained adamant that there had been no other traumatic incidents in her life.

In the next session Sue said she had been speaking with her husband and he had encouraged her to talk about her previous relationship. She doubted the relevance of this since it had ended more than twenty-six years ago.

Nonetheless she began to speak of how she had lived with a very violent man who had often physically attacked her, wrongly accusing her of having relationships with other men. Significantly she felt powerless to escape and one of his stock abusive phrases included the words 'fat slag'. It was not until she was in the safety of the session that the connection between the two situations entered Sue's awareness. As it did so she began to contact the terror of that situation and also her deep sorrow over the abortion of her baby during that time. Sue spent many of the next sessions grieving for her lost child. Allowing me to be present with her as she did this. Most of the time Sue couldn't bear to look at me and so I simply reminded her of my presence with heartfelt words of contact, 'I'm here', 'It's so painful', 'I see your sadness'. During this time there was 'something' in the quality of Sue's grieving which led me to wonder about her own childhood, yet there was no indication of why this should be, so I held this to myself. Whilst Sue's general life situation improved the relief she experienced was short-lived and her symptoms returned.

At this point it seemed that Sue entered a new phase in her counselling. Her symptoms intensified until she could barely speak in sessions, weeping inconsolably for long periods of time. As safety and depth in the counselling relationship develops it is not uncommon for the PTSD symptoms to worsen. Sue was eventually able to explain that something terrible had happened to her as a little girl but she could not tell me because of what I might think of her. Sue was fearful of being judged. This fear formed a central part of Sue's transference and was connected to the childhood fear of what might happen to her if she spoke of her experience. We spent many of the next sessions deepening safety and building solid foundations of trust before approaching what was for Sue the most dreaded thing.

Eventually Sue felt able to speak of her abuse at the hands of her uncle from the age of four until nine. She described vividly two instances that she had until now put out of her mind. On one occasion she had tried to escape his clutches by getting out of his car and running away. She was just a child and alone in the middle of the countryside; she had nowhere to go so her attempt to escape was thwarted. In another instance when older, she walked to work with his wife in an attempt to stay safe. When she was sent back to the house he was with some friends and she believed that if she went to her room this would keep her safe, but it didn't.

Both recollections contained elements similar to her most recent traumatic experience. As in these childhood assaults she had attempted to flee to safety but was unable to make herself secure. Likewise her attempts to place herself in the care of protectors had also failed. On two occasions Sue had attempted to escape but her instinctual flight response had been overwhelmed. This had created a belief that she could not effectively protect herself as she was. Sue's abuser had also used a typical manipulation, threatening that if Sue spoke of the abuse it would break her mother's heart and split up her family. As a child, Sue trusted this adult reality and protected her mother and family by embracing silence. Sue was thus in a double-bind, needing someone to rescue her but unable to speak. She had warded off anxiety about no possible escape and her family collapsing by making a strategic decision to develop a tough persona: she didn't 'do' feelings and was a strong person. The recent adult trauma had disrupted this defence leaving her unresolved childhood vulnerability raw and exposed. In working together it was important for me to facilitate Sue's little flights to safety in looking away or not wishing to speak at times about her childhood abuse. This was soft work paced over many weeks.

One way in which Sue's vulnerability showed itself in sessions was in a reflex action connected to shame about her childhood experience. Each time she would begin to speak about her abuse she would seize a cushion and cover her face. Her sense of humiliation in the face of my supposed judgement once again prevented her experiencing the presence of a supportive and caring other, in a way akin to her childhood experience. Sue remained focused on self-protection and was therefore unable to contact the feelings related to these early incidents. Using a body-centred technique I assisted Sue by holding the cushion for her. By supporting her defence and honouring its absolute rightness she was able to contact whatever else was present. Sue wept in sadness for her lost childhood, for her aloneness in the abuse and in anger for the mistreatment she had suffered. This was a significant turning point in Sue's counselling.

Having understood the connection between her recent and early experiences, reconnected with her embodied pain in the presence of a supportive ally, Sue began to re-evaluate the meaning of her life, freer from the influence of her traumatic incidents. This was not an instantaneous 'Aha' experience but a gradual emerging of awareness and integration. One of the principle decisions she made was to not return to her previous work. We explored this as a possible leftover avoidance but it quickly became clear that this was not the case. It transpired that as an adolescent Sue had acted out her distress at school causing her to withdraw from education early. She was in fact a bright woman with a good talent for complex administrative work. Sue spent many sessions struggling over whether or not she could do a different type of work but as her self-esteem grew she secured a new job within her company.

Other dilemmas of meaning also emerged for Sue. Her husband was clearly a very supportive and loving man. Twenty years her senior he had been a protector who had helped her leave the destructive battering man who had so wounded her in her youth. As Sue became more able to protect herself, her need for him to do this diminished and as she became more aware of the potential in her life unforeseen tensions developed in their relationship. Making the necessary adjustments to this transformation was a vital part of Sue finding personal meaning in her life.

Sue's story is a wonderful illustration of how the integrated model may work, however clearly not every case will develop in this way. Some people may simply need to understand their reaction whilst others may need to explore the wider meaning of their life in relation to a trauma. As is evident here, assessment needs to be an organic process which moves with what-ever issues the client is able to be in contact with. Sue's experience, whilst unique to her, is not an uncommon one. Her reaction does not show predisposition (she had been verbally and physically assaulted many times before with no after-effect) but how this particular assault was laden with individual significance for her. This is true in most cases of post-traumatic reaction.

What is shown here is that trauma can create a fracture in the self and in the defences. With this and the thawing of frozen energy and reassociation that occurs as a trauma is worked with demands in many cases more than a single technique or intervention but a skilful blend of many interventions.

The fervour to help evoked by catastrophe, alongside potent methods of treatment, can create a zealous approach to trauma counselling. The com-bination of over-confidence, which can offend those in most need, and the creation of apprentice magicians with magical techniques is a major problem in trauma counselling. The integrated model is designed to take the 'specialness' out of trauma counselling and return it to its rightful and ordinary place. This is not to say that trauma counselling is indistinguish-able or that those with post-traumatic reactions do not benefit from particular interventions. However the propensity of trauma to crack open long-held defences, to raise questions of meaning and existence, and to activate processes of deep grieving, demands that those working with the traumatised have more than a passing familiarity with the broad range of these issues. This is necessary even for those working with single-incident adult trauma. Despite some knowledge and reliable treatments, trauma counselling still holds a feeling of swimming into the darkness. Just as the client must give up the security of their symptoms to find healing, the counsellor must surrender the certainty of his or her theory and launch into the unknown depths of this person if he or she is to be of help to them.

To be able to do so the counsellor must have developed good self-support and be well trained. Above all I am reminded of the depth of courage and gentleness of both counsellor and client demanded in trauma counselling.

Chapter 2

Trauma assessment

Thom Spiers

Assessment has been likened to solving a puzzle, a process through which the counsellor works to unravel the mystery of the client's difficulties and formulates a plan of action to help remove distress. Effective counselling assessments therefore usually result in a working hypothesis about what is going on, a treatment plan or a referral.

Understanding the patterns and the possible causes of a person's difficulty is of great value. However, assessments which focus only on 'knowing what is going on', may lose the vital ingredient that the puzzle-solving metaphor conveys: the joy and wonder of getting to know the person who is sitting with you, bit by bit, until they are revealed as a complete person. It is this regard for knowing the individual that transforms the assessment meeting from an information-gathering session into the first opportunity of forming a healing relationship.

In this kind of relationship-building assessment, the counsellor adopts a particular attitude. It is experimental in that although it may follow a certain course it does not have a predetermined outcome. It is a kind of open knowing, well informed about the patterns of human distress but not blasé about their application. It does not seek to judge or change the person's experience, or to assert that we 'know' or worse 'know better' what is going on for the client. It is an attitude which trusts that the individual knows their own experience best and invites counsellor and client into a collaboration in which the client is helped to find a better understanding of his own experience and in which the counsellor can use tried and tested ways of working.

Most counsellors are able to recall times in their work when technique, theory or assessment forms obstructed their relationship with their clients. Rather than assist them it became an obstacle to the growing relationship. What occurs at these times is that the assessment process becomes a barrier to acceptance. The client's need to be loved, accepted and understood is replaced by the counsellor's need to have a history and symptom checklist. The singular experiencing of the individual is replaced by the counsellor's 'need to know', which subtly communicates the message that 'the details of your life story are more important than you are' (Johansen and Kurtz 1991). This plays into the client's fears of being blamed, abandoned and rejected (Salzberger 1970: 11ff.). If these feelings are not made explicit in the way the client relates to the assessment they will certainly be experienced in the counsellor's countertransference. The counsellor may feel angry at having to use an assessment, he[1] may believe it has no value or that it obstructs the process of knowing the client, he may feel the client made little connection with him or indeed that he himself was distant during the session. Without the crucial attitude of acceptance, which first and foremost prizes the client and not his details, any assessment and indeed the counselling relationship itself may flounder.

The story of John's assessment shows how things can go awry.

> John, a train driver, came to counselling two months after a passenger had ended his life by throwing himself under John's train. John jumped in his seat when his counsellor spoke his name as he approached him from behind. The counsellor apologised and imagined he had simply taken John by surprise. As the session progressed John appeared a little agitated. He couldn't see the point of counselling, he had always coped with things in the past and couldn't see why things were different now. The counsellor noted John's objections as possible resistance to or unfamiliarity with the process of counselling. He began to probe what John meant by having 'coped with things in the past' and what 'things' exactly he was referring to. John spoke of the death of his mother around the same time the year before, and the deterioration of his current relationship. He then began to list other experiences, many of which could be described as traumatic. As he did so his face flushed and he began to sweat. The counsellor asked if John's reaction had been the same each time. John's replies became increasingly belligerent, the counsellor enquired softly, 'You seem angry'. John exploded, 'Of course I'm bloody angry, some fool jumped in front of my train and ruined my life. God this is useless. I'm off.' John stormed out of the room leaving the counsellor stunned.

This example illustrates three things. Assessment can be a springboard for action; however if we accept that PTSD is a self-supporting response to a

---

1 Throughout this chapter the counsellor is referred to as male, although the material applies equally to female counsellors.

traumatic event we must surely be somewhat reticent about encouraging clients away from their self-protection. In short we need to monitor the extent of a client's arousal as their avoidance diminishes during assessment. Second, we must acquire familiarity with the symptoms of trauma to ensure it is readily recognised. Lastly we must remain conscious of the individual over and above their symptoms. Clearly in this case the nature of John's symptoms became paramount and as his hopes, fears and distress lost precedence he therefore could see no value in continuing with counselling.

The case for assessment

For some counsellors, assessing for a particular type of disturbance is an alien concept. It may appear to run contrary to the non-diagnostic person-centred philosophy underlying many counselling approaches. So it seems important to outline why it is useful to do this. The history of trauma, as described in Chapter 8, shows the notorious legacy down the centuries of the monumental failure to identify and retain knowledge of post-traumatic symptoms. Repeatedly those suffering from what we now know as PTSD were discarded, dismissed or disciplined because of their distress. In the face of this cruel disregard for human suffering the admission of PTSD to the DSM-IV is a huge achievement. By enshrining PTSD as a central tenet of psychological understanding it is hoped that this awareness of human reactions to life-threatening events has been faithfully preserved forever. The proficient use of the PTSD diagnosis can ensure people are informed about the normality of their own reactions and practitioners using this will not overlook the impact of trauma on shaping people's whole lives.

Eve Carlson (1997) has developed a comprehensive process for assessing trauma and presents persuasive arguments for the development of effective assessment skills. Not least these arguments include acknowledgement of the fact that PTSD duplicates the symptoms of many other kinds of human distress. For example sleep disturbance, loss of interest in hobbies and withdrawal from others may be indicative of depression, whilst irritability and hyper-vigilance may indicate anxiety. Because the symptoms of PTSD may appear regularly in other guises, it is possible that without a clear and broad understanding of traumatic responses these symptoms will be misidentified. Consequently the core need or wound is not being attended to and the client's distress remains unchanged at its source (Carlson 1997: 11).

As we begin to know the symptoms of trauma we are more likely to identify them when they are present in the lives of our clients. Carlson (1997: 16) argues that this familiarity will enable us to distinguish between what is traumatic and what is more usual distress. In John's case, for instance, it is possible that without familiarity with trauma symptoms the counsellor could adopt a more psychodynamic understanding of John's fury and relate it to the death of his mother. That, in effect, his grief was chronic and perhaps arrested at its angry stage. Alternatively, had John emphasised his relationship difficulties the counsellor might well have assumed that John had poor interpersonal skills and lacked the ability to communicate his feelings effectively, hence his anger and storming out might parallel how he was in relationships with others. The mix of feelings and experiences present in John's quite straightforward case, illustrates the value of using a definition which considers clusters of symptoms and their interaction with each other as a way of making sense of a client's experience.

It is often the case that trauma symptoms are missed because of the resulting personal and interpersonal distress that arises out of them. The PTSD definition enables the counsellor to see through the veil of symptoms that shrouds the client's life and view with clarity the core traumatic issue.

Drawing out the variety of issues facing John also raises another salient point. There is great value in having a definition that provides a way for counsellors to conceptualise about the client's experience. In this instance we could conceptualise about John's attachment issues, or John's position in the stages of grief and most usefully in my view about the impact of the trauma on John's marriage and life. Conceptualising about a client's experience is, however, always a matter of interpretation and so it is important to enter into dialogue with the client to remain as true to their perception of life as possible.

Moreover, establishing the nature of a person's difficulty can enable the counsellor to discern whether trauma counselling alone or longer-term psychotherapy interwoven with trauma work is required to best assist the client. The client who has experienced a recent adult trauma, who prior to this related well to others, and can use insight about his own experience may be more suitable for counselling. The person with multiple traumas stretching back into childhood, who is too distressed to begin to speak about his experiences, may require a different type of work.

The strongest criticisms of diagnostic approaches are that they are biased toward meeting the needs of the counsellors using them (Littlewood and Lipsedge 1989: 106; Box 1971: 15). In effect they are seen as ways of boxing clients into neat diagnostic pigeonholes. Diagnostic labels usually convey with them a sense of social disapproval, and, as a result, once branded negatively clients become disadvantaged in other areas of life. Any definition including the PTSD description is therefore arguably of no benefit to the client. However, it is hoped that the advantages of the diagnostic criteria that are expressed here, which include taking away isolation and normalising responses, are convincing. Nonetheless it is useful to hold in mind that diagnosis is a two-edged sword and must be worked with responsibly.

Using the PTSD definition therapeutically involves the client in a process that promotes self-understanding. Again, if we look at John's case as an example: if in this session John had the opportunity to understand that his angry confrontations with his partner over what had previously been minor irritations, his loss of sexual desire for her and the distance he felt between them, were in effect symptomatic of his traumatised state he may, as is often the case, have been deeply relieved. Until this point however he had simply felt out of control, acting as a man possessed and then denigrating himself for it.

In a sense John was possessed. He was held in the grip of his enduring traumatic reaction, overwhelmed by an experience that he felt was greater than him. Yet as in the story of Rumpelstiltzkin, had he known or been given the name of his tormentor he could quite possibly be free of its power. By knowing the nature of his distress he could gain a foothold of insight which placed him mindfully outside his experience. Thus rather than his reaction being greater than him, it would be reduced to being a part of him which was contained by his own understanding.

Eve Carlson also describes how using the PTSD definition can help the client make a connection between past experience and his current difficulties. She illustrates this by using the example of a woman abused as a child by her dark-haired Italian father whose reason for seeking counselling was to help manage panic attacks and poor work performance. It transpired that the attacks usually occurred at work and then always in the presence of her manager, who is, incidentally, dark haired and of Italian extraction (1997: 18). Although the trigger for these attacks may appear obvious to the counsellor, this arousal response may be so familiar and distressing to the client that it has become habitual and therefore the connection between the two situations may be beyond the client's awareness. An understanding of how emotional distress and physiological arousal may be experienced when in situations that strongly resemble the traumatic experience can be incredibly reassuring for the client. Once aware of how trauma symptoms may be affecting his behaviour the client is once again in a position to use his own insight to notice the reactions that occur when similar situations are encountered. Hence, as before, the client's insight is reinstated and the possibility of control over his reactions, lost in the original traumatic situation, is restored.

The client and counsellor therefore may both benefit from the use of the PTSD definition. In the case just cited, the client clearly came to counselling with the desire to be rid of her panic attacks. Yet the counsellor's knowledge allowed him to see that the origin of these attacks lay in her early traumatic experiences with her father. On the surface at least the client and counsellor would appear to have differing therapeutic goals, one wanting to manage panic, the other to explore childhood trauma. This could create difficulties in forming a relationship. The PTSD definition however, clearly allows the counsellor and client's worldviews to meet without either professional judgement or client need being compromised. In the DSM-IV definition, the core traumatic event and the symptomatic anxiety reaction co-exist, indicating that trauma counselling needs to be a blend of addressing both immediate symptoms and the activating traumatic wound. Used wisely the definition can assist the counsellor in establishing the therapeutic relationship by identifying with the client the source of her distress and which symptom to address first.

As a further remark on the value of the DSM-IV definition, it is useful to note that there is often great debate, particularly in workplace settings, as to whether or not an incident can be defined as traumatic. Whether or not we perceive an experience as traumatic is entirely subjective. What dictates that any experience is traumatic for a particular individual is dependent upon a complex interaction between the individual's personality, the traumatic event itself, and the degree of social support available to the person at that time (Carlson 1997: 62–73). The DSM-IV definition helps by limiting trauma to life-threatening incidents or those perceived as such, in which the person responds in very specific ways which include fear, helplessness or horror and subsequently develops symptoms of intrusion, arousal and avoidance. In defining PTSD these symptoms must persist for at least thirty days and in doing so impair a person's ability to live and work as they usually would.

This is not to say that a traumatised person will always show his distress in this way or that if he does not he is not in fact traumatised. The point is that by using this narrower definition we place a very specific meaning on the word trauma, to separate it from its everyday use where it can mean all things to all people. Indeed, to counterbalance a rigid application of the definition it is useful to hold in mind that first and foremost we are assessing the client's response to the incident and not whether the incident itself was traumatic.

The onset of a post-traumatic reaction is determined by the degree of arousal, the personal meaning of the experience and the extent of support available to the person at the time.

The individual

Vulnerability studies (Hodgkinson and Stewart 1991: 20) have identified traits which it is suggested are useful predictors when considering an individual's susceptibility to developing a post-traumatic reaction. These include being male (because males are more likely to experience a traumatic event), being female (because once females have a traumatic experience they are more likely to develop trauma symptoms), prior victimisation (such as childhood sexual abuse), having some pre-existing form of mental ill health or a history of psychiatric disturbance in one's family, being neurotic, introverted, having a tendency to withdraw, being sensitive and having an external locus of control. This list may seem to be expressed somewhat facetiously. This is not in any way to devalue the significant understanding of traumatic reactions which personality studies have provided. In some cases, these elements undoubtedly contribute to the onset of trauma symptoms. However, rigid adherence to a profile of who will develop trauma symptoms is pointless. This is because individual personality factors are only part of what contributes to a person experiencing an incident as traumatic. An exclusive focus on personality factors is therefore meaningless because it is an incomplete perspective. Indeed, emphasising individual vulnerability has historically been of great cost to those who are traumatised. Accusations of cowardice, feebleness of mind and lack of moral fibre have all been the results of an overemphasis on individual vulnerability (Herman 1992: 21).

If instead we recognise that as people our defences are permeable, our emotional resources limited, and our reactions to trauma instinctual, then the search for who is susceptible becomes irrelevant. We can be led by compassion and see that in fact it is the case that anyone, given a particular set of circumstances, may be traumatised.

What personality studies may show us most clearly is that, when faced with traumatic experiences, people will often revert to their most familiar ways of managing their distress. Thus when assessing traumatic reactions confusion has often arisen because little attention is paid to determining what are the characterological and what are the traumatic elements of the response. Since each of these may require a different emphasis in terms of method, focus and time span, it is important when assessing to make a distinction between them.

Developmental wounds

Developmental wounds are those wounds that occur in our relationship with family and the world. Brimming with needs and dependent on others to meet them, we burst into life, filled with an energetic desire to know and to experience living. As we do so, we meet with the wants and needs of others: parents, siblings, friends, society, and in this clash of energies we are shaped, creatively adapting to the environment around us. The skilful way in which we adapt to our environment has been called our character strategy. Ron Kurtz (1990) has a non-pathologising way of describing character and how it forms which is paraphrased as follows:

> Character patterns are the result of an ongoing interaction of the growing child with its environment. The child develops certain emphasised strengths to get through its childhood. These are good, adaptive responses to difficult, often traumatic situations. These strengths can also foster a complementary underdevelopment on the other side of each developed strength (i.e. I can learn to withdraw from some quality

of harshness in the environment. A consequence may be little practice or my ability to join in or participate freely) . . . So, character can be viewed functionally as a strategy based on particular emphasised strengths and dysfunctional as underdeveloped complementary aspects of our growth and development.

A person's character is therefore in a sense a history of their relationship with their environment. Successful patterns of obtaining satisfaction of needs or of thriving on compensatory emotions are retained as it were in the form of a survival guide, which slips over time below the surface of consciousness. When faced with any new struggle with the environment these time-tested solutions are reactivated. In this way we can understand people's responses as not just normal but also useful. Yet more than this, people are not their responses but rather use their responses to adapt and survive (Kurtz 1990: 43).

This is an important shift in paradigm. Kurtz writes that people's 'symptoms' seen this way become a functional emphasis of strength and dysfunctional only in that they represent an underdevelopment of certain skills. The individual can thus be seen as a unified organism not in conflict with symptoms which must be removed but in effect an individual whose symptoms are beneficial, in that they create safety and protection.

Freud, (Sainsbury 1986: 42) Klein, (Sainsbury 1986: 44) Erikson, (Jacobs 1985: xiii) Lowen, (Rowan 1988: 144ff.) and others have all identified a series of stages through which we pass on our way to adult maturity. Each developmental stage involves learning about oneself in relation to the world, for example, 'I have the right to exist', 'I am wanted', and 'I am supported'. If the tasks inherent in these stages are not successfully completed a person will be left with certain limiting beliefs about themselves and the world, such as, 'I do not deserve support', 'My needs will not be met', 'I must do everything for myself'. These limiting beliefs will define an individual's overall perception of the world and are typically the focus of counselling (Ogden 1997: 167).

Traumatic wounds

Traumatic wounds can occur at any time to anyone. These wounds are the result of witnessing or going through what are perceived to be life-threatening experiences. These situations primarily evoke a physiological response that energises us to take flight or to do battle. The failure of these responses in effecting our escape or victory may lead to the development of a post-traumatic reaction (Levine 1997: 11). The symptoms that indicate this reaction are essentially physiological, in turn creating psychological responses.

Developmental traumatic wounds

Developmental traumatic wounds arise when in the course of natural development the environment has been so unsafe that it may be perceived by the child as life threatening. Rather than being a question of whether or not 'my feelings are acceptable', it is more vitally, 'if I don't get the feeling right I will be killed' (Early 1993: 12ff.).

Implications for assessment

It is hence possible that a number of scenarios may emerge during assessment. A client may have been living a symptom-free life and then experience a post-traumatic reaction as the result of being in a life-threatening situation. Or he may experience intensification or the overwhelming of his usual strategic responses. This may compel him to re-evaluate his strategies and lifestyle because of his inability to protect himself, thereby creating an opportunity for personal growth. Alternatively he may experience a reactivation of old traumas unresolved for many years and cracked open by this new experience. What is clear is that whilst it is useful to name the different aspects of traumatic and developmental wounding, both the developmental wounds which lead to character formation and the symptoms of trauma will often be present in counselling following a traumatic event.

Patrick's case illustrates the interplay between developmental and traumatic wounds.

Patrick's manager referred him following an assault. He had been punched and spat on by a member of the public. He had little or no feeling about the incident, describing it in a matter-of-fact way. He appeared to be depressed and spoke briefly about his failed relationship. He was living in a barely habitable bedsit; he ate poorly and was not wearing warm clothes despite it being winter. Yet he had no debts, money in his bank account and a good salary with few outgoings. Overall he gave the impression of being a neglected child. As he spoke he was self-critical, explaining how he should really pull himself together and get on with life. His counsellor felt ignored and that she was not really needed in the session as he was doing 'it' all for himself. The counsellor was aware that Patrick had had a previous assault in which he had been badly injured. His counsellor asked whether he had had any other experiences in which he was beaten. Patrick began to recount a long list of violent incidents within his family when as a child he was beaten by his step-father. Again he did so with little emotional response.

Patrick clearly had had a recent traumatic incident to deal with. However, he showed few of the immediate signs of post-traumatic reaction. Patrick's self-criticism and the counsellor's countertransference seemed to indicate that developmentally Patrick had needed to become self-reliant to get through his abysmal childhood. However, his ability to care for himself was limited by his lack of experience of being adequately cared for, which perhaps explained his current living conditions. Whilst in the background he had a history of unrelenting physical abuse, Patrick had clear memories of the incidents but little understanding of what they meant to him, little feeling about them, and though he spoke of being angry had no accompanying body sensation or physical arousal to match the anger he spoke of.

It appears possible that in these violent situations in childhood Patrick, because of his youthful dependence, knew at some instinctual level that he could neither overpower nor escape his violent step-father, and consequently dissociated from the experience to manage his overwhelming arousal. Dissociation occurs when a person feels overwhelmed. He cuts off from conscious perception, blocking out the overwhelming stimulus. (We will look at dissociation in detail later in the chapter.) The residue of these unresolved traumatic experiences therefore remained active in his present life. We can hypothesise that in an attempt to manage his arousal Patrick had at an instinctual level narrowed his range of feelings so as to minimise the risks of arousal being triggered, and thus he presented with the low affect of someone depressed.

Evidently with Patrick there is an interweaving of developmental and traumatic wounds. He has dissociation and some re-enactment, which indicate unresolved trauma. He also has a deep-seated fear that the support of others will not be constant enough and so it is better only to trust himself. The issue of trust is fundamental to safety and to reconnecting with the traumatic incidents and so this will be a constant issue in any counselling with Patrick. It is possible that the developmental injury that Patrick has experienced will limit his ability to trust his counsellor readily and therefore restrict the pace at which he works in counselling. The likelihood then is that his symptoms will persist as a result, at least in part, because of his character style. This would seem to bear out research findings which suggest that personality factors contribute more to the perpetuation of symptoms than to their onset (Hodgkinson and Stewart 1991: 21).

In the process of assessment it is therefore important to be aware that a person's character style will be present in his reaction to the trauma. The extent to which relationship issues or developmental traumas are the focus of the work help the counsellor define which intervention will be most helpful to the client. Pat Ogden teaches that when trauma counselling gets stuck it is useful to scan for evidence of either developmental or traumatic wounds. She suggests as a guide that when the client's belief system and the relationship between counsellor and client are central to the counselling, and the client's arousal is low, the focus can usefully be placed on developmental counselling. Conversely, where the traumatic incident is the focal point and the symptoms of PTSD are present, indicating the client is clearly aroused, then the heart of the work is likely to be trauma counselling. With developmental trauma it seems as if previous traumatic experience leaves an indelible psychological imprint as a pattern to warn us of new and present danger. The client may therefore appear disproportionately aroused and at the same time lack the interpersonal skills to obtain support (Van der Kolk 1998). In this case it may be more suitable for the client to receive longer-term psychotherapy which may over time allow for healing of both developmental and traumatic wounding.

The trauma

Another element which Hodgkinson and Stewart identify as contributing to the formation of a traumatic reaction is the actual event itself. The general view is that a direct correlation exists between how intense and threatening an event has been and the likelihood of a person developing a post-traumatic reaction (Hodgkinson and Stewart 1991: 23). How threatening or intense an experience may be, is to some extent a matter of individual subjectivity and any reaction must therefore be considered in relation to the other events that create the traumatic response.

What is significant is that some qualities of traumatic incidents arouse the energy to fight or flee more readily, for instance, when a person experiences sensory deprivation through noise, heat or darkness; or when a person encounters a situation for which he is totally unprepared such as suddenly being struck by someone who is smiling and appears amenable; or when an event occurs beyond his usual range of experience (Carlson 1997: 61) i.e. someone jumping in front of the train he is driving. Indeed some experiences are so overwhelming because of the immensity of their destructive force that it is a near certainty they will activate an aroused response.

The environment

The third element considered by Hodgkinson and Stewart was the recovery environment. They quote a number of studies (1991: 23) which draw together the features of support which have been cited as 'buffers' to the development of a traumatic reaction. However, the existence of a good support network in which the person feels well connected and accepted no matter how great his distress, will not in itself necessarily prevent the onset of a post-traumatic reaction (Thoits 1982).

However, anecdotally at least, it is clear that those who encounter traumatic incidents regularly can develop a post-traumatic reaction if their usual support network has been disrupted in some way. When assessing it is useful to consider changes in the person's level of support over the last year and to notice changes perhaps through bereavement or the ending of a relationship. The degree to which a person feels isolated may directly affect his ability to manage distress whilst the restoration of connection with others appears to increase the speed at which he regains his sense of self-control. Thus a principle task of assessment must be to establish what support a person has and to identify ways in which wider support can be accessed.

A complex interaction

On a general level assessment with people who are traumatised needs to be more comprehensive than a mere consideration of the individual's symptoms. As is clearly shown here, a post-traumatic reaction is the result of an intricate relationship between the individual's internal view of the world, the accessibility of his support network and the content of the traumatic experience itself. Designing a way of working with someone who is traumatised therefore needs to include an estimation of how the client usually deals with his distress, his traumatic history, if there is one, and the impact of this particular traumatic experience.

Broadly speaking it is useful for the counsellor to hold in mind some wide-ranging questions such as, what is the impact on the person of this event? How does this experience fit into the rest of his life? Subsequently more detailed but equally important questions may be asked such as, how is this person reacting just now? and indeed, what can be done to help restore him to living in a way with which he feels comfortable?

The individual's make-up, the traumatic event and the support environment must therefore be considered when determining how to assist the client. Appendix 2 of this book contains a comprehensive trauma assessment form designed for use at London Underground Counselling and Trauma Service. The form is not set up as a model of excellence to be used in rote fashion but as an example of how an assessment can embrace the range of experiences which need to be considered when assessing a person's traumatic reaction.

Re-enactment

When working with some traumatised clients there is a fascinating phenomenon that often emerges. This is the remarkable and repeated occurrence of strikingly similar traumatic incidents in their personal history.

Freud identified this and gave it the name 'repetition compulsion' (Freud 1926: 290). He described this as the process whereby individuals attempted, through recreating an experience similar to an original overwhelming traumatic event, to regain mastery over that experience. Over time this phenomenon has been shown to be present in children's play, in accidents, and in the choice of partners and roles played out in relationships. The high incidence of childhood abuse amongst workers in the sex industry is often cited as a clear illustration of this and indeed Patrick's case also shows this.

Freud saw repetition compulsion as an essentially healthy attempt to resolve an early emotionally harmful experience. However, on the whole it failed to achieve healing because it was an unconscious or 'out of awareness' process. In this sense it was a pre-set programme which was followed without deviation. Without awareness it is impossible to identify the underlying need which when satisfied would create healing.

Levine (1997: 174) suggests that re-enactment is a legacy of our animal history. When faced with life-threatening experience animals will run or fight. When they have survived they will then discharge the physiological arousal used to energise this fight or flight response. There will then follow a period of review when the experience is re-enacted to master the survival skills. Levine suggests that when the energy of arousal is not discharged it continues to 'power up' the re-enactments which we as counsellors work with as acting out. The introduction of awareness of the connection to other or core development is essential for healing and completion.

Noticing previous similar experiences can give the counsellor a clear sense of whether he is working with developmental or single incident trauma, whether the client's experience is new trauma or re-enactment.

The assessment interview

On the simplest of levels assessment is first and foremost about deciding whether a person is in distress at all. Often it is presumed that because a person has had a traumatic experience he or she will have a traumatic reaction. This is not necessarily so. Such a reaction is, as we have seen, the result of a combination of particular factors that together infuse the event with traumatic significance. All too often it is assumed that people will react symptomatically to a traumatic event, and this has resulted in some controversy particularly in the use of generalised approaches such as non-assessed group debriefing. In some cases those with little or no reaction to the event may be distressed or come to believe they should be through hearing others' negative experiences.

A commonly used measurement in the assessment of individual response is the Impact of Event Scale (IES). This is a psychometric self-report test. It simply measures the frequency and type of experiences individuals say they are having following a traumatic incident. The questionnaire itself is made up of sixteen statements which distressed people are most often heard to say following major life events (Rick 1998: 40). Although it covers only some of the symptoms of PTSD it has been widely used with civilian and combat populations and is seen to be a very reliable therapeutic and research tool. It is a short test that has been used effectively in different cultural settings and has been translated into many languages. The IES is particularly useful in measuring the intensity of both intrusion and avoidance symptoms, and its brevity ensures that it is not too demanding to complete for those who are very distressed. As with any part of the assessment the counsellor must remain mindful that simply responding to questions about the frequency of intrusions may in fact evoke them. So it is inadvisable to leave the client alone to complete the questionnaire and it is useful to monitor the client's arousal as they fill it out, intervening to support where necessary. The IES (Weiss and Marmar 1995) is in Appendix 1 of this book.

Those who do not see themselves using a psychometric questionnaire in their work, such as the Impact of Event Scale, may find a structured clinical interview more helpful. The model described below is the work of Daniel Weiss (1993) who draws on an interview design created by A. Spitzer and his colleagues at the New York State Psychiatric Institute and the clinical research team of the National Vietnam Veterans' Readjustment Study.

There are certain ground rules around structured interview technique:

- The questions should be asked in a logical and consistent way.
- There should be an order in which topics are covered.
- A specific kind of information should be sought.

These rules aim to ensure that any counsellor conducting the interview with a particular client will arrive at a similar outcome. Accuracy and dependability are particularly useful in trauma assessment. An accurate result ensures appropriate treatment. Much therapeutic failure can be attributed to not properly matching treatments to clients' needs. Clients who have unsuccessful treatments may develop feelings of despair, possibly coming to believe that there is no hope of recovery. For this reason reaching an accurate diagnosis which gives clear direction on how to intervene is vitally important.

A dependable interview structure is crucial in that it enables the counsellor to create a benchmark against which to assess distress and measure recovery. This structured interview helps the counsellor pay particular attention to prevalence and incidence of symptoms. Once the extent and frequency of a person's distress is known the chronicity of his condition may be determined. With information about the strength of reaction and the person's fragility the counsellor can then decide what might be a helpful approach for the client just now, e.g. a very aroused client might not find it useful to talk about the incident.

One of the greatest benefits of the structured interview is that the client is able to tell his story without interruption. Once familiar with the symptoms of PTSD the counsellor can use the questions as part of an informal conversation that helps the client to articulate his experience. Clients do not have to be familiar with the jargon of flashbacks or intrusive thoughts but can instead tell their experience in their own words. The counsellor should be captivated by the client's telling of his story and allow the assessment to flow from this in easy conversation. This is a practical example of ordinariness in which the counsellor, unable to know empathetically how the client feels, must begin to relate in a normal way to reduce the extra-ordinariness of the client's experience. At the very least this is critical to therapeutic engagement. Most of those involved in traumatic incidents have previously been getting on with their lives; it is unlikely that they would discuss their difficulties beyond immediate friends and family. Counselling may be understood more in terms of paying to talk to a stranger than the supportive relationship we hope it will be. With this in mind the more ordinary the form the relationship takes the better.

For many clients, though, separating the symptoms from the experience is not always straightforward. The assessment can for some be very distressing. By observing the signs of arousal the counsellor can notice when the session has become both physically and emotionally too strenuous for the client. It is important to notice the intensity of arousal, to ground or establish a sense of safety with the client and to adjust the length and depth of session according to his or her ability to manage arousal.

It is useful if the client can tell the story of their experience and allow the assessment to flow from this. Simple questions: 'What has it been like for you since the incident?', 'What's happening, physically/emotionally to you when you think about the incident?', 'How are you at home and at work?', What's worrying you and how is that showing itself?' are all useful ways of exploring and gathering valuable information without sanitising the experience.

In assessment following a traumatic event we have many tasks. Primarily we need to create a relationship of safety, which in turn allows people to rebuild the broken connections that have been created within them and with the world. In time we hope that this will lead to integration of their experiences. One part of this process is to clarify and deepen clients' understanding of their experience as they describe their reactions. It is hoped that through explanation clients will more fully comprehend for themselves their own experience. Yet this is only part of the story. If someone comes looking for direction he usually asks in the hope that the person he asks will know the way and give him some useful guidance; so clients come with an expectation that we know what is happening to them and how it can be stopped. As we gain familiarity in working with traumatic responses we begin to recognise the usual way in which things go. Or at least to know the way things have gone for us in working with others in the past. Even if we are uncertain we can be committed to travel with distressed clients on this part of their journey to their healing. This can give us confidence about recovery which can then be conveyed to the client and it allows us to begin to discriminate what is usual or familiar in a person's experience and what is not.

Working with traumatised people can be upsetting and at times scary. Having good assessment tools and a diagnostic label can give the counsellor a feeling of security that may also reassure the client. However it is crucial to remain open to following and observing the client's own experience. If we hold too rigidly to PTSD as a response we may stop hearing what people are actually saying about their experience. Our clients may understandably become resistant, if their hope of a compassionate ally in the midst of their distress is lost. The simple use of valuing the client is particularly poignant in trauma counselling. The straightforward validation of the individual's perception (having at times lost faith in their judgement) is empowering.

Identifying a traumatic reaction

As we have seen, whilst there are a range of ways people might respond to traumatic experiences there is a common human pattern to traumatic reaction which is outlined in the DSM-IV definition of PTSD. Following a life-threatening or perilous experience symptoms of **intrusion**, **avoidance** and **arousal** interplay to resolve the experience and return the person to equilibrium. When the experience cannot be easily integrated these symptoms persist and disrupt the person's everyday life. Intrusion works to find meaning, replaying the experience again and again until some purpose or significance can be found. As the distinction between physical and symbolic reality is limited the imagined replaying ignites the arousal energy which fuels the fight or flight response. Unable to bear the strain of maintaining the energy required to sustain a continuous emergency response, avoidance strategies are introduced to divert the individual away from triggers that activate the arousal. A dynamic interplay then begins between the arousal response designed to accelerate the person to run or do battle and the avoidance response designed to put a brake on the frequency and speed of arousal (Levine 1997: 28).

The DSM-IV diagnostic criteria are outlined below taking one cluster of symptoms at a time. To make the diagnosis more accessible Weiss (1993) drew out several important qualities that help distinguish the symptoms as specifically part of a traumatic reaction. Since the symptoms of trauma are probably best illustrated through casework, where this is necessary each symptom will be demonstrated by using a case example.

Intrusion

The traumatic event is persistently re-experienced in one (or more) of the following ways:

i   Recurrent and distressing recollections of the event including images, thoughts or perceptions.

ii Recurrent and distressing dreams of the event.
iii Acting or feeling as if the traumatic event was recurring: flashbacks.
iv Intensive psychological distress at exposure to internal or external events that symbolise or resemble an aspect of the traumatic event.
v Physiological reactivity on exposure to internal or external events that symbolise or resemble an aspect of the traumatic event.

i Recurrent and distressing recollections of the event including images, thoughts or perceptions

The repetitive thinking which often plagues the traumatised person has certain defining characteristics. It is almost exclusively about reviewing their experience *vis-à-vis* the trauma.

It is widely agreed that the composition of a person's thinking often indicates the type of distress he or she is experiencing (Weiss 1993: 182). When someone is depressed, for instance, his or her thoughts tend to be self-deprecating, commonly expressed as, 'I am worthless.'

Characteristically the make-up of a traumatised person's thinking, in addition to being about the incident itself, also tends to seek a meaning in or understanding of the incident. This may be summarised in the phrase, 'If only'. It is this quizzical reviewing of the incident which further identifies the thinking as a traumatic response.

Other features which characterise traumatic thinking are that it is recurrent, intrusive and distressing. **Recurrent** means that the thoughts are repeatedly experienced by the client, not in a now and again sort of way, but at least weekly, often daily, and perhaps several times a day depending on their severity. **Intrusive** indicates that the thoughts encroach spontaneously and unbidden into consciousness. The traumatised person therefore has no control over when or how they will emerge into his awareness. Typically they occur when the person is driving, reading or watching TV, thus violating what are for some important means of rest and recovery. Understandably this is an emotionally **distressing** experience. The following example illustrates recurrent intrusive thoughts.

Bill was referred for counselling following a confrontation with a burglar in his own home. He wasn't concerned about this but another part of his life had become less manageable. Bill explained that he had been a national service recruit. He had served in Indo-China where he was part of a troop assigned to retrieve the bodies of dead rebel soldiers killed in action. As he lay down to sleep each night thoughts and images recalling scenes of the young men's bodies being roughly treated flooded his mind, evoking deep feelings of sadness and regret.

Often in counselling past memories are recalled, for example the death of a parent or the end of a relationship, and these may evoke very deep feelings. As they emerge, old memories can be assessed for traumatic charge by considering whether they are recurrent, intrusive and distressing.

ii   Recurrent and distressing dreams of the event

Losing sleep is common when people are distressed. There are a number of reasons why the traumatised person's sleep is particularly disturbed, one of which is the vividness of dreams about the incident. As with intrusive thoughts, it is the frequency of these dreams which is peculiar to trauma. Yet it is not simply the recurrence of the dreams alone which defines them as traumatic. It is specifically their content which does so. Unlike recurring dreams of falling, being lost or caught naked in public, traumatic dreams singularly replay the traumatic incident itself or contain symbolic representations which depict the life-threatening incident figuratively (Weiss 1993: 182).

Tony worked as a security officer. As he replenished a cash dispenser in a particularly notorious area a youth shone a laser pen in his eyes. He was momentarily dazed as his eyes naturally averted from the light. Having sought medical advice there was no significant risk of damage to his eyes, however Tony still feared that his eyesight might have been permanently harmed. That evening and for several nights thereafter he dreamt vividly. The same dream recurred each time. He would be waiting at the side of a busy road near a tunnel. Suddenly a security van would emerge from the tunnel at great speed and he would see himself driving with no eyes in his sockets. He would awaken gasping for breath and terrified.

iii   Acting or feeling as if the traumatic event was recurring: flashbacks

Many people nowadays have some familiarity with the language of trauma. The idea of the 'flashback' has entered everyday speech and is often incorrectly used to describe intrusive thinking. Because the presence of flashbacks may indicate a higher degree of arousal and therefore a greater possibility of dissociation, it is important to make a distinction between them. When a person is experiencing intrusive thoughts he remains conscious that he is in fact thinking back to the incident and recalling the details of his experience. In a flashback the person understands himself to be *in* the experience. The distinction between there and then and here and now disappears so that the incident is not an event which has occurred in the past but is currently happening.

Another feature which separates the two is that whilst intrusive thoughts can occur at any time, flashbacks are usually activated by a trigger. This trigger is commonly sensory and may be simply a smell, sound or physical sensation.

> Mel and her friend were walking home from the shops on a warm May afternoon. The birds were singing and the sounds of children's voices from a local primary school could be heard in the distance. As they turned the corner into her road, the shadow of a male passer-by fell across the ground at Mel's feet. Instantly she was as a four-year-old. She was with a stranger, her feet were like lumps of lead, and she was filled with a strange indescribable feeling. She knew something wasn't right but she had no words to express it. Her head was filled with the desperate thought: 'Where is Mummy?' Suddenly, as though far in the distance someone was calling her name over and over again: 'Mel are you alright?' Mel looked down. She was dragging her shopping bag along the ground – she had walked the last twenty yards completely unaware of anything around her.

In working with clients a useful means of separating out flashbacks and intrusions is to ask the question: 'When you have these 'flashbacks' are you remembering or are you right back there?' The description of the process of what happens will indicate to the counsellor if the client is experiencing flashbacks or not.

iv   Intensive psychological distress at exposure to internal or external events that symbolise or resemble an aspect of the traumatic event

iv   Physiological reactivity on exposure to internal or external events that symbolise or resemble an aspect of the traumatic event

The final two categories of this collection of symptoms may be described together. Essentially these descriptions refer to the physiological arousal and psychological distress that occurs in response to anything that reminds the person of their traumatic experience. Interestingly what is seen to prompt arousal is expanded to include not only representations of the original experience but also specific aspects of it. Bessel Van der Kolk (1998) explains that following an encounter with danger, humans appear to have the capacity to retain the pattern of circumstances surrounding the experience as a record of a threat to life. It is as though we have an indelible mental imprint which warns of danger. This is not a novel premise, Gestalt psychology has long asserted that fixed Gestalts or set patterns of behaving and responding have been the basis of emotional disturbance. What Van der Kolk appears to suggest though is that these responses are an evolutionary psycho-biological mechanism designed to ensure our physical safety. Simply expressed, where enough similar elements come together in configuration, or a single attribute strongly points to the original traumatic incident, a person's tendency to respond in a self-protecting patterned way is great.

By its nature symbolism can be opaque and so what the client determines as a reminder may not be immediately obvious.

Phil came for counselling after he was mugged at knifepoint. He thankfully had not been physically injured during the incident but had both his wallet and his trainers stolen. He was forced to walk home some distance in his bare feet, which was both painful and humiliating. When he came for counselling Phil was experiencing significant symptoms of arousal and was unable to sleep. He could however talk freely about the mugging and could not understand the strength of his reaction. Perplexed herself, his counsellor explored the possibility of previous incidents but Phil could not recall any past or similar traumatic incident in his experience. A week later Phil arrived forty minutes late for his session. As the session began he was clearly aroused and very upset. He explained that his car had broken down on the way and that he had tried to call three times, but twice the pay phones were out of order and the third time a shopkeeper had refused to allow him to use the telephone. Phil said he had walked all the way to let the counsellor know he was 'alright'. A sudden realisation flooded Phil's mind. He had gone to see the match on the day of the Hillsborough Stadium disaster. He had seen some terrible things and afterwards he couldn't find a phone. He knew his mother would be 'worried sick and for some reason I locked on to the idea that it was faster to walk home'. The recognition of the similarity in all three events enabled Phil to begin to reconnect with his earlier traumatic experience.

Avoidance

Avoidance responses can be understood using the metaphor of having toothache or sensitive teeth. To avoid the pain of contact with the tender area we might eat on the pain-free side of our mouth or change the kinds of foods we eat, staying away from hard foodstuffs or very hot or cold drinks which might cause us pain. Some of this 'avoidance' will be conscious whilst some will be beyond awareness. Trauma avoidance is similar in form to how we might deal with dental pain but obviously much greater in its degree. The traumatised person both actively and involuntarily stays clear of any triggers that ignite their arousal. For those energised to take action in the presence of reminders of the incident, avoidance is a practical self-management tool. By immediately withdrawing from the perceived threat, arousal, which is often experienced as distressing, diminishes rapidly. Paradoxically though, avoidance may contain an undermining message which in the longer term confirms the person's belief that their arousal will always be beyond their control. Fearing that their arousal will continue to spiral upwards they increase the parameters of their avoidance, thus reducing the likelihood of their arousal being activated at all.

Deliberate efforts to avoid thoughts and feelings associated with the event

Avoidance following a traumatic incident is often characterised by the client's 'deliberate and intentional' evasion of thoughts, feelings or conversations about his experience. Not only is the person distressed about the experience but also the distress is such that he actively recoils from any reminder of it. In practice this may be noticed as deflection away from the trauma in the session. A client may close discussion down by saying that he puts things to the back of his mind, or he may be more direct in his refusal to talk about the incident. As with most deflection it is useful to take note that it is occurring and perhaps describe what is happening. 'You don't seem to want to talk about what happened just now – how does that help you?' is a far richer vein to explore than attempting to break down avoidance. Acknowledging the value of avoidance in keeping clients safe allows them to see how they work for themselves, and creates a permissive ambience in which clients feel free to explore their fears and concerns about reapproaching the trauma. Fundamentally then, whilst avoidance is designed to create safety, the creation of safety within the session will in fact reduce avoidance behaviours. When avoidance is present the emphasis on honouring the client's need for safety must be paramount. Indeed there appears in my experience to be some correlation between the degree of avoidance and the level of distress the client experiences when reconnected to the event. So avoidance can be used as a barometer for the extent of a client's distress and its decline as an indication of a client's increasing ego strength.

Trauma-related avoidance is clearly best observed in lifestyle changes. For example, following a train crash, the client may only travel by bus, or after a mugging refuse to go out at night. The shunning of certain places or activities can be a clear indication of avoidance and so it is useful for the counsellor to ask some basic exploratory questions about what happens in thinking, in feeling and bodily sensation when the client relates an incident.

Beyond a blanket refusal to speak about what has happened to them a person may divert themselves away from their traumatic pain in other ways. Drugs and alcohol may be used by those unable to maintain avoidance at a level sufficient to numb their psychic pain. Indeed where a person's ability to temper his or her arousal using avoidance strategies is diminished there may be a reliance on substance abuse to regulate distress. Awareness of this is important since exposure-based techniques for treating trauma will themselves actively work to reduce avoidance. Where an individual does not have the resources to manage the subsequent arousal the possibility of substance misuse as a modulating response to treatment may arise (Hodgkinson and Stewart 1991: 155). It is possible too that the person may disconnect from feelings and thoughts by throwing himself into work. Operating from the premise that if he keeps busy he will not think about the incident, avoidance is observed in the constant state of frenetic hard work. This single-minded obsessive response may, like other avoidance, be an attempt to restore control by running away from the dangerous incident – a process that may have been impossible to complete at the time of the incident.

It is the active avoidance and accompanying distress when escape is not possible which qualifies this as a traumatic response. In this way 'avoidance responses' can be separated from other responses such as depressive social withdrawal. This might also be present following trauma but is more related to a conservation of energy.

Jitesh had witnessed a person jump in front of a train on the station where he worked. As he described his journey to the counselling session he explained how he could not bear seeing the front of trains. He would begin to perspire as he approached the station and think about what would happen if he saw another person jump. He believed he 'couldn't take it' and 'would go to pieces'. To make the journey he would stand at the head of the station stairs and listen for a train's arrival. Once he knew it had entered the station he would run down the stairs and on to the train and sit with his eyes firmly shut counting the stations until he arrived at his destination.

Where the trauma is recent then the extent and manner of avoidance may be apparent. However over time this avoidance may become embedded in the person's lifestyle and so is only noticeable in subtle ways, for example the child who escapes a house fire who in later life always unconsciously registers the nearest exit from any building they are in.

Inability to recall an important aspect of the event

The loss of the whole or fragments of memory may be the result of a sensory overload. Unable to process the amount of incoming information the brain instinctually prioritises awareness focusing on self-preservation. The information is taken in but not as a unitary recollection. So thoughts, feelings, sensations, smells and sights about the same memory may be split off and return later as intrusions or are experienced as gaps in experience which cause the person great distress. This whole response is often referred to as psychogenic amnesia, which simply means that the cause of this amnesia is psychological and not physiological. This distinguishes psychogenic amnesia from other conditions such as alcohol blackouts or head injuries, where the cause is defined as organic.

Markedly diminished interest in significant activities

It seems that when the threshold of security and the normality of everyday life is broken, ordinary life itself is diminished in value. When trauma strikes, the flow of life seems to be disrupted, what was before and what is after the event may both be permanently changed. What previously existed may be idealistically held up as a serene and acceptable existence, and may be set in sharp contrast to what the client's life has now become. At times there appears to be a fundamental shift in perception where the client no longer feels able to usefully control and plan his own destiny. Even where he believes it is possible to create a new life there may be no sense of certainty of it protecting him from suffering. This seems to resonate in some way with the transpersonal understanding of midlife transition and the idea of the ego identity project (Washburn 1994: 187). It is suggested that to fend off the deep feelings of isolation and disconnection as he separates from parents, the individual seeks completion through succeeding in his life goals. For most of his life this identity project will give the impression of integration and cohesion until at last, either through failing to achieve his aims or in reaching his goal, the project is unmasked as illusory since either way the 'soul remains dissatisfied'. What re-emerges then is a need to address the profound disconnection from the self, as deep feelings of alienation, long ignored, are reawakened. Trauma appears to destroy the ego identity project prematurely, giving rise to a midlife transition-type crisis in which the person experiences loss of faith and disillusionment in life and all its ordinariness. In particular there may be an abandonment of the things which have been lovingly created because they are no longer seen as either necessary or useful ways of achieving fulfilment. Instead the person may become preoccupied with what they have negated or despised in themselves or feared about the world and those in it.

Often it is lifelong religious convictions, hobbies and passions that are lost to this estrangement from the 'old life'.

> Reg had kept racing pigeons from when he was a boy. Racing was a well-established family tradition and he had won many prizes with his birds. Following his stabbing at work he lost all interest in them. He couldn't bring himself to feed or care for the birds. All he could think about was that although they could fly away they were still 'trapped' because they had to come back to him. He explained to the counsellor that similarly he was trapped in that although he could run away from work for a while, he still had to return in order to pay his mortgage.

This loss of interest should be taken along with the other trauma definition criteria to ensure it is not confused with the loss of pleasure that is often symptomatic of depression. Depression can be assessed separately by either using the Beck Depression Inventory or interview.

Feeling of detachment or estrangement from others

The idea of detachment from others carries on the theme of alienation. Although not uncommon in many forms of psychological distress it is delineated in this instance by the fact that it is preceded by a traumatic experience and that the extent of this detachment is markedly increased subsequent to the trauma. The person themselves feels this detachment acutely and this is most commonly expressed as 'no one understands me . . .' or 'no one can understand what has happened to me'. Perceiving this to be the case it is understandable that being with others is experienced as a strain rather than a support, and little benefit is gained from social contact.

> Gary was known as a buoyant and outgoing person. He had been a soldier with tours of duty in Northern Ireland and the Falklands, where he saw his friend killed in action. At first after returning home

things were fine, until the headaches started. The doctor said they were stress related. Gary began to get irritated by people as they talked to him, growing angrier 'the more drivel they spoke'. He stopped answering the telephone, letting the ansaphone take all his calls because he couldn't be bothered and started to go to the gym in the afternoon to 'avoid the rush'. Whilst acknowledging the clear reasons Gary gave for making these changes his counsellor noted that they were certainly significant changes in how he once had been. Gary agreed, saying that there was no point because 'people who hadn't been there couldn't understand what it was like, and anyway they weren't much interested.'

Restricted range of affect

One of the ways in which traumatic arousal is managed is through narrowing the range of emotional responses. In the wake of a traumatic experience a person may be aroused by his or her own self-protective fight or flight responses. This means that they are already brimming with arousal. Emotion has itself been described as energy in motion. This description seeks to capture how emotions are in effect embodied, with each emotional response creating a degree of physical arousal. When the person is already aroused any additional arousal from usual emotional responses is perceived as a threat because it feels likely that it will be overwhelming. In a way it is like being on a small rope bridge. When one person walks on it the bridge begins to bounce. As another joins the bridge the bouncing increases so that the person fears they will be flipped off. In response he may crouch down or become still to prevent this. Similarly a person already aroused may work to restrain his emotional responses thereby reducing the risk of being overwhelmed. Consequently he may experience a more meagre emotional existence.

Sense of foreshortened future (e.g. does not expect to have a career, marriage, children or a normal life span)

As with other avoidance strategies the sense of foreshortened future reflects a wounding to the very value of life. The reasons for this have already been outlined above. However it is useful to be aware of how this curtailment of life expectations might show itself. Fundamentally, there is an abandonment of any anticipation of the future. Whether there is a positive or negative expectancy appears to be irrelevant, what is clear is that life has lost purpose and zest.

Daniel was the son of a successful and now retired stockbroker. In his session he related how his father had offered to send him on holiday and offered to buy him any car he wanted. Money was no object; he would do anything to see his son 'right again'. But nothing interested Daniel, there was nothing he desired and he wanted to think about it even less.

Arousal

The DSM-IV categorises arousal as persistent symptoms of increased arousal (not present before the trauma) as indicated by two or more of the following:

i   Difficulty falling or staying asleep
ii   Irritability or outbursts of anger
iii   Difficulty concentrating
iv   Hyper-vigilance
v   Exaggerated startle response

i   Difficulty falling or staying asleep

Although quite obvious as a symptom, it is helpful to know what identifies this as a particularly traumatic response. Obviously arousal is about energising the person to seek safety. When a person is functioning from a vigilant and active place, sleep becomes an anathema. Falling and staying asleep run counter to the physiology of keeping safe and so naturally diminish. Indeed, traumatic sleep disturbance differs from that of depression in that getting off to sleep and the lightness of sleep tend to be more problematic than early waking.

ii   Irritability or outbursts of anger

Irritability and anger may be understood as part of the defensive fight response activated following traumatic incidents. The person continues to be energised to do battle and so minor irritations can and often do elicit explosive anger. Many people find this very difficult and may hide their anger or present it apologetically (Weiss 1993: 183). This is because such anger is usually out of character or in the client's mind reprehensible and therefore brings with it feelings of guilt and shame. Fear too is present, as anger may for some represent being out of control. It is often those closest to the client – partners, children and colleagues – who are recipients of this anger, which has implications for the client's wider social support. In assessment it is useful to explore how clients are when relating to others and to explain the normality and function of irritability as part of the arousal to fight.

iii   Difficulty concentrating

Having difficulties concentrating is part of what demarcates traumatic response. Several things may influence problems with concentration. The person may have his flow of thoughts constantly interrupted by intrusive memories and may find it hard to concentrate without his thinking being disrupted. Indeed he may also be so aroused and vigilant that his thoughts fly constantly from one observation to another, testing the safety of their surroundings and making any reflective thinking impossible. Other symptoms such as lack of sleep may also compound poor concentration. Recent research (Van der Kolk 1998) also indicates that following traumatic incidents brain function concentrates on primary needs, the neo-cortex that manages concentration is therefore less capable for a time of facilitating intensity of thought. This has important implications particularly with regard to the use of some of the larger psychometric tests. A traumatised client's ability to complete these may be greatly reduced if his attention is disrupted.

iv   Hyper-vigilance

Weiss (1993: 183) describes this as 'Excessive attention to external stimuli beyond realistic appraisal of external threat.' This is a useful description but may imply some judgement about the individual's perception of reality. What is perhaps a more understanding view is that evolution has equipped human beings with a response to threat, which allows us to become alert to danger very quickly. When danger is perceived to be present this very sensitised watchfulness is activated. Following a traumatic experience intrusion may create a sense of present danger and therefore the world is scanned constantly for threat. This may be noticeable in a person's staccato movements, references to 'always looking over my shoulder', or insisting that you walk in front of them.

v   Exaggerated startle response

As described above this startle response is a helpful evolutionary development, useful when danger is present. Although danger may have past, the person may remain aroused by other symptoms so that they act as though there is a real and present danger. This may be noticeable in the client's jumpiness or appearing to be easily surprised by usual sounds such as their name being called in a waiting area.

An important defining component: duration

The DSM-IV categorises a post-traumatic reaction as one in which intrusion, avoidance and arousal symptoms have had a duration of more than one month. Additionally, the disturbance causes significant distress or impairment or social, occupational or other important areas of functioning.

- Acute PTSD: symptoms are present less than three months but more than one month.
- Chronic PTSD: the symptoms persist for more than three months.
- PTSD with delayed onset: if onset of symptoms is at least six months after the stressor (event).

Clearly what we define as the symptoms of PTSD are helpful survival responses. It is their persistence into habitual responses that disrupt everyday life which qualifies them as a 'disorder'. The one-month period can appear somewhat arbitrary but it attempts to convey the transition from what may be an 'expected' course of distress following an incident and what is becoming an enduring response. Hence understanding the timing of the acute stress disorder and the PTSD diagnosis is important. Up to one month after the event, experiencing one of each of these symptom clusters and having a feeling of being depersonalised or cut off from life is described as acute stress disorder. Beyond this it is given the name PTSD, listed above in three time-defined forms.

When using the definition it is important to hold a general overview of what a person is explaining to you and to follow and explore the symptoms he describes allowing them to fall into place naturally. For example if you notice a client appears tired you might ask about how he is sleeping. The client may say his sleep is very disturbed. You might then explore if the client's difficulty in getting off to sleep is restlessness, or early waking. You can explore if dreams disturb your client's sleep, what these dreams contain and if he had such dreams and disturbed sleep before the incident. It is vital that no single symptom is used to define a traumatic response but that the clusters are considered in conjunction.

Assessing for exposure-based work

Several types of trauma counselling have embraced exposure-based methods, which gradually work to remove post-traumatic symptoms through a managed reconnection with the traumatic event. For many clients these are often extremely effective. However, methods such as Eye Movement Desensitisation and Reprocessing (EMDR), Traumatic Incident Reduction (TIR) and Direct Exposure Therapy (DET) and even Debriefing can create such rapid change that they can come to be seen as 'magic bullets'. Where any technique is applied without cognisance of the individual with whom it will be used it can become a harmful rather than a healing procedure. It is vital to assess an individual's ability to safely use re-exposure otherwise we run the risk of inadvertently retraumatising the client.

Assessing ego strength is an important consideration when deciding to use exposure-based methods of treatment. Symptoms of acute and post-traumatic stress disorder can, as we have seen, fulfil a protective and self-supporting function. Avoidance or dissociation may exist to help the individual cope with what is for them painful and incomprehensible. Encouraging a person to revisit a traumatic incident therefore involves a judgement as to their ability to manage strong feelings and safely integrate an experience without once again being overwhelmed. Stephen Johnson (1985) has developed a creative way of thinking about ego strength, which is helpful when determining whether or not a person is resilient enough to manage exposure therapy. Although his work is primarily designed for use with developmental wounds it has a great deal to offer trauma counselling. Some of the features he considers when defining a strong ego are used here to help the counsellor assess individuals' suitability for exposure-type work.

Self-representation

Self-representation is a useful first consideration. This simply means: is the person able to hold a clear sense of his own identity, is he able to present a cohesive self which remains constant over time? Johnson (1985: 250) suggests several reflective questions that can help clarify this, which include:

- Is the person able to make a balanced judgement about his own strengths and weaknesses?
- Does he see himself as neither all good nor all bad?
- Does he hold some consistency?
- Does he seek to merge with others or is he in pain about his separateness?

Following a traumatic experience a person's sense of self may be deeply disrupted. He may be extremely self-critical, deeply ashamed, respond erratically and 'out of character', focusing on his inadequacy rather than his abilities. It is important that his sense of self is well stabilised before he reapproaches his traumatic experience otherwise he may be retraumatised by the experience.

Relationship to others

How an individual relates to others is another area that can usefully be explored when determining a person's ego strength. Enquiries Johnson (1985) identifies which can help determine this include:

- Does the client see others as they actually are or as he hopes or fears he may be?
- Is there a sense that those with whom the client has relationships hold a constant value for him which is unaffected by swings in his mood or needs?
- What quality of relationships does this person have with lovers and friends?

Johnson rightly suggests that ego is in part about an individual's ability to stand separately. In trauma counselling, whilst it is useful to know the extent of a client's robustness in this way, the client's ability to self-support is only part of the equation. Equally important is the client's ability to feel safe and develop trusting relationships. Forming a trusting relationship is crucial if the client is to approach his traumatic experience with you. This involves not only seeing how the client relates to others but also to you the therapist.

Anxiety

The way in which a person manages anxiety can indicate their ego strength. How does this person handle anxiety? Do they rise to meet everyday challenges or are they overwhelmed by the basic tasks of living? A traumatised person who is in a state of high anxiety may feel unable to cope with everyday tasks. He may not have the ability to draw upon his visual coping skills because they do not appear adequate to the tasks they now face. Where this is the case it is clear that exposure work would further submerge the person under the traumatic experience. Instead it would be more appropriate to increase his resources so that the anxiety level is diminished or becomes more manageable.

Containment

Egos that are stable can contain strong feelings. Is the client therefore able to hold intense feelings of grief or anger when he has suffered loss or frustration or do you have a sense that he is unable to deal with his present situation? Until an individual has some ability to move in and out of deep emotion with some fluidity it is not possible to carry out exposure work. The client will have emotions which will be experienced as too great or too frightening and will dissociate out of the exposure therapy to modulate their arousal.

Adaptive functions

Johnson writes that the well-developed ego has certain adaptive functions that include the ability to delay gratification, reality test and create solutions to difficulties. Some exposure-based therapy actively works toward a cognitive shift in the person's view of events, which implies the person is able to set up a disputational dialogue either with a counsellor, or within himself or herself. The ability to do so requires a strong enough ego to support such a dispute. Naturally where a client is unable to clearly check out perceptions or think creatively such work should be avoided. Likewise the ability to delay gratification is important in exposure work. Most clients will experience some level of psychological distress as they reconnect with their traumatic experience. In a way, in order to feel better they must first feel much worse. This being the case the ability to endure discomfort for the gratification of feeling better is a crucial skill. Clients without this ability will need to spend some time learning to tolerate discomfort and manage their distress before undertaking exposure treatments.

Regression

Can this person regress within a session and satisfactorily return to his adult part at the end of the time with the counsellor? The nature of most counselling is that it is bounded by time. After completing a session a client must travel home and be with family members who are perhaps unfamiliar with trauma symptoms or he may be alone with little or no support. The client must have the ability to sustain himself through the ongoing processing which accompanies some exposure techniques without ready access to the containing presence of his counsellor. This being the case, if a person is unable to regress and then return to adult competency within a session, it would be unwise for him to undertake exposure-based therapy.

Dissociation

In working with trauma it is essential to be aware of the purpose and function of dissociation. Dissociation is neither unusual nor pathological. It is in fact an innately human skill that enables us to become lost in our daydreams, absorbed in a book or engrossed in some everyday activity that we enjoy. It is a state of 'double consciousness' (TACT 2000) where we appear both conscious and yet unaware of our surroundings. It is in a sense our way of giving 'selective attention' to what interests us. Indeed dissociation can in its mildest form be a useful part of the counselling process where the counsellor himself is able to observe his own actions and responses as he works with clients.

Dissociation can be more profound and feel less controlled when it is part of an instinctive self-preserving response to a traumatic experience. In these situations we experience more 'stimulation' or incoming information about an experience than we have the ability to integrate, and we may 'phase out'. Blocking out the external world or locking on to some particular aspect of the incident or a tiny detail on the periphery of our awareness is a means by which we can limit the stimulation. Dissociation can be the result of either external stimulation when what we see, hear or sense is overwhelming, or internal stimulation when what we feel or come to know is too much to comprehend.

As a way of surviving dissociation is a great tool, however when a person uses dissociation habitually and it interferes with their ongoing relationships with others, then it is clearly unhelpful.

Making a connection

In outlining the four-session model Alison Dunn (Chapter 4) describes a pivotal point in the first session. We call this 'noticing' (see p. 103). This is a moment critical to engagement and ultimately to recovery. Here the counsellor bridges the self-protective psychic barrier surrounding the client and initiates the journey toward reconnection with ordinary life. Others have written about this more fully. Ron Kurtz (1990) calls this 'making contact' whilst Eugene Gendlin (1996) describes it as focusing in his extensive work on 'focusing-orientated psychotherapy'. Essentially both Kurtz and Gendlin noticed that successful therapy occurred when clients were assisted to notice meaningfully their present physical, cognitive and emotional experience. Turning away from narrative and giving attention to embodied feeling the therapist is able to capture in a statement the client's 'here-and-now' experience. This 'felt sense' usually has a physical expression and by noticing this the therapist draws in from the periphery of the client's awareness the barely conscious and unarticulated present needs. The story of Ade illustrates this:

Ade came to counselling following an assault. Initially he made little eye contact and talked nervously about his journey to the session. It was as though he was preoccupied, wanting to be present and yet distracted in some way. As he began to explain why he wanted to see me, he stoically recounted the story of the vicious assault he had undergone. It was as though he was alone in the room, lost in his own world. As he described the first blow he received, he took a sharp intake of breath and his shoulders began to squeeze together as if constricted. As he continued to speak, he began to squirm in his seat, moving his shoulders apparently to release the tension from them, and yet all the while he continued self-absorbed in his story, seemingly unaware of his physical discomfort. There was a pause and I interjected, 'As you say all

this you stop breathing and have terrible pain in your shoulders.'
There was an immediate freeing of breath and his shoulders released.
Ade looked up and replied, 'You noticed.' He then began to describe
his general physical discomfort since the assault, his poor appetite and
sleeplessness. As he spoke he was able to follow the rising tensions in
his body and importantly was able to relate these to me.

This extract describes 'noticing' which is a moment of intimate connection.
It commonly occurs in first trauma counselling sessions. It is the beginning
of the dissolution of the psychic defences necessary at the time of the
trauma. The protection, which dissociation initially affords but which by
remaining active creates individual distress, begins to melt in the face of
person-to-person contact. With noticing, the counsellor conveys that the
client's distress is recognised, acknowledged and may be freely discussed. It
is a process whereby the client appears to show his traumatic wound and in
which the counsellor, if vigilant, is presented with an opportunity to show
his empathy. Essentially it is where the client is seen to be bigger and more
important than his traumatic experience. Establishing this type of rapport is
more important than gathering facts and will of itself enable the counsellor
to glean relevant information in a way which is helpful to the client. It must
therefore take priority when assessing.

*

So what is hoped for here is that assessment becomes, in essence, a
collaborative decision-making process about what is needed by this particular client just now. Counsellor and client together must determine this,
and if they are uncertain, the counsellor can draw on knowledge of what
has been helpful to others in the past. Following a traumatic experience this
can be many things including: the need to keep warm, have food, shed
tears, sit in silence, receive information, be with family or friends, and,
should they wish to talk about and explore the impact of this incident on
their lives, the opportunity to speak to a counsellor. All of this may appear
elementary yet it is amazing how the simplest knowing may be swept aside
in the face of traumatic events.

To conclude, there is a simple and yet profound difference between
assessment based on relationship and the straightforward collection of
information. Rafael Campo (1997), the physician turned poet, captures this
difference when he speaks of the distinction between listening to a patient's
heartbeat and listening to the patient's heart. Assessment is a complex and
heartfelt process. There is much information in this chapter to take in. If

there is an expectation that you should now be able to 'do it' perfectly then you set a high goal for yourself. However if through practice you hold on to the basic belief that the relationship with the client must always take precedence and information must be thoroughly and thoughtfully gathered, then effective assessment will be the ultimate result.

Chapter 3

Resourcing the trauma client

Emerald-Jane Turner and Francesca Diebschlag

Connections

Imagine the intricate web of perceptions, sensations, relationships and actions that connect us to life: the feeling of the sun on your face, your feet touching the earth, the memory of a favourite grandparent, the smile on your child's face. Recall the tasks that give structure to your day and your life: feeding the birds, pruning the roses, walking the dog, going to work.

An unresolved traumatic event can break these connections and alters our sense of belonging in the world, and even in our bodies. We may find our hearts racing, or the appearance of strange and distressing symptoms like breathlessness or migraine, experiences we don't associate with our 'normal' selves. We feel alienated from ourselves, strangers in a strange land, where life is pervaded by an unreal or nightmare quality.

For many people, their only wish is to return to their old, 'normal' self, for things to once again be the way they have always known them, and for the restoration of some sense of their familiar place in the world.

Trauma is a natural part of the human condition. It is an aspect of suffering, and, at its most profound, an opportunity to discover and embody compassion for ourselves and others. The person who has suffered trauma knows – perhaps reluctantly – that one day we all will die. Innocence is lost and 'terrible knowledge' is gained.

When a person comes to see us as counsellor, it is often to pick up the frayed and broken threads of life again, to make sense of and find meaning in experiences that have severed them from their familiar relationships with themselves, other people, and an orderly world. Traumatization is not an individual experience; it inevitably impacts on relationships, families and the society in which we live. It can be passed down through generations. An individual's healing can likewise produce ripples with far-reaching consequences in family, social and even global structures.

In some societies the negotiation of this passage is ritualized; the initiation into the state of knowing is organized and deliberate, and the transition from one state to another is supported by tradition and community. Sadly, for both individuals and our society as a whole, we in the West have few such opportunities for initiation.

In the model that we are about to propose, the chaos that swirls in the wake of trauma is not an unruly symptom to be eradicated; it is the turbulence of a phase change, an opportunity to allow a new and more complex organic order to emerge. To wilfully attempt to impose the old order on this new phase is a form of violence; moreover, it is rarely successful, and even then at a terrible cost. Let us assume that catastrophes can present themselves as growth points, not in some 'New Age' sense that everything happens for the best, and that we must only 'positively affirm' their benefit, but rather in the sense that calamity can open us to the possibility of deepening our understanding that chaos and order, good and evil, do indeed exist side by side, and that life is, in the words of Jon Kabat-Zinn (1996), a 'Full Catastrophe'.

Recognising developmental wounds

When clients present themselves, they may do so with a specific event or trauma in mind. However, for many people developmental and traumatic wounds overlap and we find ourselves as counsellors needing to know how to respond to and contain their experience in appropriate ways. Developmental issues are those that involve incomplete or unsatisfactory negotiation of particular issues during the process of maturation.

A body-centred approach that recognises this originated from the work of Wilhelm Reich, further developed by Alexander Lowen as Bioenergetic Analysis, which is described in detail at the beginning of Chapter 5 by Carrie Jess. As she explains, the past two decades have seen this work expanded in various directions by individuals such as John Pierrakos (Core Energetics), David Broadella (Biosynthesis) and Ron Kurtz (Hakomi Body-Centered Therapy).

The map of character 'defensive strategies' that is now a significant part of Hakomi Therapy finds its roots in Lowen's character types. Over twenty years, Kurtz and his colleagues have evolved a way of understanding developmental wounding and consequent defensive strategies through character types that are reflected in the physical form as well as many other aspects of a person.

Looking at the animal world may help us to understand the purpose and meaning of strategies. A moth may be seen to have large spots on its wings so that when viewed from above by birds – potential predators – they may resemble the eyes of a bigger animal. This exemplifies a strategy which is aimed at fooling or deceiving others into thinking that you are bigger, stronger or more powerful than you really are, thus keeping potential threats at bay. Strategies serve the purpose of protecting us from experiences that are perceived as life-threatening or unbearably painful, and over which we have no control. Some typical strategies are taking the shape of a body that looks tougher than it is, or a body that is designed to keep busy in order not to feel worthless, or a collapsed body that has little energy and appeals to others to look after it. There is also a stage of development where developmental and traumatic wounding cannot be separated, and dissociation is an integral part of the character strategy.

The character strategies are based on certain key developmental issues during maturation, particularly from the pre-natal stage to roughly the age of seven. As we negotiate each stage of development the issues change, so that safety, support, autonomy, responsibility and the right to be loved are each addressed as we progress on our journey. When for some reason a stage is not successfully completed, for example, when a mother is unable to support or nourish the child fully, or the environment is unable to welcome the newborn in a safe and loving way, then the child develops strategies to cope with what may be experienced as intense pain or a threat to its very being. For a full description of the map of character strategies it is useful to refer to *Hakomi Body-Centered Psychotherapy* by Ron Kurtz (1990: 24).

To help clarify how this translates into life experience it may be helpful to refer to Chapter 1, in which Thom Spiers describes his work with Sue (see pp. 30–34). As we read his case study of Sue, we become aware of how unprotected she was as a child, yet as a grown woman she describes her body as strong. The strength of her body gives no apparent clue to the vulnerability and shame inside her. Indeed it has become so much a part of her that Sue herself believes that she is able to withstand many difficult experiences. Her body has organized itself in a way that offers its own protection and has an ability to endure ongoing abusive situations. At what he sees as a turning point in the work, Thom is able to provide the missing experience for Sue by taking over protecting her and allowing the exiled child to return.

As therapists it can help to have a map in order to see beyond strategy in a compassionate way. Focusing on childhood development, we can view strategies as strengths that a child develops as a way of dealing with their particular life situation; therefore they can be viewed as functional rather than malfunctional. However, every function that is overdeveloped leaves another underdeveloped, and will eventually result in an inability to respond with flexibility to life, leading to unconscious and automatic behaviour. With this in mind, we can look to some aspects of strategy as strengths and resources to be called upon consciously to help us become more resilient or to cope better. For example, someone with the strategy of withdrawing might tend to find their resources in fantasy or intellectual pursuits.

In Sue's situation her strength and endurance had become her only option rather than something to be called upon when appropriate. Saying 'no' would be another possible option, and it can be seen that as therapy progressed many others started to present themselves. Her unconscious strategic behaviour had led to her habitually making particular choices in her life, around relationships and work for example, in an effort to keep herself safe, while at the same time they limited her. Over time, this is what can happen as we become fixed into a particular pattern; our inability to go beyond what we know prevents us from flowing with life.

In times of stress or danger, strategies are allies that get us through; they are automatic and appear to be our best hope. Thus when a client comes to us in a time of crisis their characteristic developmental strategies are usually in operation. This is apparent in Carrie Jess's case study of Emma (see pp. 142–155). Emma is described as carrying around an 'unspoken slogan', 'Nobody's support can be relied upon or trusted, better only to trust myself.' Using the Hakomi character map we would read this as a 'core belief' concerning nourishment and support, arising from particular circumstances in Emma's early development. This belief would more than likely have influenced many of Emma's life choices, but becomes very obvious in the circumstances leading up to, and following, the trauma of her sister's death. Emma's breathing is mentioned as being 'shallow', an observation that can be viewed in terms of strategy, in that even her ability to take in nourishment through breathing, our most fundamental relationship with life, is limited. It appears that the strategy that has been most effective in her life to protect her against the unbearable pain of needing (but not getting) support and nourishment has been one of doing things herself and relying on no one. This would be one way of dealing with a lack of nurturing, but is often found to be punctuated with periods of collapse and hopelessness. Stephen Johnson (1985) writes about this very descriptively in his book, *Characterological Transformation, the Hard Work Miracle*.

Although developmental and traumatic wounds often overlap, work with character requires a fundamentally different approach from work with trauma. It is essential that counsellors take great care in compiling a personal history and distinguishing between developmental and traumatic wounds.

So, how are traumatic wounds different?

Trauma is held in the body

In his research and experience in the field of trauma, Dr Peter Levine (1997: 18) looks to the animal kingdom to understand the physiological process and implications of trauma and shock. He describes shock as being 'in the nervous system, not the event'. As counsellors this is a very important concept to understand, otherwise we may find ourselves caught up in the compulsive retelling of events and the reliving of violent emotions, becoming unwitting agents in a process of retraumatisation in which an already overwhelmed nervous system continuously revisits the very situation that led to its breakdown.

Our model draws from the model of the 'triune brain' articulated by McLean (Koestler 1976: 277–278) and further developed by Jantsch, Ledoux and others. To state it very simply, there are three distinct anatomical parts of the brain, which roughly correspond to three distinct types of function.

In all vertebrates, the oldest part of the brain, both in terms of evolution and individual development, is the 'reptilian' brain. In primitive animals it is the highest centre available for coordinating behaviour. It handles the vegetative involuntary functions, which include sensation, movement and sensory perception. It has relatively fixed modes of operation, which we share with reptiles, fish, birds and other mammals, and it has very little capacity for choice: it has a job to do and it does it. In terms of individual development, this area develops first; it functions even in the womb.

As we develop emotionally, the lower mammalian brain, or limbic system, plays a fundamental role in emotional behaviour. It has a greater capacity than the reptilian brain for learning new approaches and solutions to problems on the basis of immediate experience. But, like the reptilian brain, it does not have the ability to put its feelings into words. The human limbic system is much more highly structured than that of lower mammals, but its basic organization and chemistry are very similar.

The neo-cortex, developing between the ages of two and three, gives us the capacity for symbolic logic and language. The neo-cortex allows us to process information in the ways characteristic of the self-reflexive mind.

We start our lives processing our experience through the reptilian brain, from the 'bottom up', as it were. As we mature, we eventually switch to 'top-down' processing, in which the cortex takes over and our thoughts run our life. Although the three parts of the brain interact in complex ways, generally for most of us, cognitive processing takes precedence over emotional processing, which in turn takes precedence over sensory-motor processing.

In an emergency, however, the reptilian brain takes over, and initiates an automatic, involuntary sequence of physiological responses, which we know as the 'fight or flight' response. This response is actually a complex sequence of actions which can be easily observed in animals; it includes arousal, hypervigilance and muscular and chemical changes which enable the animal to defend itself or escape. Once the danger has passed, animals will discharge the arousal by running and/or shaking; they then sleep and their systems reorganize and return to normal.

But as humans, all too often we don't return to normal. When we survive a life-threatening experience, the content of the experience and its meaning become inextricably tangled up with our physiological response. We are rarely supported in discharging the nervous arousal; with few exceptions, we are prevented from doing so by circumstances or a sense of propriety. So we live with it, and hyperarousal becomes part of our sensory-motor patterning, ready to be triggered by any external or internal stimulus which shares any element of content with the traumatic event.

As the reptilian part of our brain is all about survival and our ability to respond to what it perceives as life-threatening situations, it does not, for example, distinguish between a surgeon's knife and a physical attack. In both cases it activates the central nervous system in order to cope with this threatening event. Our natural reaction to being cut with a knife would be either to flee, or to fight for survival and defend ourselves in some way. These instinctive responses mobilize a tremendous amount of both physical and emotional energy, but our higher cortex also comes into play, imposing cognitive responses which may cause us to belittle the event or try to suppress our feelings. If the natural process of trembling or shaking occurs, as it would in another mammal, we may try to control or stop it; well-meaning friends or medical personnel may distract us from the process and encourage us to 'pull ourselves together'.

In circumstances where fight or flight is not possible, or if the individual's defensive response to the event was unsuccessful, or if the arousal is maintained longer than the body can sustain it, the nervous system falls back on another instinctive response and 'freezes'. When energy mobilized for defence cannot be expressed it becomes bound up in the nervous system, creating immobilization and dissociation. Animals 'caught in the headlights' cannot move; other animals 'play dead' when threatened. It is important to realize that freezing is a highly charged state. It contains all the energy that would have been expressed in fight or flight, and the process of recovery from a state of immobilization requires the discharge of this hyperarousal.

The ability to fight or flee are resources that can save our lives. If the situation is one in which they can effectively be employed, then we survive. The recovery process can then unfold: we may experience trembling or shakiness followed by euphoria, elation and an upsurge of energy. As we return to a baseline state, we bring with us newly gained knowledge and experience; we know that we have survived, and that can strengthen our resources for the future.

Not every traumatic event results in traumatization. Indeed, if the individual is successful in meeting the perceived threat, such experience can ultimately be life-enhancing: the person has proved her competency, and gains both physical and psychological confidence. In short, she has learned something and her life is richer for having survived the experience. If the inner resources of the individual are sufficient, and appropriate familial, social and, where appropriate, medical support are provided, the nervous system arousal resolves and the person regains a healthy capacity for flexible responsiveness.

If, however, the recovery process gets interrupted for any number of reasons, then hyperarousal remains undischarged from the system. The physical signs of such arousal – for example, increased heart rate, dry mouth, trembling and feelings of panic – are normal and give us a survival edge in life-threatening circumstances. When they become chronic, lingering on long after the event, it is quite a different matter. Freezing can likewise become a chronic state when the recovery process is not completed, producing chronic or episodic feelings of paralysis, flat affect or 'spaciness'. Post-traumatic stress disorder commonly features both states, with the traumatized individual swinging between a sort of glazed numbness and emotional outbursts of inappropriately violent anger or fear. Over a period of months to years, the person may identify with these symptoms; they seem to become part of their personality. Under the influence of long-term nervous system arousal, physiological responses change over time, predisposing the person to chronic physical problems. So much of the person's energy and attention are caught up in the chronic arousal and freezing that their ability to deal with present-day challenges is compromised; furthermore, their strange behaviour patterns undermine both intimate and professional relationships. In this way, post-traumatic stress disorder sets people up for retraumatization.

Dissociation

When the parts of the self – body, emotions and intellect – are mutually associated and aligned, we have a definite sense of self; our thoughts, feelings and sensations are congruent and fluid, and we can respond appropriately to both inner and outer experience.

Dissociation is a breakdown in the continuity of a person's felt sense, resulting from a partial loss of function of one or more of these parts, or from a lack of congruence between them, so that some parts of the self are not present to the whole. It is essentially a lack of presence, a gap in consciousness, and usually occurs when we are unable to tolerate some aspect of experience. Traditional cultures considered this to represent the loss of some part of the soul. To the extent we are dissociated, we are less alive.

In traumatic circumstances, the psychic numbing of dissociation is an important survival mechanism in that it provides us with the means to cope with overwhelming stimuli when an experience exceeds our capacity to integrate and assimilate. It allows us to endure extremes of pain, terror and hopelessness that are beyond endurance. Indeed, the violence of trauma is compounded when dissociation is denied the victim, as in the case of a torture victim who is forced to remain conscious.

There is a direct relationship between dissociation and resources, since it is our resources which determine our capacity to process and integrate experience. The more other resources are available, the less need there is to fall back on dissociation, either in one's response to the original event, or in its aftermath.

Dissociation can manifest in many different ways. One individual may demonstrate more or less complete amnesia of a traumatic event (a disruption of cognition), while another may recall the event itself, but be disconnected from any feeling about it (a numbing of emotion). Sometimes dissociation can manifest as euphoria, which may feel like a spiritual or ecstatic state, but is ungrounded.

A typical feature of post-traumatic states is an apparent compulsion to re-experience the trauma, both within the context of therapy – for example rushing headlong into traumatic memories which bring on hyperarousal and dissociation – and in life. (In fact, it often appears that life conspires to provide us with opportunities to renegotiate traumatic situations.) It is a very important part of the work to know when to slow someone down and stabilize them, even if it means that the story does not unfold immediately.

Most victims of trauma suffer some degree of dissociation from physical sensations and impulses connected with the traumatic event. There is in fact a cultural bias in developed countries to distract ourselves from sensations and impulses. Even in physical and psychological health, many if not most of us are largely unaware of bodily sensations much of the time. Physical trauma compounds this cultural tendency, because physical pain and injury tell us that the body is not a safe place to be. Working with trauma through the body, by gradually assisting the client to reassociate with physical sensations and impulses, is an important approach to healing such wounds.

We have all suffered injuries and accidents. Most people recover from injuries, accidents and even horrors without persistent symptoms. Why do some individuals fail to recover fully?

It is the degree of dissociation that makes the difference between resolution and healing on the one hand, and post-traumatic stress disorder on the other. With parts of the self missing, how can we possibly process and integrate the experience? Dissociation may appear to be a survival resource, but if we don't come back, time stops. We can remain locked for years in a time warp in which every moment is *that* moment, and every stimulus is potentially threatening.

The traditional shaman, in retrieving the lost soul, calls it back to the body. How can we do this?

Resourcing

A resource is 'Something that can be turned to for support or help . . . An ability to deal with a situation effectively' (American Heritage Dictionary

1969). In the context of trauma work, resources are those awarenesses, abilities, objects, energies and connections that support a person not only in surviving, but also in maintaining a sense of inner integrity and relationship in the world, a sense of one's 'place in the family of things'.

There are many kinds of resources; they may be external or internal, and are often context-specific. On the physical level, our bodies may be strong or weak, healthy or sickly, attractive or not. External physical resources include things like housing, transportation and economic security. Emotionally, we may have resilience and optimism; externally, we may have a network of compassionate support. Intellect, knowledge and the ability to think clearly and quickly help us to flourish; this requires access to education, teachers, books and so on. Transpersonal resources may be particularly important in trauma, and range from a felt connection to God, spiritual guides, or Nature, to meditation practice or participation in a spiritual community such as a church or group rituals.

Everyone who arrives in our treatment room brings with them resources, things that have enabled them in their lives. It is from this viewpoint that we can start to become curious about the person and how they carry with them the seeds of empowerment. Resources are the material that lead to empowerment. The concept of empowerment is of great significance when working with clients who have not sufficiently negotiated a traumatic experience. With disempowerment comes a risk of becoming overwhelmed, with nothing to draw on but our reptilian brain sending messages of 'fight, flee or freeze'. Resourcing helps deactivate post-traumatic states such as hyperarousal or freezing.

As counsellors, we all have the ability to find resources, and we need to develop a fine nose for smelling them out, encouraging them to rise to consciousness and framing them to open up new options and choice for our clients. Invoking resources skilfully helps minimize traumatization; if a client can remember and thus connect with them when freezing or hyper-arousal start to activate, they can provide an experience that differs from the original one. Resources can be the simplest things and yet, under extreme life circumstances, can keep the thread of hope alive.

Resourcing in action

The therapist's attitude and intention

Our intention and attitude as therapists have a profound effect on the therapeutic process. Our beliefs, our need to get things right or to please, to know or be in control, all these attitudes and a multitude of others enter into the relationship with our clients.

As practitioners of Hakomi Body-Centered Psychotherapy, we apply certain principles that are seen to support both the therapist and the client in this process. These principles are rooted in spiritual traditions, particularly Buddhism and Taoism. They take much of the effort out of working and allow us to sit in deep trust and awareness; the journey is then allowed to become one of partnership, cultivating an attitude of curiosity and a sense of openness to outcome.

The principles can be described as: non-violence, mindfulness, unity, organicity and holism of body/mind and spirit. They combine to bring about a compassionate way of relating.

It may be useful to examine how these principles actually translate in a session with a client. Most therapists take for granted that non-violence is present when they are working, but some of the subtle ways that this principle may translate include letting go of agendas, allowing the client to be their own expert, and seeing defences or 'resistances' as offering valuable information as opposed to presenting the necessity for getting through or overcoming them.

Unity and organicity are about embracing all parts of ourselves, the dark and the light, going with the flow, having trust in the inherent wisdom of the organism to move towards healing, not feeling we have to fix someone. It is finding the place that can acknowledge that we are all interconnected, we all share suffering, that it cannot be measured but is simply part of the human condition. When we apply these perspectives the work takes on an atmosphere of adventure rather than being a job to perform. Relating aspects of body, mind and spirit to each other brings about integration and deepens the process.

Finally, mindfulness is the container that holds all the other principles. It is the ability to bear witness to yourself and another without judgement, bringing spaciousness and presence to the process, and is possibly the most profound tool that a therapist can cultivate.

To sit in these principles and apply them to ourselves as therapists as well as to our clients is not an easy task. It requires perseverance and humility. It takes a lifetime to practise, and perhaps the greatest gift is that our work affords us this opportunity.

Recognising and establishing resources

Using this model, when someone arrives in our office we want to know how they have got this far and what is *right* with them. What was important when they were growing up, and what makes life meaningful now? All of this information is essential to understanding how we can support the healing process.

One of the marks of a skilled therapist is the ability to sniff out our clients' resources, to bring them to consciousness and integration. How do we develop a 'nose' for resources? How can we recognize them when they appear in a session?

Resources facilitate presence. They support the return of our souls to the here and now. We can see our clients begin to arrive back in the room by changes in facial expression, a softening and expansion, a deepening of the breath and centre of gravity, a sense of settling. When they make eye contact they are inhabiting their eyes – there is someone home. Establishing resources is the cornerstone that supports the process of unfreezing and reassociation in trauma work. Bringing to consciousness the way that people already resource themselves can affirm empowerment and choice.

One way of establishing resources in the very first session is to ask the client if he or she can imagine or remember a person, place, object or favourite activity that gives him or her a feeling of love or wellbeing. Having identified this, it is then important to support the client in tracking the associated sensations into his or her body, grounding the experience in the here and now. Encourage the client to spend time with these sensations, to become really familiar with them and to practise recalling them so they can be easily accessed.

An example of this could be as follows:

THERAPIST: Just take a moment and notice if there is anything in your life at this time that helps you feel good. It may be a place you like to visit, a person or animal it feels good to be with, or an activity you take part in.

CLIENT: I really like walking on the Downs with my dog. I do that just about every day. (*As she says this, a small smile appears and her shoulders drop a little.*)

THERAPIST: It makes you feel good, huh?

CLIENT: Yeah, it sort of calms me down.

THERAPIST: So maybe you can recall walking with your dog right now. Imagine the view and let your body feel the movement in your feet and legs. Take your time. (*As the client does this, the therapist tracks her body for signs of relaxation, such as a deepening in the breath, softening of the face and body, skin colour changes, etc.*) Just become aware of sensations in your body as you recall this.

CLIENT: I notice that my stomach sort of relaxes . . . my breathing feels easier, I feel sort of warm and tingly and I can feel my back against the chair.

THERAPIST: See if you can stay with those sensations right now and really get familiar with them. There may be others you notice too . . . Just allow yourself to slow down and let your body have the experience of this . . .

After taking some time on this, it then helps to practise recalling the sensations. Spending time in this way, setting up a really grounded and resourced place to work from, creates options and fluidity in the process of therapy.

Coming into present time

In shamanic cultures when a person had been through some kind of over-whelming experience, a moderately difficult task, such as climbing a mountain to give offerings or thanks to the spirits, might be set for them to undertake. What was important was that the task would be one at which the participant would be likely to succeed, but it would require concentration in order to do so. When we think about this in terms of time and space, it is not the task itself that is important but the fact that in order to complete it the person would have to come into present time and inhabit their body. When working with trauma this is a fundamental requirement.

When someone has experienced trauma or overwhelming stress it is difficult to stay in present time as aspects of psychic and physical energy are frozen and trapped in the past. Consequently, there are distortions in the perception of time and space, and it is difficult to envisage a future that is different from the past. Time gets lumped together, which can precipitate feelings of anxiety and despair. Working with present experience is a valuable way of teasing this apart and facilitating the process of unfreezing. Yael Danieli (1998) notes that 'One needs to be present with the past long enough to allow integration of traumatic responses that have remained frozen in time, that is, those responses that have been operating outside of conscious awareness.'

When working with traumatized women, Dr Aangwyn St Just (1999) uses a variation of Jean Houston's 'yardstick of time' to introduce the idea that we have options in our perception of time and reality. The exercise involves choosing a stick and marking it into three zones representing the past, present and future, then becoming aware of the zone in which we spend most time. Clients are then invited to spend time in each zone for a set period. This gently introduces the idea of moving at will between the past, present and future, and returns a sense of fluidity to the normal flow of life.

As therapists, cultivating the ability to be present and mindful is essential if we are to encourage our clients to be here. There are several ways to aid clients in this process.

Developing a witness

In Hakomi Body-Centered Psychotherapy, Kurtz identifies a state of con-sciousness known in the Buddhist tradition as the principle of Mindfulness. It is a state in which we can be a non-judgemental witness to our experiences without adding to them or taking anything away from them. The capacity to do this enables us to create a sense of space and allows us to stand back a little. When working with trauma it is a powerful tool that helps uncouple emotion from sensation. It also aids empowerment.

Mindfulness helps support clients by focusing them on present experience, even as they are talking about past events. It allows them to report on feelings, thoughts, insights and sensations, helping to distinguish experiences from interpretation. When someone lacks the ability to witness – in other words, tends to identify totally with experiences – it is important to go very slowly and explore ways to support and develop this capacity.

The importance of slowing down

Developing mindfulness and slowing down go hand in hand. By slowing down we can allow awareness of subtleties and connections that would pass us by if we continued to travel at our everyday pace. Life happens very quickly for most individuals, and the opportunity to lower internal noise and take the time to listen to ourselves on many levels can feel strange for a lot of people.

Moreover, when we are uncomfortable or anxious most of us tend to increase the speed of our speech or move quickly on to something to distract us. While this may sometimes be a useful strategy, within the therapeutic context we can offer a different way to help bring the client's awareness back to present time. The ability to slow down and enter present time is essential in trauma work if we are to notice when the system starts to move toward overwhelm.

Because the nervous system becomes activated instinctively and instantly in response to distress, traumatic memories – along with all the feelings and dissociation that accompany them – can be triggered very quickly, catapulting the client into the past. Slowing down and taking things in bite-sized bits is essential if you and your client are to track dissociation. It is helpful to break down information and make it specific by asking questions that require attention to present time experience, such as, 'Just take a moment right now, and notice your breathing.' If you think about doing this as you read it, you may notice that you have to stop and mentally turn inward, while momentarily suspending your habitual patterns of attention.

This sort of intervention allows some space to develop in the process over a period of time. Slowing down mends broken connections and fragmentation. It also allows you as a therapist to keep checking that the person has access to their resources and is therefore not dissociating and pushing the trauma deeper into the system.

The art of tracking

Tracking is a skill that most of us employ unconsciously in our daily interactions with others. The chances are that part of what we refer to as our 'gut' feelings about another person are the outcome of tracking all the little things that are outside that person's consciousness, such as their breathing, skin colour, habitual gestures, tone of voice and a myriad other things. When we enter into ordinary conversation we can become entranced by words or the content of the story; tracking gives us another perspective and an opportunity to respond to what is happening in the present moment, paying attention to those signs that give us clues as to what that person's experience may be, beyond the realm of words.

When practised, tracking becomes an art form, helping us move into a level of relationship that reaches beyond everyday interaction. Training people in this practice on Hakomi workshops, we might have them close their eyes and track the quality in the client's voice, or we may have them move across the room so that they can see a session in progress without actually hearing anything, relying solely on body information. There is a wealth of untapped information waiting to be noticed that enables us to enter into meaningful communication. Ignoring these signs often results in therapy that can feel stale and lifeless.

In the field of trauma, tracking is invaluable, giving us clues to involuntary signs that indicate overwhelm is close by or happening at that moment. Changes in skin colour and moistness, eyes glazing over, lack of movement, shallow or increased breathing, dilation in the pupils – these are just some of the bodily signals of the nervous system starting to become activated, which can then alert us to slow the client down and bring them back into present experience. By tracking for such signs we can also encourage the client to learn to track for themselves and eventually start to interrupt the cycle that is so debilitating.

Teaching ourselves to become trackers can be fun. Try turning down the sound on the TV or listening with your eyes closed; become aware of people from a distance and notice what goes on in everyday interactions with new eyes.

Working with sensation

If, as we have said, trauma is in the nervous system rather than in the event, then working with physical sensation is the key to resolution. Focusing on bodily sensation gives us a link to present time. Emotions and thoughts take us into the past and the future; sensation is right *now*. A person who is traumatized is to some degree stuck in the moment of the traumatic event, and has lost her connection with *now*. The mind and emotions are caught up in the past; establishing a connection to immediate bodily experience, even if the experience is one of a racing heart, grounds the person in the present. By staying with sensations, slowing down and keeping a sense of spaciousness, the body can start to process traumatic shock.

The problem, of course, is that physical sensation is tangled up with emotion and cognition. The mind groups experience, so that the racing heart = terror = car crash. PTSD is a loop in which the cognitive faculty interprets *any* nervous system arousal as fear or rage, and the emotion in turn stimulates an intensified physical response. By the time this loop has gone round a time or two, instinctive survival responses have overridden the cognitive function, a state of panic or rage prevails, and there is no chance of the ordinary enjoyment of everyday life, much less the processing of the traumatic memory.

We can begin to tease apart these elements of experience by asking for specific information. Perhaps the client presents with a 'feeling' (affect) of terror. So we can ask a question like 'What sensation in your body is telling you that you feel terrified?' The actual *sensation* may be good or neutral, a rush of adrenaline. We invite the client to check out her present time experience, here and now, in an attitude of curiosity, of interested self-study without judgement or interference.

An attitude of 'wilfully passive' self-observation allows us to expand the experience, to notice *what else* is happening. After all, most of our body is functioning exactly as it should. By learning to focus one's attention gently and patiently on inner body sensation, it is possible to 'unhook' the *sensations* of arousal (such as rapid heartbeat, sweating, dry mouth, nausea, shaking) from the *affective* and *cognitive* elements that normally accompany them. This breaks the positive feedback loop of physical sensations of arousal giving rise to strong emotions and/or intrusive thoughts – which in turn intensify the sensations – and replaces it with an attitude of curiosity and benign self-study.

As the client stays present with sensation and follows it in mindfulness, the body may start to tremble or shake as the system discharges some of the shock of the trauma. It is important not to interfere with this process, but simply to allow it to occur, while tracking for signs of dissociation or overwhelm.

Our culture has trained us to keep things *happening*. There is generally no support for attention to sensation, which is often subtle and invisible to the outside observer. But sensation is precisely how our bodies inform us of inner states, of our relationship with the external world, and of what we need in order to heal. Even emotions have their roots in the felt experience of bodily sensations. Our bodies have a lot to say to us, if only we can learn to listen.

We're often drawn to try to understand and explain sensation so we can do something about it. We are also culturally conditioned to ignore and work through pain. Just being with uncomfortable sensations, letting awareness rest on them without trying to change or avoid them, can allow those sensations and impulses to move and change spontaneously and organically, revealing healing impulses toward recovery.

The experience of pleasure is, for many people, less familiar than discomfort. You don't have to go out and find pain – it announces itself loudly enough. Pleasure is a difficult experience for some people, and particularly for those locked in a traumatic memory which is telling them they are in constant danger. To begin to reinstate the resource of pleasurable sensation, we can ask something like: 'Is there a place in your body you like/trust/feel good in?' If there is none, there might be a place that feels better than the rest.

Finding and giving attention to pleasant or restful sensations can return a world of lost experience to such a person.

Creating choice and options

One of the key factors that makes an event traumatic, rather than merely painful or unpleasant, is that choice is taken away and we lose our ability to say 'No!' In working with trauma, we try to re-establish that choice. We can start this process within the therapeutic relationship by asking questions such as 'Where do you want to sit?', 'Do you want to do this at all?' You can ask your client 'What would you tell other people in a similar situation, that could really be helpful for them?', 'What would you tell a therapist about how to work with someone in your situation?'

Give your client as much opportunity as possible to self-regulate. Ask her if what you're doing is enough, too much, or not enough; once she can ask herself these questions, she's attending to herself, and more than halfway to being able to modulate her own arousal. Clients need to know, too, when they need to be more resourced.

You can teach clients to recognize their own dissociation, and contract with them to tell you when they feel themselves starting to disappear. They have a choice – they don't have to leave! If the traumatic memory is overwhelming, you can talk about the weather, or football.

Joni got very activated whenever she thought about an event that had occurred in early childhood. I worked with her for some time to teach her to recognize the physical sensations of arousal. The next time she started to experience these sensations, we took 'time out' and talked about gardening, which she finds grounding and nourishing. As her panic symptoms subsided, she suddenly looked up and said, 'I see what you're doing! I don't have to go into this!' This was a major turning point for her and, in her next session, she reported that since the last session, not only had she not experienced the symptoms of panic, but the bodyworkers she had been seeing had commented on a change in her posture and energy patterns.

Another basic resource often lost in trauma is the sense of containment of the self. Confidentiality is an important starting point in re-establishing containment. The therapeutic relationship is itself a container in which the therapist takes responsibility for the boundary. The more the client trusts you, the more she will be able to trust herself, and her own process.

When the client is unable to modulate her own levels of arousal and dissociation, the therapist can take over this function, and help to keep the client present in order to prevent overwhelming restimulation. Trauma work must sometimes be more directive than developmental work; it is sometimes necessary to interrupt a client who is on a fast track to hyper-arousal and dissociation, and bring her back.

Ultimately, the way to return to the client a sense of containment is to teach her to modulate her own arousal. She can learn to track her own body for the first signs of arousal, before it becomes overwhelming, and to break the loop by consciously shifting her attention on to something that is stabilizing and soothing. Just knowing what your triggers are, and that you can do something to avoid being overwhelmed, can in itself be empowering.

Finding resources

In the section that follows, we describe several types of resources. External objects (such as amulets) and events (such as ritual) can be seen as symbolic of inner states. It is these inner states that are the *real* resources, and this is why it is so important to work with the client's 'felt sense' of them, as described above in the section on 'Recognizing and establishing resources'.

The body as a resource

The body itself is our main resource for a sense of self, of presence and information about and relationship with the world. Our culture is not one that encourages the enjoyment, or even the awareness, of physical sensation. Many of us never fully develop a somatic sense of self, and physical trauma tends to undermine what body awareness we do have. In the wake of trauma, the body may become a place of pain, a reminder of the failure of physical defence; we may feel that our bodies have let us down, or cannot be adequately protected. Withdrawal from a place of physical and emotional pain is a natural impulse. Reinstating the body as a resource is an essential early stage of healing from trauma.

Dr Aangwyn St Just (1999), the Director of the Colorado Institute for Social Trauma, is a Rolfer as well as a psychotherapist. She has experience of working with many women who have been sexually and pelvically traumatized, which has led her to establish that women who have suffered in this way withdraw awareness from the lower halves of their bodies, and particularly away from the pelvic region. 'The lack of awareness in the legs, and lower legs in particular, is often a remnant of a thwarted fight or flight response, where the women could do neither and froze. This lack of awareness in the lower body and lower legs specifically leaves women vulnerable to further trauma.'

When working with women in a natural environment, she realized the importance of the pelvic floor in grounding women, observing that they instinctively found ways to ground themselves through the pelvic floor by sitting, squatting and making contact with the earth. It is an important part of work with women that we find gentle and empowering ways to restore awareness in the lower half of the body.

Exercise programmes can help to discharge arousal, but certain types of exercise can also be grounding, and can help to re-establish awareness of positive embodied experience. Any *mindful* exercise, in which one is conscious of the working of the muscles, and of one's changing relationship to gravity, establishes a nourishing connection with the body. Yoga and Pilates, in which movement is done slowly and consciously, and coordinated with breathing, are good examples.

Although these approaches are a preparatory step to actually processing the traumatic event, they are profoundly therapeutic and may be sufficient in themselves to resolve many post-traumatic symptoms; they serve to reinstate the body as a source of information and pleasure, and open the way for reassociation. The magic of resourcing through body awareness is that we all carry it with us, everywhere and always, and can tune into it at any time as a resource. Listening to the body is literally attending to yourself.

Dissociation as a resource

People have all sorts of mechanisms for not being present in the moment. For a person suffering from the symptoms which accompany chronic hyperarousal, substance abuse, eating disorders and self-mutilation may be not only effective ways to dull out or rivet one's focus on to something else, but may be subjectively preferable to experiencing these symptoms. To the individual suffering from post-traumatic stress disorder, these behaviours may appear to be the only alternative to hyperarousal, and may thus come to be perceived as resources.

Stripping a person of these perceived resources without offering a healthier alternative, compounds the problem and does violence to the adaptive adjustments of the psyche. The overwhelming nature of trauma robs us of *internal* resources, such as confidence in our bodies and our capacity to deal with challenges. People become traumatized precisely *because* their internal and external resources were insufficient to allow them to recover on their own.

Humour as a resource

For some people humour is a lifeline that helps them stay connected and allows them a sense of space in the midst of overwhelming feelings. This was an important discovery for me when working with a client who frequently found herself 'frozen'.

Trying out different ways of resourcing and recognizing options around this frozen state, her ability to see the humour in life consistently brought her back into present time and relationship. What follows is a vivid description of the part that this resource plays in her healing process.

Laughter feels to me like a life force that bubbles up in the darkest moments. When I went to see a close friend recently who is very ill, the first night she was talking about wanting to end it all. The second night we were reading some self-help book on illness, taking the symptoms literally. We started laughing and laughing and laughing, it felt like all the darkness that had been there, all the despair just evaporated in that moment, as if we were turning from death to life.

It is such a physical response with a strong energetic change – from a heavy stuckness to a light, free-flowing, tingling aliveness. It is to me as cathartic as having a good cry. I don't think anything should be too sacred or too serious not to have humour in it.

Humour seems to strike very suddenly. As if I'm trudging along staring fixedly at my feet sinking into the mud and then I'm tripped up on my back in soft grass, looking up at the spacious blue sky. I'm in the same place, but how different it looks!

When I'm stuck in a frozen place I cannot connect with others. They seem alien painful presences intruding on the edge of my consciousness. Eye contact feels unbearable. But then laughter can suddenly trick me into contact. It's hard to laugh alone. And it feels a profound connection, a shared feeling/experience, that comes from the gut not the head.

It would be impossible for me to have a therapist I couldn't laugh with as well as cry. I think I would be buried under the weight of my own darkness.

As therapists it can be of great help to participate in a client's humour, recognizing when to engage appropriately, so that the sense of overwhelm recedes and a feeling of strength through humour can emerge. In the story of Demeter and Persephone, when Demeter had reached the end in her search for her beloved daughter and felt she could no longer carry on, along came the little belly goddess Baubo making lewd jokes and shaking her belly until Demeter could no longer resist, and through joining in the laughter once more found the strength to continue. Humour can make it possible for us also, to move from those paralysing or anxious states and reconnect with a part of ourselves that is strong and grounded.

Wearing our resources

Traditionally, amulets and talismans are objects which confer protection on the wearer. Most of us have favourite articles of clothing or jewellery that have what we might call 'sentimental value' – they give us, for whatever reason, a feeling of safety, comfort and connectedness. We cherish wedding rings, heirlooms, a favourite sweater, lucky shoes, photographs of our parents and our children, old love letters – souvenirs of times when we were rooted in joy, grounded in belonging.

When a client comes into the room, take a look at the kind of jewellery and colours they are wearing. Ask them to tell you something about them and notice the related sensations in their body. As they talk, track for signs of relaxation and warmth.

One woman I worked with was on the edge of becoming overwhelmed when I noticed a beautiful pair of heart-shaped earrings she was wearing. I asked her to tell me about them, and she started to describe how they represented her son and daughter. As she talked, she reached to touch them; her breathing calmed and she developed more space around her. Although it might seem that I was jumping away from important feelings by changing focus at that moment, it was important that she stay resourced and present. Drawing her attention to her earrings was a tangible way of doing this, and bringing her awareness to the meaning they held for her enabled her to use them to maintain a sense of connection at moments when she felt panic start to envelop her.

Another client wore a string of vibrant blue beads. When asked about them, she said they reminded her of the blue of the ocean where she had swum with dolphins. Talking about this experience and following the sensations evoked by it enabled her to stay on the edge of panic and move gently between safe and unsafe places, creating choice rather than overwhelm.

Neither of these two women consciously chose their jewellery as resources, but when asked about them they were very clear. Perhaps it would be interesting for us as therapists to look at the way we resource ourselves when working, making conscious choices to wear a particular colour, scarf or brooch that evokes connectedness and strength.

Sometimes objects that have the quality of amulets or talismans seem to find us by chance. This was the case with a woman I work with, who after a number of sessions appeared wearing a statuette of an African woman around her neck. This is how she describes her:

She was 10p from a charity shop although she looks African exotic. I put her on one day and she stayed tied to me. She is all woman, wholesome, nourishing and wise. She is in touch with all the natural cycles and moves between the realms of the spirit world and the natural world with intuition and ease. If you hold her and ask questions she has answers. They are direct, no room for doubt or procrastination. Her energy flows, unlike my stiltedness. She helps me when I'm raw. I dream about her. She is my Black Madonna.

This client, who was adopted at birth, has since discovered that the Black Madonna is the patron saint of abandoned children.

When my son had to go into hospital for major surgery several years ago, we bought him a beautiful crystal, and I made a little brocade bag for it. He clung to it during his stay in hospital and made a speedy recovery. Now he keeps it tucked away in his room, but it still comes out from time to time in moments when he feels the need for extraordinary support.

If, as the poem goes, we are all children of the universe, then these are our transitional objects.

The use of ritual in resourcing

We all have the ability to imbue actions or objects with symbolic meaning. The act of shaking hands, the marriage ceremony, drinking out of a special cup, any of these acts are rituals in that they are instilled with an inner meaning. Rituals can involve the community or be performed quietly alone. They may be highly stylized and developed as part of a culture or religion to be performed at set times, as in Holy Communion, or they may be an intensely personal and unique experience.

Rituals do not have to be exotic or require specialized knowledge. In their simplest form they require intent and attention. They are, however, a means to acknowledge, bring to consciousness, or lay to rest those things that call to us.

In her book *Women Who Run with the Wolves*, Clarissa Pinkola Estés (1998: 365) writes about *descansos*, little crosses or flowers that mark a spot where a death has taken place. They can be seen on the roads in Mexico, and similar places also spring up in this country. These informal shrines allow us to acknowledge that something has happened that has changed life forever. There comes a point in our lives when, having dwelt on the pain and been haunted by the images, we can start to heal and transform our experience. Ritual has an important place in this process.

As therapists we may feel wary of approaching this aspect of work, feeling that it is the territory of shamans or specially trained individuals. There are times when this is undoubtedly true, but if we listen to our clients we can support them in following their intuition, helping them ritualize simple actions, such as planting a tree or special rose, or, as in the case of one client, using the sea and pebbles as a way of integrating a traumatic experience. She describes how this transformed things for her after the loss of an unborn child:

> I was very apprehensive about what using ritual meant – some dark and dreaded thing I would have to do. It wasn't. Naming and sexing my child helped to actualise her presence. This done, I let my instinctive love of the sea and the pebbles help me to enact a simple ritual. I went alone to stand on the water's edge and called out her name. I said goodbye and said hello, picked up some pebbles and brought them home.

Performing this ritual allowed a feeling of peace to emerge and lay the trauma to rest, giving it a place to exist in the tapestry of this woman's life.

The Medical Foundation for Victims of Torture has a 'Garden of Remembrance' in London, which plays an important role in providing a safe space in which to perform rituals. Here there is a bread oven and the weekly ritual of baking bread is continued, gardens are planned, people and ways of living are remembered. Rituals take place involving planting herbs or making mosaics, as well as others that acknowledge the horror and terror that these people have endured and survived, thus enabling them to mourn for loved ones who have disappeared or never been buried. Experiences that go beyond words and understanding can be expressed and shared through ritual.

Community

In his book, *Ritual – Power, Healing and Community*, Malidoma Patrice Somé (1993: 69) describes his experience as a member of the Dagara tribe:

> A true community begins in the hearts of the people involved. It is not a place of distraction but a place of being. It is not a place where you reform, but a place you go home to.

Pat Ogden, who developed Hakomi Integrative Somatics, suggests that there are three factors which determine how easily a person will recover from any traumatic experience. The first is the person him or herself: how well resourced and integrated they are, what is their past history of trauma, how well they are supported by their belief system.

The second factor is the severity of the event itself: how profound the injury was, how long the event lasted, was it a single discrete event or an ongoing situation, what relational factors were involved, etc.

The third, and equally important, factor, is the presence or absence of active family and community support in the aftermath of the event. A child who escapes abuse and is then returned to the 'care' of the abuser is further traumatized by the lack of support. The trauma of a battered wife, who is forced by an unsympathetic community to continue to endure abuse, is compounded. The rape victim who faces accusations of having 'provoked' the rape may be more traumatized by these accusations than by the rape itself.

It is difficult to confront suffering, and there are many ways in which we can fail to do so. We fail when we blame the victim, when we make unrealistic demands that they 'get over it' quickly, when we imply that an injury or attack was deserved, and when we simply fail to respond with active compassion.

In her book *Trauma and Recovery*, Judith Lewis Herman (1992: 214) advocates the group as a powerful resource in the recovery process:

> The solidarity of a group provides the strongest protection against terror and despair, and the strongest antidote to the traumatic experience. Trauma isolates; the group re-creates a sense of belonging. Trauma shames and stigmatises; the group bears witness and affirms. Trauma degrades the victim; the group exalts her. Trauma dehumanizes the victim; the group restores her humanity.

Groups come in many different shapes, such as women's groups, psychotherapy or spiritual groups, and survivors' networks. Clients at a mid-stage of recovery may benefit from sharing experiences with others and can gain tremendous relief and mutual empowerment.

A supportive and sympathetic familial or social network can provide a deep sense of connection and belonging, a 'place to go home to', which is the context within which recovery is possible.

Nature as a resource

Nature is the ultimate resource. It is the great web of birth and growth, death and destruction, rebirth and regeneration, an endless font of creativity. Nature has its own rhythms of ebb and flow, bloom and decay, a regularity of activity and rest that resonates with our animal bodies and soothes wounds. So many of us are separated from this powerful resource, living as we do by the clock, surrounded by manmade shapes, with a desperate sense of alienation. Spending time in the elements can calm the nervous system and allow natural rhythms to re-establish themselves.

In 1990, the Medical Foundation for Victims of Torture pioneered a project for the treatment of trauma, which involved acquiring allotments for clients who were often from farming backgrounds but found themselves living cut off from nature in urban tower blocks. This was the beginning of the Natural Growth Project, which now has a large number of allotments and the Garden of Remembrance mentioned above. In these places people are encouraged to see that the sun, the earth and the elements are the same as the ones they have left behind. Tending the gardens evokes many metaphors for the human condition and both the old and new lives clients are struggling to come to terms with. 'The project is about destruction and disillusionment as well as growth,' says Jenny Grut, resident psychotherapist and project coordinator since its inception. However, it also reminds people 'that the earth here is the same earth that they come from'. One of the residents describes vividly how being in nature is a resource in an otherwise shattered life: 'When I garden I feel I have a pain-killer medicine to make me strong.'

Many of the refugees do not speak English, but, unlike other areas of the Foundation, Jenny does not rely on interpreters; the garden itself becomes the translator. Its capacity for exploration and connection is vast, and people work with failure, relentlessness and abundance, recognizing what *can* thrive, as distinct from what they may wish to be there. When someone stoops to weed a plot, their body may remember being incarcerated in a small cell; over time, tracking and working gently with sensation, the body may begin to allow new experiences to take place, and a sense of becoming more present may arise.

In *The Faithful Gardener*, Clarissa Pinkola Estés (1995: 66) writes eloquently of her uncle, a survivor of some of the worst horrors of the Second World War. When confronted with yet another grievous loss, he set a ground fire on his plot of land and let it lie fallow so that a new forest might seed itself:

> I am certain that in every fallow place, new life is waiting to be born anew. And more astonishing yet, that new life will come whether one wills it or not. One may try to uproot it each time, but each time it will re-root and re-found itself again. New seed will fly in on the wind, and it will keep arriving, giving many chances for change of heart, return of heart, mending of heart, and for choosing life again at long last . . .

Nature is not something apart from us; we are as much a part of the natural world as the trees. Contact with nature, particularly with wilderness, can remind us of 'that faithful force that is born into us, that one that is greater than us, that calls new seed to the open and battered and barren places, so that we can be resown' (Estés 1995: 67).

Resourcing the therapist

In his book *Becoming A Full Human Being*, Chogyam Trungpa (1985: 126), a well-known Buddhist teacher, says:

The basic work of . . . psychotherapists in particular is to become full human beings and to inspire full human beingness in other people who feel starved about their lives.

This idea speaks to us of resourcing ourselves as therapists and of making this our main task in our work. Working regularly with clients who are traumatized can restimulate our own feelings of overwhelm. It is essential that we have knowledge of and access to those things that strengthen us and bring us back to the joy of being alive. Hattie Berger describes in detail the complexities of maintaining the stability and spaciousness necessary for this work in Chapter 7, 'Trauma and the therapist'.

Spending time listing our own resources and calling up the 'felt sense' of them is a worthwhile activity, as is time spent developing new resources. It is also helpful to study what really happens when we go into overwhelm, so that we can recognize warning signs and give ourselves appropriate attention.

Our own therapy – the exploration of our inner worlds, our motivation for working in this field, and its impact on our lives – is essential. Without it, we can ourselves become dissociated and cut off from our clients. Each of us has our limits in terms of how many clients we can stay present and associated with at any given time. This may mean that it is necessary to limit the number of our clients, to say 'No' to a prospective new client, or at times to take a break from work completely.

Carrying on regardless in times of overwhelming stress may feel necessary, but in the long run is a process of diminishing returns. Supervision can help us recognize the places in ourselves that are disconnected or unresourced, and a relationship with a capable and experienced supervisor can itself provide safe haven in a storm, as can the support of understanding peers and colleagues. It is helpful to have a supervisor with specific knowledge of traumatic transference, as described in Chapter 7.

Balancing our work with providing physical, emotional and spiritual nourishment for ourselves lets clients observe and model this possibility for themselves. Allowing one's practice to fluctuate and reflect the demands of one's life at any given time requires extraordinary trust and willingness to act on the greater picture. Knowing when we need to be out in nature, to spend time with family or friends, to engage in spiritual practice or to immerse ourselves in a creative venture demands that we listen and relate to ourselves with as much sensitivity and compassion as we give to our clients. Developing a regular discipline such as journaling or meditation can be of great value in keeping our own needs in the picture.

Trauma as transformation

Trauma is a descent into an unknown world, where the familiar landmarks have lost their meaning. Descent is an essential part of human experience in general, and of the 'hero's journey' in particular. Robert Bly (2001) adopts the term *katabasis* for the sudden sinking through the floor, the way 'down and out' that separates the questing hero from his companions and their support, and propels him forward in his growth.

But *katabasis* has its proper time in an individual's life. It properly comes not at the beginning of his journey, but only after the hero has been initiated into his quest, and has received gifts that will sustain and guide him through the trials and tests along the way. There are many versions of these gifts. Here is one possible map.

The first gift is the willingness to inhabit one's body, to experience the myriad sensations that arise in sometimes mysterious ways from physical embodiment. To be alive in one's body is to hear the symphony of notes, tones and timbres produced by the movement of muscles, ligaments, bones, organs, fluids, breath and energy. Listening to the wisdom of our bodies, the legacy of millions of years of evolution, allows us to be informed by messages telling us of the position of our limbs, the movement in our joints, our relationship to gravity, the flow of bodily fluids, the movement of our breath, songs of pleasure and of pain, of impulses to run, to fight, to stretch, constrict, relax, dance.

The second gift is the willingness to feel, to embrace the full range of emotions: to be stirred by the ardour of passionate love, to suffer pain, to be sensitive to the poignancy of loss, touched by intense joy, and moved by vehement anger. It is indeed a precious gift to be strong enough to contain the heat of emotion without losing oneself in it. It is the foundation for social relationships, for cooperation and community.

The third gift is the capacity to think, to handle concepts, to name things. It includes the functions of language, of logic, decision making and will. Cognitive competence allows us to modulate the other aspects of experience so as to create coherence and focus in our lives. It lets us play chess, invent spaceships that fly to the moon, and will ourselves to work through pain, panic and grief to rescue a friend from a burning house. It is the channel through which we endow our world with meaning.

The fourth gift is the willingness to be aware of suffering, that bears witness to the events of our lives without identifying with them. It gives us ears to listen to our dreams and intuitions. It is also the divine guide within us, our genius, our essence, and the invisible presence of the ancestors, or guardian angels. It is eternal, and it can never suffer damage. This gift puts our experience into the context of the journey, and elevates our lives to the quest for true humanity.

When we possess the gifts of body, emotions and intellect, we have a definite sense of who we are, where we begin and end, and a tolerance for our own sensations, impulses, feelings and thoughts. We feel present in the world; we take up space in a comfortable way. We are able to receive and be nourished by the beauty of the world: the fragrance of summer, the touch of a friend, a breeze through the trees, and by music, poetry and our own good work. We are outraged by injustice and can take appropriate action. We can appreciate that other things and beings are different from us, and we can enjoy that difference without feeling threatened by it.

From this state of preparedness, we can negotiate the descent, learn the lessons of the depths, and move on, stronger and richer in human experience. But what happens when a person is thrown into the descent with such suddenness, force and impact that he is robbed of the four gifts? Worse yet, what becomes of the person who is catapulted into the descent without initiation, and without having received the gifts in the first place?

Even a well-resourced individual can lose some degree of aliveness, some degree of association with body, heart, mind and soul through trauma. These are lost resources; they are still there, really, but we may need to be reminded of them, to make their acquaintance afresh, and to appreciate them in a new way.

Early childhood trauma, occurring before we have learned fully to inhabit our bodies, has a profound impact precisely because we have not yet learned to negotiate the somatic, emotional or cognitive/spiritual realms. The resources to do so were not developed in the first place; they are not merely lost, but missing. In such cases, the role of the therapist must also extend to helping the client discover, stabilize and integrate entirely new experiences of embodiment, feeling, thought and transpersonal connection.

There is a balance to be struck between processing the wound and building on the vitality and strength that is already there. Many schools of natural medicine recognize two distinct approaches to treatment: the first being to clear the illness, the second being to strengthen or 'tonify' the vitality of the organism in order to support its own healing process. It is with this second approach that we have concerned ourselves in this chapter. As living organisms we cannot be 'fixed' in the same way as machines; we do, however have the awe-inspiring capacity to heal ourselves when the conditions are supportive. If I break my leg, then in order for it to heal optimally, I need it aligned and stabilized to provide the appropriate support while my body then gets on with the task of regenerating the damaged tissue. The truth is, we never 'heal' anyone else. All healing comes from the reassertion of the organism's pattern of self-organization, the same process of self-generation that created the organism in the first place, 'that faithful process of spirit and seed that touches empty ground and makes it rich again' (Estés 1998). In the same way, when working with trauma, we can provide an appropriately supportive environment for regeneration, and trust in the innate wisdom of the body-mind to find healing in the way most appropriate for itself.

Bring your troubles onto the path

> Nothing can be sole or whole
> That has not been rent.
> (From 'Crazy Jane Talks with
>   the Bishop' by W.B. Yeats)

There are many approaches to spirituality and spiritual practice. One approach – that which lies at the root of Buddhism, Taoism and yoga, and which we find also in the works of Emerson, Thoreau and Whitman, and in Native American wisdom – is to try to become progressively more present, to apply ourselves to the task of meeting every event consciously, mindfully, with patience and compassion for ourselves and others. And when we are fully present, we are in the presence of something greater than ourselves.

One Buddhist scripture advises us to 'Bring your troubles onto the path', that is, to use the difficulties – indeed the catastrophes – that sometimes befall us, as a focus for this work. Working with trauma, particularly in a way that resources the client to transform dissociation into a grounded, conscious presence that can embrace the complexity and mystery of human suffering and joy, lends itself to such a path.

Chapter 4

Trauma aftercare
A four-stage model

Alison Dunn

Introduction

This chapter will outline and discuss a newly developed four-stage trauma aftercare model for working with clients individually, following a traumatic incident. I will outline the context in which it was developed, and explain the model fully, discussing the theories and experience on which the model is based. The reader will be guided through the model stage by stage, with reference to individual client reactions and different client needs.

This model was developed by a counselling service based in a large transport organisation with experience of working with traumatised people over a number of years. Company employees sometimes experience work-related traumatic incidents such as assault or fatal accident, and of course they experience individual personal traumas like anyone else. Working with traumatised employees after a major incident in the 1980s focused the team on trauma and its impact, and the question of how to provide effective help. Since that time, the service has been constantly developing its approach to trauma with a view to providing the best possible service for traumatised employees. Through this process, the four-stage trauma aftercare model has been developed as an approach to working sensitively and effectively with employees in the first weeks following a traumatic incident.

Current context

Working with trauma is often approached by professionals as if it were different to other client problems, and requires a specialist approach. The word 'treatment' is often used along the lines of the medical model, rather than the word 'counselling', for example. I believe that counselling is what is effective, together with a good understanding of the nature of trauma and its impact. Training in specific techniques for working with post-traumatic stress disorder is a useful addition to these skills.

Many approaches to working with trauma are based solely on cognitive and/or behavioural approaches. Cognitive therapy involves identifying maladaptive cognitions before and as a result of the trauma with a view to enabling the client to modify them apppropriately. Behavioural therapy is based on the theory that repeated re-exposure to the original stressor (the trauma) will decrease sensitivity resulting in a reduction in arousal symptoms, and thereby counteract the development of avoidance behaviour. This re-exposure may be carried out in various ways: repeatedly talking through what happened, taping an account of what happened and listening to it regularly, writing an account and re-reading it, revisiting the physical location of the trauma, etc. It is less distressing for the client if this is carried out in a step-by-step way. For example imaginal exposure (getting the client to tell their story) can be followed by in-vivo exposure (revisiting the location of the incident).

Tarrier and Humphreys (2000), comparing the effectiveness of imaginal exposure and cognitive therapy, conclude that although exposure is an effective therapy for those who can tolerate it, some post-traumatic stress disorder patients cannot cope with it and therefore receive no benefit. Rick and Briner (2000) also conclude that exposure work can be problematic for some clients. In my own experience, while exposure work is very effective for some clients, others are in such distress that they cannot bear to revisit the trauma – even imaginatively. For some clients, exposure work can heighten their distress to a point where they fear being completely overwhelmed by and out of control of their feelings. Where this overwhelm happens and there is no intervention in the process to bring the arousal level back down, this effectively retraumatises the client who is likely to drop out of counselling rather than face going through it again.

Much of what is written on cognitive-behavioural therapy with post-traumatic stress disorder suggests that clients need to be strongly encouraged to revisit their traumatic experiences – for their own benefit. Moore for example, suggests that 'many therapists and their PTSD clients (tacitly) agree not to confront such incidents head on' (Moore 1993: 124). The suggestion seems to be that counsellors collude with their clients' avoidance, although confronting the experience is what the clients need to do. It is possible however, that the counsellor may have assessed that there is a risk of overwhelm which would make exposure unhelpful for a particular client at this point in time. Moore's approach assumes that ultimately all clients have the same needs. It also comes from the 'expert' position – that the counsellor knows best what will help the client. If this is put into practice, elements of the traumatic experience, for example the lack of control, risk being replicated in the therapy. I use my judgement before asking a client to talk about what has happened to him, and I will often ask him outright how comfortable he feels about telling his story.[1]

---

1 I shall refer to the client as male throughout this chapter, although the model applies equally to female clients.

Some clients can't wait to talk through everything that has happened to them in order to have their experience heard and acknowledged. At the other end of the scale are those very distressed clients who are unable to face the thought of talking through and facing what has happened to them. A fundamental part of this model is the belief (based on experience) that clients know best what they need to do to heal themselves. It follows that pushing someone to tell their story when he is finding it difficult to face, cannot be the best thing to do. Exploring the discomfort and the fear may be an option, but in my view the client's wishes should be respected totally.

Another current debate being waged in the counselling world concerns the effectiveness of psychological debriefing in helping clients following a traumatic incident. Mitchell (1983) developed one of the early critical incident stress debriefing (psychological debriefing) models in the 1980s. This is a seven-stage model forming part of a comprehensive approach to working with people following a traumatic incident. It is designed to be used by trained debriefers, with groups, including mandatory attendance for all those involved directly or indirectly in the incident. Debriefers are urged to follow the model exactly. The seven stages of Mitchell's model are:

1   Introduction – boundaries and introductions.
2   Facts – each person describes his or her role and experience of the incident.
3   Thoughts – each person describes his or her thoughts as the incident took place.
4   Reactions – integrating thoughts and feelings with a focus on the perceived worst parts of the experience.
5   Symptoms – people describe what they have been experiencing since the incident.
6   Teaching – the group is advised on how to manage their symptoms, and how to find support.
7   Re-entry – including consideration of the future, a focus on positives, summarising the debriefing, reminding about boundaries, and allowing for individual contact after the group ending.

It can be seen that psychological debriefing contains elements of normalisation, promotion of support, encouragement of normal processing of the event, as well as exposure through recounting facts and exploring feelings. Debriefers are advised not to deviate from the model. When the model was first developed and used, it was believed that psychological debriefing was an effective method that would prevent the development of post-traumatic stress disorder.

More recently, Parkinson (1997) has developed a more flexible model for debriefing, based on earlier models. The stages of this model are:

1   Introduction – purpose, rules, procedure.
2   Facts – before, during, after.
3   Feelings – sensory impressions, emotional reactions.
4   Future – normalisation, information and support.
5   Ending – final statements.

Parkinson advocates that debriefers are selected and trained, using a specific debriefing model and a structure. He suggests that potential participants should be assessed initially, with negotiation rather than self-selection. He argues that debriefing should form only one part of a wide range of support offered to people after a trauma, including individual sessions, and that ongoing monitoring and support is essential.

As Wesley, Bisson and Rose (1998) report, there have been very few systematic studies evaluating the effectiveness of psychological debriefing. However this examination of those few suggests that there is no clear evidence supporting its effectiveness. The results of some of the studies suggested that debriefing might actually be harmful. There seems to be no evidence that debriefing can prevent the development of post-traumatic stress disorder.

The report commissioned by the Health and Safety Executive on workplace trauma (Rick et al. 1998) suggests that reviewing the research on debriefing 'must raise serious concern about its use'. Rick and Briner (2000) also suggest that debriefing may be detrimental for some people in the group who can be traumatised in a secondary way by listening to the accounts of other members.

However, Irving (2001) points out that when much of this research is compared with Mitchell's criteria for good debriefing practice, they can all be seen as falling short in some way, which raises questions about the validity of the conclusions drawn. Moreover, Irving points out that the evidence suggests that individuals appreciate and benefit from debriefing and that their voice is an important one.

I believe that if group debriefing is being considered as an option, attendance should be voluntary. Potential participants should be assessed individually first, as those in considerable distress or who have had other issues triggered, may feel very unsafe in a group. It is important that individual support is available as an addition, or an alternative to the group.

My experience of working with people who are traumatised leads me to believe that developing post-traumatic stress disorder is not something that can be prevented by the right 'treatment'. Post-traumatic stress symptoms are natural reactions to life-threatening events, and only become problematic when they do not resolve naturally. The persistence of these symptoms is linked to factors such as the nature of the incident itself, individual character style and history, quality of support, previous exposure to trauma, etc. These are largely determined before the client receives any support.

However, counselling support for those clients who appear to be experiencing a severe reaction is still useful. Not only can it provide some containment for their distress but it also helps to build the foundations for future work.

THE TRAUMA AFTERCARE MODEL

The trauma aftercare model is designed to be used by counsellors who have had professional counsellor training, as advanced counselling skills are needed. For example, it is essential that counsellors can identify what is happening for the client and how best to respond. The ability to sense accurately what is going on for the client is essential, as client needs will vary a great deal according to who they are, what has happened to them, and the nature and severity of their symptoms. Sometimes, it may be that the client merely needs someone to be with in their distress, rather than to try do something about it. Arguably this is a more challenging need to meet. The trauma aftercare model involves searching for therapeutic explanation, but will not necessarily involve retelling the story of what has happened to the client. The most crucial element involves the establishment of a safe therapeutic environment for the client, for which advanced counselling skills are essential.

The trauma aftercare model is an integrative model in that it is not based solely on one theoretical approach (see Chapter 1). This model is based on the premise that all of the major traditional theoretical approaches have something useful to offer the field of trauma counselling and it integrates those elements. The model is based on a person-centred approach to working with clients; building a safe therapeutic relationship using traditional Rogerian skills of empathy, unconditional positive regard and congruence is fundamental to it. The psychodynamic tradition of acknowledging and working with the impact of the past is woven into the model. The past may include previous traumatic incidents as well as long-established patterns of relating, responding, defending and coping. The cognitive-behavioural technique of exposure (where appropriate) forms a part of the model, as do the techniques of identifying and adjusting unhelpful beliefs which assist the client to process the incident on a cognitive level.

The trauma aftercare model owes a great deal to Herman's three-stage model for working with trauma (Herman 1992). Although this is designed for working with what she calls complex post-traumatic stress disorder, I see the stages and tasks as being crucial to all trauma counselling to some degree. The stages Herman outlines are safety, remembrance and mourning, and reconnection, and she argues that recovery can only take place within the context of an empowering relationship that enables the necessary work to take place. The task of establishing safety (both mental and physical) is primary and must be achieved before any therapeutic work can begin. Telling the story is seen as essential for integration of the experience although the need to balance this with safety is stressed. Mourning the losses resulting from the trauma, whatever they may be, is seen as an essential part of reconstruction. The final stage is reconnection – with other people and with the world.

This trauma aftercare model has a framework, yet is designed to take account of the fact that all individuals respond very differently to different incidents. Within the framework, the counsellor, using his or her skills to respond to the individual, can work in a way that is appropriate to the client's needs. For example, the model can be used for assessment only, for short-term acute stress reaction counselling, and/or for preparation for longer-term post-traumatic stress disorder work.

Although no two clients are the same and all their needs are different, for the purpose of this chapter it is useful to group traumatic stress reactions by type and severity. It may be worth noting at this point that a small percentage of people involved in a traumatic incident will experience no stress reaction at all.

a   Normal short-term acute stress reaction
     This group includes clients who are shocked and upset by their experience, but are fundamentally stable. These may be clients who have good support, good self-esteem, with no additional current difficulties in their life. They probably have no previous major trauma to be triggered, and no psychiatric history. They may feel satisfied with the way that they responded during the incident and maybe the event did not feel too personal. These clients may only need assessment, normalisation and advice. Many clients just need to be reassured, to know that some distress is normal, given the situation, and to be given advice on how best to cope until the symptoms subside. Some clients, however, will need a bit more support and help to manage their symptoms – there may be aspects of the incident or their reaction to it that need to be worked through and made sense of, for example.

b   A strong reaction is evident – may develop into post-traumatic stress disorder
     The second group are those who are clearly very distressed and finding it hard to bear. These clients may be having trouble functioning on a day-to-day basis, it may feel that life has been turned upside down by what has happened, their beliefs about life and their way of being in the world, may be shattered. Previous unresolved traumas may have been triggered, or there may be a history of depression or other mental health problems. These clients are more likely to develop post-traumatic stress disorder and will need intensive sensitive support in the first few weeks, and preparation for longer-term post-traumatic stress disorder counselling.

c   Trauma is not the real issue
Sometimes a small number of clients present for counselling following a traumatic incident, even though post-traumatic stress is not the real issue. It can be an acceptable way of accessing help. This can be an unconscious process – the traumatic incident may trigger other issues that are not fundamentally linked to it. For example, one client attended counselling after an incident at work, believing that this was the cause of his distress. When we explored his reaction it became apparent that the incident had highlighted the fact that he had little support, and was lonely. Having discovered this, we agreed to work on this issue instead for a couple of sessions.

The trauma aftercare model takes account of these possibilities and offers ways of working with all of them within the same framework. For simplicity it is outlined as taking place within four sessions, however it is freely acknowledged that depending on the individual, more or fewer sessions may be appropriate.

Session 1: Making contact

Establishing the working alliance: creating safety

In the first session, establishing a therapeutic alliance, creating an environment for the client that feels safe, and beginning to build up the client's resources, are the priorities.

Assessment – finding out what happened to the client and what impact it has had on him may be the stated aim of the session (see Chapter 2). Working out what is going on for the client will be an ongoing process beginning from the very first contact, maybe even before the first session has begun. If the first contact is by telephone, for example, the counsellor will begin to pick up clues about how the client is reacting and coping.

It is important that the counsellor is attuned to the client from the very beginning, as the first session may be crucial in demonstrating to the possibly very distressed client that they can cope with coming for counselling, and that it might be helpful. Most clients are, at the very least, apprehensive about coming for counselling for the first time. They do not know what you will be like, or what you will be 'doing to them'. A client who is in severe distress and having trouble functioning may be terrified about coming for counselling and confronting the cause of his distress and difficulty, and, ultimately, his own vulnerability. If clients are to come back, it is crucial that the counsellor's approach is responsive to their needs, and is sensitive and accepting, encouraging them to return for further sessions.

The importance of a safe therapeutic environment has already been discussed. So many things can make clients feel unsure about reaching out that establishing a sense of safety is essential. For example, people who have been through a traumatic experience can feel very cut off from others around them who have not been through the same experience. They may feel ashamed of how they are reacting. Clients are also aware that talking about what has happened to them will be painful.

In session one therefore, establishing a sense of safety for the client is of primary importance. Safety needs to be considered not only on the therapeutic level but also from other perspectives in order ultimately to enable the client to undertake the necessary work. You need to consider your client's safety outside of the counselling setting as well as within it: is there an anxiety or fear that is likely to get in the way of your work together, for example is your client vulnerable in any other respect? A client's sense of safety may be enhanced by giving practical information about the physical environment, for example does he know where the toilets are? It may be useful to reflect on the nature of the trauma that has been experienced by the client in order to work out what information might help him to feel safe. For example, a client who has been involved in a fire may need to have fire exits pointed out, and the evacuation procedure explained.

The traumatised client will also need to know all the usual information that counsellors tell their clients on first contact. Sometimes trauma work feels different and more urgent than 'ordinary' counselling. Sometimes a sense of urgency may be conveyed by the client or their representative during the referral process, so that the contract and boundary-setting part of the process is set aside or rushed in order to get on with the task of helping the client to feel better. Trauma clients need this information as much as other clients, if not more so. They need to know how to make and change appointments. Is it OK for them to come back if they have missed a session? How often will you meet, where and for how long? What are the options and possible outcomes to your work together? If referral on to another worker or agency is an option, when might this happen, where will you refer them and how will you make this decision? How can the client have an input in this decision? What are the particular rules of your setting that the client needs to know? Is it possible for the client to make telephone contact between sessions?

Confidentiality is of course of crucial importance. The client needs to know how your confidentiality policy works in practice, who might you have contact with in what circumstances, and what will you say? Duty of care makes complete confidentiality impossible for most counsellors, and I find that most clients seem to understand that. It may be that clients feel reassured to know that their counsellor is monitoring their personal safety and will take action if he or she perceives there to be a risk. However, they need to know exactly how your confidentiality policy works. In order to provide some sense of control for the client I believe that it is essential the counsellor contracts with the client to inform him in advance of any contact the counsellor might have with others about him. I always make this agreement with my clients: I tell them in what circumstances I might pass on information about them, and reassure them that I shall always talk with them about it in advance. If I make contact in writing, I always show the client a copy of what I have written.

The next step is to talk to the client about the aim of the session, what will happen, and exactly what you plan to do in the session: whether you will be asking questions; whether you will be writing anything down. (If so, what will happen to your notes, who will have access to them?) Tell your client about the work that you will be doing together: explain your understanding of trauma and its impact and how you will be putting this into practice as you work together. Invite your client to discuss his hopes and fears regarding counselling so that these are out in the open and can be addressed as you work together.

Ask your client about how it feels to be coming for counselling. What did it feel like anticipating the session, the day before, or on the way to the session? How does it feel now? Was it his decision to attend or was he referred by someone else? If so, does he want to be here now? This information will help you to assess your client's motivation, and give you clues as to how to respond as you proceed with your assessment. By now you will be beginning to form judgements about how robust or distressed your client is, how he is coping with what has happened to him. You will be thinking about what responses from you will be most helpful for your client, what you will need to be especially attuned to as you begin your work together.

Control is another important issue, because most post-traumatic stress reactions involve some sense of being out of control, and some clients feel completely out of control. It is therefore crucial that the counselling process begins to restore the client's sense of being in charge of his life, and does not mirror the out-of-control nature of the trauma. It is important to foster an atmosphere of partnership in the work and to make it clear to the client at a very early stage that he has a say over what happens in the session. I always ask my clients, for example, what they would like to talk about in the session. If clients at some level know what they need to do in order to heal, then the counsellor's role is to encourage them to access that part of themselves. Restoration of a sense of control is empowering for the client – an important part of the recovery process.

The counsellor's approach to the client is of crucial importance. The approach should ideally be a holistic one. All of the usual person-centred conditions need to be present, but with important additions as guided by the counsellor's intuition. Most readers will no doubt be fully aware of the Rogerian core conditions of empathy, congruence and unconditional positive regard. However, I will say a few words about each in relation to working with traumatised clients. An empathic response when working with a client following a traumatic incident will be about trying to get a grasp of the impact on the client – how did it feel to be the person involved in the incident? How has it felt to be that person since it happened? How does it feel to be that person now?

Congruence – honest responding – and integrity will help the client feel safe and to begin to develop trust, which is essential. For example, it needs to be acknowledged that there are no easy answers to the client's questions about the incident or quick fixes for his distress. It also needs to be acknowledged that no one else can truly understand what it felt like to experience that traumatic incident, or how it feels now. I sometimes remind myself that knowing something about trauma in general does not necessarily mean that I understand my client or know about his experience – I try to be careful about presenting myself as an expert. Initially it is useful and reassuring for the client to hear that you know about the impact of trauma on people and to have his own symptoms normalised, and to be given advice on how to reduce them. Ultimately, however, I believe that it is more helpful for the client to be helped to access his own expertise.

Unconditional positive regard when working with traumatised clients is about accepting them as they are, accepting their feelings, their thoughts and their actions. It also involves supporting rather than trying to break through whatever defences they are employing to help them cope, even if they are avoiding something that appears to need confronting. Being supportive and accepting however, does not mean colluding with the avoidance; the use of the defences and the purpose they serve can be acknowledged and explored, but not attacked. This will help to build trust and enhance the client's sense of control, while not colluding with the avoidance. In addition, Herman points out that while the counsellor working with trauma needs to be completely accepting of the client, this does not mean that they should be completely non-judgemental (Herman 1992). In her view, the client needs to hear any injustice acknowledged, and his struggle with the issues raised shared. In my view this is also linked to being congruent with the client. Herman talks of the counsellor as an ally, a compassionate witness to the client's recovery process.

There are many different ways of making contact with clients, and counsellors can take their cues from the client. Ordinariness seems to me to be particularly important when working with traumatised clients, as this is something that has probably vanished from their lives temporarily. I might, for example, ask the client about their journey, I may make comments about something in the immediate environment, or about the weather. If there is an opportunity to bring normality and ordinariness into the session, I will usually take it. The client may take this cue, thus a message is given and received that normality can and will return. Keeping the client grounded is also something to bear in mind, especially with hyperaroused clients. If your client becomes particularly agitated, you might suggest that he walks around the room, touching objects in it. Alternatively, talk to him about his family, or a hobby he enjoys, a favourite pastime, a place he likes to be or food he likes to eat.

Use your judgement about the pace of work that is suitable for your client. A hyperaroused client will benefit from a very slow pace, which will help him to learn to manage his aroused state. A client who is using dissociation to cope with what has happened will benefit from a different approach. It may be useful to try to access some arousal, for example through gentle challenge, to begin to work with what he thinks, feels and senses about the experience.

The holistic approach also takes account of basic human and physical needs. Is the client eating properly and how is he sleeping, for example. May he benefit from a visit to his GP? Does he have support at home, if not how might he begin to access support between sessions?

Above all, the counsellor's approach, while not dismissing the seriousness of what has happened or the depth of the client's distress, needs to be positive. The symptoms of post-traumatic stress reaction are normal and part of a healthy response to a traumatic incident. The counsellor can offer support and advice in the short term, which is usually sufficient for most people's symptoms to ease. For the small percentage of people who develop post-traumatic stress disorder, trauma treatment is available and it is effective. Normality can be resumed.

Beginning work: reassurance, resourcing and exposure

Part of the task of this first session is to assess how the client is, in response to the traumatic incident. This information can be accessed in different ways (see Chapter 2). Initial clues may include the client's appearance, manner of dress, etc. If asking about symptoms, encourage the client to go into detail, for example, if the client reports experiencing nightmares, ask about the content of the dreams. A useful question to ask is: 'What's different about you that people around you have noticed?' Other useful questions include: 'How does it feel to be here?', 'How did you feel when you thought about coming here?' The information gathered will already be contributing to your sense of what is going on for the client – whether there is a particularly strong reaction for example.

An early task of the session is to normalise the client's reaction to the trauma and the symptoms they are experiencing. Clients get anxious about the fact that they are experiencing symptoms that are distressing and that they do not understand, exacerbating the problem. Many clients are very reassured to hear that what they are experiencing is entirely normal given the circumstances. It is important to explain that stress symptoms are a normal (even healthy) reaction to a traumatic incident, and that they generally fade within four to six weeks. Metaphors may be useful to illustrate the point, for example comparing the stress reaction to a physical wound that will heal in time.

Giving advice is usually something that most counsellors are cautious about. However, it is an essential part of trauma counselling in that people need to know how to manage their symptoms effectively. Stress reduction techniques are particularly useful for working with post-traumatic reactions. For example, it will assist the client's recovery if they are looking after themselves on a practical level as far as possible. I have noticed that traumatised clients seem to benefit from following a good daily routine that includes regular meals, rest, exercise (swimming, walking or cycling are best), an activity that they enjoy, etc. I also suggest that clients set themselves a daily goal, something that is important for them, and add it into the routine. Planning going-to-bed and getting-up times may seem a bit over the top, but following a routine as regular as this does seem to help by providing a structure. The routine can not only help with managing symptoms such as sleeplessness, but also help clients to feel that they are regaining some control over their lives.

The quality and amount of support available to your client has a significant impact on how he reacts following a trauma, and how he moves forward. It is therefore very useful to explore this with your client. Connection with (supportive) friends, family and colleagues should be encouraged, and ways of extending your client's support network explored. It helps if those around him can understand a bit more about stress reactions and how to help, so a leaflet given to your client that can be shared with the people around them may result in more effective support.

Exposure work can begin as early as the first session, if your client is willing and able to talk about what has happened to him. Some clients will want to begin talking about what has happened to them before the door to the counselling room has been closed, whereas others will be very reluctant to begin to confront what has been a very painful experience. You may already have a sense of where your client is between these two extremes, however it is worth checking how your client feels when he talks about his experience before inviting him to tell you what has happened. If he does decide to tell you about it, it may feel safer to begin talking about it by looking at how the day had been going before the incident took place. If your client runs through the incident reasonably comfortably you can check out other facts such as what happened immediately afterwards. Clues to the impact on your client will be liberally scattered in his story, for example, was he supported or did someone criticise him or lay some blame at his door for what happened or for how he responded? Does the client express beliefs that have been brought into question by the incident and its aftermath? Encourage your client to express his feelings about what happened: is he experiencing strong feelings of anger or shame for example? Where is this feeling located in his body and what is the sensation like? All of this information can be added to what you have already learned about your client, and how he is reacting. It will also help to build your relationship with your client, who will probably feel very held by the level of attention you are giving him.

The normalisation and advice that you have already given the client may well help him to rebuild his resources for coping with the incident and his reaction to it. Another way of augmenting the client's resources is to help him find evidence of strengths shown during and/or since the incident (see Chapter 3). Strengths may include feelings, responses and actions during the incident, or survival strategies since the incident. There will always be strengths and as the client tells the story it is useful to identify, acknowledge and emphasise them.

As part of your assessment process, you may ask your client to fill in psychometric questionnaires to give you more information. Chapter 2 on assessment refers to these, but if you decide to use questionnaires the timing needs to be sensitively judged. The purpose of them needs to be explained and reassurance is helpful – about what you will do with the information, for example. You can take the opportunity afterwards to explore with your client what it felt like filling them in. Some clients won't want to do them and this should be respected.

Finally, there might be other issues that need to be explored with your client, depending on the setting you are working in. For example, in an occupational health setting attention is paid to the work context – is the client off sick? Has he seen his GP and obtained a medical certificate? Has any contact been made with management? Might some contact from us be useful? Whatever the setting it might be worth suggesting that your client make an appointment to see his GP if he hasn't already done so. Medication can be a useful adjunct to counselling in the short term, for example something that enables clients to sleep better can give them a bit more energy for dealing with things. Anti-depressants are a longer-term medication although they may be helpful for some traumatised clients.

Consolidating your assessment: process analysis

After the session, you might want to spend some time reflecting on what took place, and what you have learned about your client that might guide your ongoing work with him. Think about some or all of the following issues: the nature of the interaction between you and your client, the apparent impact of his past experiences, the nature of his present reaction, and anything else that strikes you as significant.

Initially, ask yourself how you responded to your client in the session and what was going on for you when you were with him? Your client's communication with you will probably have provided some useful clues. If he is talking well, for example, this could indicate good coping skills. It could also be a defence. What do you think? Your client is probably also communicating a lot on an unconscious level – what might this be? Are you being told something else as your client speaks, for example is there something that keeps coming up or is said repeatedly? A client who witnessed an accident in which a young girl was killed kept telling me how many children he had. This suggested to me that the incident had brought into question his role as a father and as protector of his children. In a later session I raised the idea as a possibility and it proved to be useful. Reflect on these issues and think about what they might be telling you about your client and what is going on.

What have you learned about your client's past that might inform your understanding about his present experience? If your client has discussed any past traumas, what is your sense of the seriousness of these, and are there any links with how he is now? You may have noticed some issues that were highly charged when your client spoke about them, a possible indication of something unresolved. Or was there a sense of something else – something not spoken about? Is there any evidence of repeating trauma patterns in the past and, if so, might there be a link with the present incident? Have you learned anything about the coping strategies that your client has employed in the past (or is employing in the present) and how effective these are or have been?

Reflect on the main symptoms that your client is experiencing and whether they might have some significance. What defences is he using? What else seems to be significant about his reaction, for example how useful was the normalisation? Clients who don't find the normalisation helpful are often experiencing a severe reaction. Do they seem shocked to the core and if so what is it that has been so completely shattered? What beliefs about the world have been rendered meaningless? What does your client's character style seem to be and how is this impacting on his reaction? Don't make assumptions about any of the above but be curious about the possibilities and bear them in mind as you proceed.

Establishing the working alliance: creating safety
- Practical information as necessary
- Boundaries:
  what happens during the session
  confidentiality
  'rules' of the setting
  future options
- Counsellor attitude:
  holistic
  grounding
  positive
  mindful

empathic
congruent
unconditional positive regard – supporting defences
ordinary
respectful

Beginning work: reassurance, resourcing and exposure
- How is your client?
- Normalisation
- Advice
- Exposure if helpful
- Encourage expression of feelings
- Emphasise client strengths
- Questionnaires if appropriate
- Context issues e.g. work

Consolidating your initial assessment: process analysis
- Your sense of what is going on for your client
- Your understanding of their symptoms
- Your reaction to your client
- Relevant history:
  previous trauma
  repeating patterns
  coping strategies
- What else is significant?
- Shattered beliefs

Box 4.1   Session 1: Making contact

Session 2: Assessment and the way forward

The second time you meet your client, you will probably find that you are developing a real sense of the nature and severity of his reaction, and how you can begin to move forward with him. You may also be beginning to get a sense of his character style and coping strategies, and how effective these are.

Assessment

a   Symptoms are considerably reduced, the client appears quite well
   This client will be making a noticeable recovery. Symptom reduction techniques are proving to be effective in reducing symptoms, and normalisation has enabled some cognitive shift to take place. This doesn't happen often, but it has happened occasionally in my experience. As

counsellors, we may question whether a 'flight into health' has taken place, and it is probably worth checking this out by exploring symptoms and the impact of the event. In my experience, however, it is not easy for traumatised clients to fake a recovery. Instead, they are more likely to drop out of counselling if they no longer wish to continue.

b   A short-term post-traumatic stress reaction seems likely

This client has made some movement forward since the first session – the normalisation and advice was helpful, but more help is needed. This may take the form of working with the client to make some sense of what has happened, helping him to reconstruct his belief systems in a way that takes account of the traumatic incident, but is appropriate to the client and his life.

c   A strong reaction is evident which may develop into post-traumatic stress disorder

This client is still in considerable distress, and the normalisation and advice given in the first session have not noticeably eased it. His feelings may appear to be overwhelming, and you may find yourself wondering if there is previous unresolved trauma. These clients are likely to need preparation for longer-term post-traumatic stress disorder work.

d   Trauma is not the issue

You may get a sense of this if there is a lack of feeling when your client talks about the incident (although you need to consider carefully whether this could also indicate dissociation) or by the fact that the feelings expressed seem to be linked to something else. If you have a strong sense that trauma is not the real issue, you need to explore this sensation and the observations on which it is based with your client in order to work out whether something else is going on. Your decision on how best to move forward will be informed by what comes up.

Some traumatised clients use the opportunity for trauma counselling to rebuild their defences sufficiently in order that they are able to move on and begin coping again, in the way that they know best. These clients tend not to resolve the incident or their response to it. In line with person-centred thinking, I believe that if clients want to and are able to do this then their decision should be respected. It is useful to acknowledge this process with your client, however, so that he is aware of what he is doing, and can maybe learn something about his coping style. It is probably worth pointing out that the issue is probably not resolved, and that the symptoms may return at a later date, so that your client has some understanding if it does happen.

Work in the session

In this session, you need to begin to adapt your approach to your sense of what is happening for your client. Stay within a person-centred framework and be guided by your client. It is worth remembering at this stage that the need to do something is a common counter-transferential response to a distressed, traumatised client, and it may not be helpful. Sometimes, less is more, and your client may just need you to stay with their distress, to hold them.

If your client is comfortable with talking about what happened, encourage them to tell their story, in more depth this time. Try and elicit facts, thoughts, feelings, bodily sensations, smells, sounds, sights, etc. The following questions may be useful as you try to help your client explore the meaning of the incident for him. 'Is there any part of the story that your mind keeps returning to?', 'What was the worst part of the incident for you?', 'What was your first thought?'

Watch your client on different levels as he tells his story. Observe the tone of voice, for example, and any physical reactions or changes in body language. These may include nausea, dry mouth, tearfulness, sweating and changes in breathing. When do these happen? Is there a link with the story? What other clues are there about the impact of the event, for example does the client repeat something more than once? What is said with strong feeling? What questions is the client left with?

Be aware of the client's arousal level as he talks, and be aware that some modulation may be needed if it seems to be becoming overwhelming. Some clients will be able to do this for themselves, others will need you to intervene in a way that prevents the arousal from escalating further and brings it back down to a manageable level. This can be done in different ways:

- Making contact with the client, so that he is really aware of your presence and support.
- Encouraging him to move from feeling to thinking – for example by talking about the process he is in – to provide some respite.
- Changing the pace of work, maybe slowing things right down.
- Getting your client to do some slow breathing, thus encouraging relaxation and also changing the focus of attention.
- Reminding the client that the incident is in the past and that he survived it, emphasising the distance between then and now.
- Reminding the client of his own resources and showing confidence in him.
- Giving the client control of the pace, for example over the choice of when to take a break and when the session finishes.
- Affirming how well the client is doing, in order to encourage continued exploration.

It may be useful to note what seemed to trigger the move into hyperarousal, for exploration at a later date.

As your client tells the story you may begin to get a sense of what issues have been triggered for him. Often, the client's beliefs about himself and the world, developed through childhood, have been brought into question. Developmental issues may have been triggered. If during the incident, for example, your client perceived his actions or reactions as 'weak' when he holds the belief that he must be strong, then it will be helpful for the client to identify the issue, and help him to explore it. Your client will need either to try to reconstruct his belief so that it is more appropriate to his life and experience, or reframe his view of what has happened in a way that enables him to integrate the experience and move forward. The client will know what is right for him ultimately, what fits with him and his experience. Your client's view of the world as a whole may also have been brought into question. For example, 'the world is a safe place' may change to 'the world is a dangerous place' after a traumatic incident. The client's view has swung like a pendulum from one extreme to another, and he needs to find a way forward that enables him to rejoin the world effectively and safely. It can be useful to use this analogy with your client, to help him to see that neither end of the pendulum swing is appropriate or useful to all situations. He needs to find an appropriate and flexible balance, and as he moves forward this will be easier to achieve and maintain.

In addition, as your client talks to you about what has happened, you will probably begin to understand more about the defences he uses and how they work, also what his coping strategies are. It is useful to remember that defences are often formed during developmental years, and are often used unconsciously. They serve the purpose of self-protection, forming part of a repertoire of strategies for dealing with the world. They can take many forms and clients use the same defences in the counselling relationship as they use in everyday life. For example, some clients make jokes to make light of the situation, hiding their real feelings and vulnerability. Others may use throwaway lines at intervals which serves the purpose of mini-mising what is really going on and diverts attention. Some clients use nonstop talking to prevent you from getting too close to what is really going on for them. These defences (and others) have probably been quite effective in everyday life on the whole, and after a traumatic incident they will usually be heavily relied upon to protect the person's vulnerability. Some clients, however, find their usual defences have ceased to be effective, and they are left feeling very vulnerable. In the counselling relationship the defences that the client is using can be highlighted and explored. Bear in mind that defences serve the purpose of protecting the client's vulnerability and therefore they need to be supported and not attacked. If the rela-tionship feels safe enough (and supporting defences will be a factor in establishing safety) they may become less necessary over time.

Coping strategies are the ways in which we normally deal with difficult or painful situations and are often used more consciously than defences. Some people withdraw from the world to 'lick their wounds', for example, having found in the past that this has given them time to come to terms with what has happened and move forward. Some people develop the strategy of bottling things up, presenting an image of coping, hoping to reach the stage at which they really are coping. Others may throw themselves into some all-consuming activity so that there is little time to reflect on other things. All are ways of trying to avoid being overwhelmed after a painful experience, and their effectiveness will depend on many things. Unfortunately, the nature of trauma is such that many coping strategies are rendered ineffective because the trauma itself needs to be confronted. The most effective coping strategies for dealing with trauma, therefore, are those that involve facing rather than avoiding pain. For example, people whose normal response to a crisis is to call upon the people around them for support will find that this strategy does help them to come to terms with what has happened. You will be able to discuss your clients' coping strategies with them, and maybe help them to try out new and more effective ways of coping.

If your client appears to be experiencing a stronger reaction than the incident would seem to merit, you may be seeing evidence of previously unresolved trauma. It is useful to ask directly whether your client has experienced any traumatic experiences in the past, or whether he is reminded of another time. He may be able to make links for himself.

Another source of information is to examine the nature of the interaction between you and the client. Are you engaged with your client, or is he trying to avoid real contact with you? What is going on between the two of you in terms of transference and countertransference, and how can you make use of that information?

Clients who appear to be experiencing strong post-traumatic reactions may cut off, or dissociate from their experience, as a way of coping with potentially overwhelming feelings. Some clients use dissociation as a coping strategy, cutting off from the feelings they have about the experience. This effectively cuts them off from all feelings. Dissociative reactions vary: clients may appear to be out of contact with the incident, themselves and/or the world around them. Some clients may seem blank and unapproachable, so that making contact with them is not easy. Body-centred work may be useful to bring them in contact with themselves: encourage the client to identify what he is feeling in his body, in order to heighten his awareness of what is going on for him. A client may also be in a dissociative state if he seems to be outside of the story, telling it from a distance, without feeling, and he may be unable to enter into any discussion about the incident. For some clients, gentle challenge may be appropriate, to encourage them to make contact with their experience. Grounding may be helpful to enable your client to make contact with the world around him. Stay closely attuned to your client, and respect his choice if he wants to be left alone. It may be that all you can do is to point out what is happening in order to bring it into the client's awareness, empathising with the need to use the defence. Dissociation can be evidence of the existence of deeper trauma, and long-term therapy may be required.

The opposite of dissociation is hyperarousal. Clients who are hyper-aroused are unable to modulate, let alone cut off from their feelings, appearing to be overwhelmed by grief, anxiety, fear or terror, for example. Hyperaroused clients often appear to be very agitated, and it may be difficult to make contact with them because of the strength of their feelings. If this is the case you will need to find a way to gently bring your client out of this aroused state. Relaxation and breathing exercises may be helpful. Use of grounding techniques may also be appropriate, for example you could ask your client to look around the room and talk about what he can see, or ask him to describe a favourite room in his home. It is useful to talk to your client about what is happening to him, in order to normalise it, as often the overwhelming feelings are compounded by a fear of madness, or of breaking down. (See Chapter 2 and 3 for more detailed explanations about dissociation and arousal.)

Many clients will be confused at this stage, trying to make sense of what has happened to them. They may not understand their feelings, or their reaction to the incident, it may be hard for them to hear what you say to them, they may be totally wrapped up in the story, needing to talk about it over and over again. They may be asking, 'why has this happened to me?' In my experience, many clients want to find an answer to this question and some get very stuck with it. It is as though they need to find a reason, in order to help them move on. Often there are no objective explanations to be found, and some clients will turn to their counsellor to provide the answers to their questions. When this happens in a session, I find it useful to empathise with the need to find answers, being congruent about my response. It is not normally useful to get caught up in trying to provide the answers although this is sometimes tempting. Instead, your clients can think about what the experience means for them and find their own answers, and you can assist them in this process.

Continuing normalisation and education are needed throughout this process, as you stay with your client. Resourcing also needs to be con-sidered as an ongoing process (see Chapter 2).

Assessment

Client may be one of these:

a   a dramatic recovery has been made, symptoms are greatly reduced, there has been a cognitive shift

b   the client has moved forward a bit, but more help is needed

c   a strong reaction is evident, intensive support is required

d   trauma is not the real issue

Work in the session
- person-centred
- exploration of thoughts and feelings since the previous session
- telling the story in depth, if appropriate. Looking for clues to deepen understanding
- need to respond to individual client needs:
  dissociation – grounding, bring into awareness in some way
  high arousal – gentle grounding, calming techniques
  confusion – continuing normalisation and education, stay with the client
  reflection – stay with the client, facilitate their exploration

Box 4.2   Session 2: Assessment and the way forward

Session 3: Resourcing and moving forward

In this session, it might be useful to ask your client about his experience of counselling, and whether this has changed since you started. Does anticipating the session feel any different, does it feel different within the session? This is always a useful area to explore, and may tell you something about how your client is moving forward.

Continue to observe your client, what seems to be happening for him, are there further clues in what he is saying? How do these come across in the session and what is your reaction to them? Does all of this information fit together, or are there discrepancies?

Continue to respect your client's choice not to look at the incident if this persists, but consider exploring with your client the feelings and the thoughts underlying this choice, if you haven't already done so. Can the client think of a way in which these could be managed, what might help him? Support the defence until the client is ready to let go of it.

Different directions

There will be three possible ways forward, emerging from the previous session:

a   Clients who are moving forward very quickly
    Those whose symptoms have largely abated will be working towards ending. The client may be reflecting on his learning from the experience, together with finding ways of integrating it and moving forward.
b   Clients who are working through their reaction but still need more help
    Work may focus on helping your client to find meaning in what has happened, to rebuild his beliefs about himself and the world. He may

be searching for the right way to move forward with his life. There may be decisions to take, particularly concerning the area of his life in which the incident took place. Something symbolic may need to be done, in order to mark what has happened and enable moving on.

c   Clients who appear to be developing post-traumatic stress disorder
This may be a point at which you stop and consider how your client's needs can best be met in the longer term, so that you can begin to prepare him for the next step. You could consider the following factors:

- Single or multiple trauma   Clients with a history of multiple trauma are likely to need long-term therapy. It may be possible to work with single incidents in a short-term focused way.

- Psychiatric history   Does your client have a psychiatric history? If so what sort of problems has he had? What kinds of medication have been prescribed? Clients with a history of severe mental health problems, especially personality disorder, may need referring back to the medical system so that they can access the long-term support that is usually needed.

- Alcohol and drugs   How is the client using these? Clients who are using alcohol or drugs to self-medicate will probably find it difficult to engage with in-depth trauma work, and this issue may need to be addressed first. Is this a long-standing coping strategy?

- Fragility   Is your client likely to be able to cope with exposure-based work? Most therapies for post-traumatic stress disorder are exposure-based to some degree. How does he cope with telling the story? What happens when he talks about it, for example are there physical signs of discomfort such as sweating, broken eye contact, restlessness, etc? If so, time should be taken to develop the relationship, and in-depth support will be necessary to create the sense of safety needed to underpin future trauma work.

- Ego strength   What defences is the client using? How well developed is his sense of self? Observe the style and the content of your client's speech: projection and self-criticism may indicate ego fragility. These clients may need more support to help build their internal resources before undertaking in-depth trauma work.

- Client preference   How does the client feel about going on to in-depth work; what are their hopes and fears?

- Co-morbidity   Post-traumatic stress disorder reactions can be accompanied by depression, anxiety, phobic disorder, substance misuse, borderline personality disorder. These clients may benefit from specialist assessment – for example by a clinical psychologist – in order to determine the most appropriate and effective form of help.

How you move forward if long-term therapy or short-term focused work is indicated will partly depend on the options available both within your setting and locally. If referral to someone else appears to be the best option, you will need to begin working with your client to prepare him or her for this. There are many different ways of working with post-traumatic stress disorder; and it is important to ensure that full consideration is given to choosing the treatment option that matches the client's needs most closely. For example, a client who is unable to tolerate exposure work is likely to benefit from a way of working that does not involve talking through the traumatic experience, for example body-centred therapy. Clients who have a tendency to cut off from their feelings when talking about the incident may benefit from a method of work that makes this separation difficult to hold. Traumatic Incident Reduction is one such method. Clients with high levels of arousal who can tolerate some exposure may do well with Eye Movement Desensitisation and Reprocessing (EMDR), for example, because contact with the traumatic material can be managed.

Work in the session

Continue observing what is going on for your client – other aspects to his reaction may still be emerging. You will probably be aware which cluster of symptoms are causing your client the most distress, and work in the session can focus on this in order to help alleviate them.

Arousal symptoms

Consider resourcing your client in order to increase his sense of safety in the session. Ways in which you can do this include:

- Relaxation exercises, for example deep muscle relaxation
- Light and dark exercise (the client imagines that they are breathing out thick dark smoke and as they breathe out the tension leaves their body and gradually lightens to a mist, they then imagine filling their body with pure white light as they breathe in, filling their bodies with relaxation, calm and tranquillity)
- Breathing exercises
- Grounding work as discussed in Session 2
- Body-centred work as in Session 2

Intrusion symptoms

These indicate a need to address the trauma directly, and therefore exposure work should help to dissipate them. Exposure or telling the story can be done in different ways and to different degrees, according to which way suits the client. Telling the story is the first step, but if this feels too difficult, it can be broken down into chapters. For example, encourage the client initially to talk about the time before the incident took place. Go through the story at your client's pace. Consider writing, taping, imagining, telling, revisiting as possibilities and work through them as it feels appropriate, monitoring your client's arousal level, adjusting your responses accordingly.

Avoidance

Avoiding triggers and reminders of the incident is a natural part of the post-traumatic response, and will cause varying degrees of disruption to the client's life. For example, if the incident took place at work, avoidance will result in an inability to resume work, unless it is confronted. Avoidance is also worked with through the use of exposure, as outlined above. For avoidance, revisiting the physical location of the incident (in-vivo exposure) can be useful. Encourage your client to do this, in stages if necessary, with a friend for moral support. Educate your client in advance about how to deal with the anxiety that this may induce. Teach simple breathing exercises, for example, and emphasise to your client the importance of staying with the anxiety until it subsides. Walking away in a state of high anxiety will probably hinder rather than help the recovery. In-vivo exposure sometimes needs to be done more than once, although subsequent visits should provoke less and less anxiety.

The counselling relationship

As you continue to work with your client, you will notice that the expert role that is useful initially is not sustainable and the relationship between you and your client will be developing in terms of transference and countertransference. If this does not change as you might expect, observe what is happening and its meaning.

Working with a traumatised client, you are less likely to work directly with the transference, however it is useful to observe what is going on and use that information to inform your work. In their distress, many clients transfer their desperation to the counsellor: 'take this pain away from me'. This transference is likely to elicit a countertransference reaction of helplessness and/or frustration: 'what else can I do?' It is useful to recognise and acknowledge this with your client if it happens. You may find you and your client taking up positions in the victim–persecutor–rescuer–bystander cycle. If the client takes up one of these positions, it is likely that this will bring about a countertransference reaction. If however, as counsellor, you find yourself taking up one of these positions – and not as a response to the client's transference to you – you may need to take this to supervision in order to explore what is going on in the work with this client for you and enable you to make use of this information.

A genuine trauma reaction?

In my experience, few clients 'fake' trauma reactions. However it is clear that this sometimes happens, and the reasons for this vary. If you have identified some inconsistency, and you find yourself wondering whether your client is for some reason faking or exaggerating a post-traumatic response, you will probably need to address this in order to find out what is going on. This can be done in a person-centred way by feeding back your observations of inconsistency to the client and inviting him to explore it with you. The client may be faking trauma symptoms consciously, for example to enjoy a short break from work. However, the process may be less conscious and require a thorough exploration. The client may be benefiting in some way from the attention that is being focused on him for example. When the secondary gain has been identified, it will be important to acknowledge it openly in order to help the client to find a way of moving on.

Different directions

a   client is recovering quickly

b   movement forward continues more slowly

c   a strong reaction is still evident

Work in the session

Be watchful and use what you observe to help you decide on how to move forward. For example, what is going on between you and your client in the form of transference and countertransference reactions? Also look for client fragility and ego strength.

a   If the client is moving forward, continue facilitation of his search for meaning, and work towards consolidation and ending.

b   If there is a strong reaction and the client appears to be very fragile, just be there and be supportive.

c   If the client is experiencing a strong reaction but appears to be sufficiently robust, identify which cluster of symptoms he is experiencing and focus on techniques aimed at reducing them:

   • arousal – relaxation, breathing, grounding

   • intrusion – exposure work, graded and structured

   • avoidance – (while respecting client wishes) set homework on graded exposure

Box 4.3   Session 3: Resourcing and moving forward

Session 4: Ending or preparation for post-traumatic stress disorder work

If your client has been experiencing a short-term reaction that has now eased, you will be ending with him as you would with most clients. It may be worth thinking about ongoing support for your client and possible difficulties that he may experience in the future. For example, might the anniversary of the incident prove difficult? For incidents involving a death, there will probably be an inquest at which your client may be expected to give evidence. It is helpful to address such situations with him, to help him plan how he will organise support for himself at these times. In addition, you will need to address with your client the options for further contact: is it OK for him to return to see you if he gets distressed again? If not, how can he access appropriate support? Is there a follow-up system for clients who have experienced a traumatic incident and how does this work? Some clients may still be in the process of resolving something and may need a couple of extra sessions before they end, so some flexibility over the number of sessions is useful.

Clients who are still experiencing post-traumatic stress symptoms more than a month after the incident, will probably need some additional work in order to resolve them. It is useful to continue to reassure your client that post-traumatic stress disorder is a normal response, and that help is available. Give more information about post-traumatic stress disorder and explore whether something else is going on that is getting in the way of recovery. One way of lightening the process a little might be to foster their curiosity about themselves and what is going on; encourage them to see this as a learning process that will benefit them in the future, rather than as something negative. What is your client's perception of what is happening? Does he think he is better or the same? Give him an opportunity to discuss any fears that he might have. Finally, discuss the way forward: what happens, when, and what possible outcomes there might be so that your client knows exactly what to expect.

Methods for working with PTSD

Traumatic Incident Reduction

Traumatic Incident Reduction – TIR – is a guided cognitive imagery procedure developed by Gerbode in 1989 (cited in Moore 1993). The theory behind TIR is that where past traumas have never been fully faced, they retain an emotional charge, and can be triggered by later incidents. TIR is a method of enabling people to confront their past traumas by exploring the recent incident and linking back. This is achieved by going through an incident repetitively, enabling the client to engage with it and to work out links with previous repressed but re-stimulated incidents. These can then be worked through similarly. The counsellor (facilitator) creates the safe environment in which the client can confront and explore their trauma, and manages the session, by guiding the client through the procedure. Sessions have no fixed length but continue until an appropriate end point is reached.

Clients are encouraged to imagine the incident happening as if they were watching a video, then talk through what they have seen, repeating this procedure until some resolution occurs. Resolution may take the form of a cognitive shift, a distinct relaxation, or a sudden return to the present. The counsellor does not interpret what the client says, and says very little, although they listen intently, enabling the client to feel held and accompanied on their journey. What seems to happen is that clients connect with their feelings as they move through the process, enabling them to be discharged. In addition, they are often able to make a cognitive shift, achieving a different, more constructive perspective on the incident. In my experience, TIR works well with clients who can tolerate exposure, are reasonably robust and have good outside support.

Eye Movement Desensitisation and Reprocessing

Eye Movement Desensitisation and Reprocessing – EMDR – was developed by Francine Shapiro in 1989 (Shapiro 1995). It is based on the theory that there is a physiological component to traumatic reactions, that a part of the brain becomes over-excited and freezes the trauma in its original form, complete with emotion, image and negative self-assessment. The theory is that a series of rapid eye movements allows the frozen material to be unfrozen and processed, easing the post-traumatic stress disorder symptoms as they cease to be necessary. The therapist, directing a series of rapid eye movements, enables the client to confront the incident and to replace negative thoughts about himself with positive ones. It is not fully understood how the eye movements facilitate this process, although it seems possible that there is a link to the rapid eye movement stage of sleep, which appears to be the time when processing of the day's events usually takes place. EMDR also works on the principle that there may be previous experiences that are linked to the present distress, and the process is used to address all the issues that surface.

In my experience EMDR is a collaborative process that works well with clients with severe symptoms who have reached a stage where they can tolerate some exposure, and who have achieved some stability. Part of the counsellor's role is to monitor the arousal level of the client, providing appropriate support and distance as necessary (as outlined earlier in this chapter), so that the client can explore his experience without being overwhelmed by it. Caution is recommended where dissociation appears to be a problem.

EMDR and TIR are two examples of specific techniques that provide effective and relatively fast ways of working with post-traumatic stress disorder. There are other methods, all of which require additional training. However in my view the use of specific techniques should ideally be integrated within the counsellor's own psychological understanding, and use of counselling skills. It is also possible to use some of the ideas outlined in this chapter – for example on exposure – for working with post-traumatic stress disorder in the longer term.

Ending
- as usual
- review learning from the incident and from the reaction
- explore support and resourcing as appropriate

Preparation
- discuss the process and demystify it as far as possible
- explain post-traumatic stress disorder and why this is happening
- encourage the client to feel curious about themselves; ensure the client knows exactly what is happening and when
- provide opportunity for the client to discuss fears, assumptions, etc.
- ensure that the client has adequate support throughout the process

Box 4.4   Session 4: Ending or preparation for post-traumatic disorder work

---

How it works in practice

Case example 1: trauma aftercare for acute stress reaction

Danny is a single man aged thirty, who lives alone. He was referred for counselling by his manager after being involved in an incident in which a man committed suicide. As we walked into the counselling room together, I chatted to Danny about his journey to our office. When we were seated, I explained what would happen in the session, and talked about the relevant boundary issues, confidentiality for example. I was keen to know how Danny felt about coming for counselling, as he was not self-referred, and seemed a bit hesitant and withdrawn. He told me that he wasn't sure about coming for counselling as he had never been before, but he had decided to give it a go because he kept thinking about what had happened and was feeling bad about it. I suggested to him that we treat this first session as an assessment: for me to get to know him and to learn about his experience and for him to get a feel of what counselling is like, and to decide whether it was for him or not. I did however tell him that it is quite normal to feel more upset at first as he begins to face what has happened.

During our first session, we explored the impact that the incident had had on Danny. He said that he was having trouble sleeping, was finding it hard to concentrate on anything, and was feeling very fed up. Also, he kept seeing images of what had happened. He was staying in his flat most of the time, finding that he did not want to go out and face other people. When we explored this he said that he felt very alone, that other people did not understand what he was going through and that it was easier to be alone. He couldn't face going into work and had no idea how he was ever going to be able to return to work.

Throughout that first session, I reassured him that his reaction to what had happened was normal and that most people would be experiencing similar symptoms in the same situation. I talked about what acute stress reaction is and he seemed really relieved to find out that what was happening to him was normal in the circumstances and that he was not going mad. He had wondered whether there was something wrong with him, and was telling himself that he was weak for not being able to put the incident behind him. I encouraged Danny to talk about his thoughts and feelings about what had happened. He kept asking why the man had chosen to commit suicide and how come it was him who had been involved in the incident. He said that he would rather not go through what had happened in any detail, and he looked confused whenever he thought about it. I told him that I thought he was brave to come for counselling when he was so unsure about it, and feeling so upset.

Together we devised a routine for him to follow every day which would help him to look after himself on a practical level – eating, sleeping, encouraging him to begin to go out and face the world – and would include a goal for him to aim at every day. I asked him whether he wanted to book another counselling session, and he agreed that he would like to come back.

After the session, when I was writing my notes, I reflected on the session with Danny. It seemed that there were no significant incidents in his past, and I thought that he was probably experiencing a typical acute stress reaction. He did seem to be quite upset though, and I decided that I would keep a check on this, although it could simply be because he had not talked to anyone about what had happened. His usual way of dealing with difficult things – withdrawing into himself – had not helped him on this occasion.

Danny arrived promptly for his second counselling session. He seemed quiet and a bit miserable and when I asked him how he was he said that he had felt flooded by the feelings that he had experienced over the past week. He had thought even more about the incident than before, and was feeling very upset about it. He said that talking about it in the previous session seemed to have brought it all to the fore. He hadn't really been able to follow the routine that we had put together. I told him that it was normal for this to happen and I said that I thought he had done well to return for the second session. He said that he had thought about not coming back, partly because he was finding it difficult to talk about himself, and that having all my attention focused on him made him feel a bit uncomfortable. He had decided to come back because he did not know what else to do, and because he still wanted to give it a try.

In this session I encouraged Danny to talk through the incident in more detail, and he agreed to do this. As he told me everything that had happened, his voice became very shaky and he started to stumble over his words. His breathing speeded up and he showed signs of feeling very anxious. I said to him that I could see how upsetting it was, and asked him to stay with the anxious feeling if he could. I kept in close contact with him throughout, ensuring that he remained grounded. (If he had shown signs of dissociation or overarousal I would not have asked him to stay with it.) He was able however to talk it through to the end, and to begin to try to make some sense of what had happened. When he had finished telling the story, I asked him what it felt like as he was talking. I wondered whether it had reminded him of how he had felt on the day it happened – and he agreed that it had. I reassured him again that his anxiety was entirely normal, and I encouraged him to carry on talking about what had happened to a couple of his supportive friends. I suggested that he have another try at following the routine we had planned in the last session, and I also gave Danny a few suggestions concerning ways of relaxing that he could try if and when he felt anxious. He seemed keen to book a further counselling session for the following week.

After the session I again reflected on my work with Danny. He had moved forward a little as he was able to confront the incident more easily, but he still needed help to process his understanding of why this dreadful thing had happened and why his normal way of dealing with things hadn't helped on this occasion.

Danny once again arrived promptly for his third session, and as we walked into the counselling room I noticed that he appeared more relaxed and confident than he had on the previous occasions. We spoke about how he had been through the week and he said that he was getting upset a lot less often, and had been able to follow the routine that we had devised. He had been out with his friends on a couple of occasions and had been able to talk to them about what had happened. He was sleeping better, and the images of the incident were appearing less often. In the session we explored the questions that he was left with about the incident. Danny talked about the man who had committed suicide and wondered how bad he must have felt to commit suicide in this way. Remembering how upset he himself had been feeling after it had happened, he realised that severe distress might cause someone to act without thinking about the consequences for other people. At this point, he stopped feeling angry with the man who had involved him, and began to think that he was quite fortunate never to have felt that desperate. This was the shift that Danny needed to make in order to begin to put the incident behind him. He began to talk about returning to work, and how this could be managed, and we planned one final session to bring everything together. After the session, with Danny's permission, I spoke to his manager to discuss how they could best support his return to work.

In the fourth and final session, we reviewed how Danny's return to work had gone, as step by step he had returned to full duties. He now felt quite comfortable, although he was a bit more alert than usual. We looked back at what he had learned from the incident and from his reaction to it. He said that he felt he had gained a greater understanding of people in distress, and was hoping to volunteer for a local support group. Danny talked about how counselling had helped him: he had learned that talking things through may be more helpful than withdrawing. He had also learned that sometimes he might need support from others and had experienced how he could get that for himself. Danny believed that he had enough support to carry on without coming for more sessions at this stage. I explained that he could return at any time if he needed to and that I would in any case write to him at intervals over the next year to follow up his progress – a usual procedure.

Working with Danny reminded me that confronting the traumatic experience can release more distress initially, and that it is reassuring for clients to have this explained in advance. I was also reminded of the need to allow clients to teach you what you need to know about how they interact in the world, and what they need to do to heal. Danny is a good example of how quickly some clients can move forward once they have begun to let their feelings go, and have begun to make sense of what has happened to them.

Case example 2: trauma aftercare for post-traumatic stress disorder

Ken is a man in his fifties, married with grown-up children. He was referred for counselling after being assaulted by a member of the public who without warning hit him in the face causing serious physical injury. This had happened two months previously, but Ken had not wanted to come for counselling until now.

When I went to collect Ken from the waiting area, I noticed that he was sitting on the edge of his chair and his eyes were darting around the room. He appeared startled when I approached him. He sat on the edge of his chair in the counselling room, appearing nervous and edgy. He immediately asked how long the session would last. My perception was that he felt trapped and I thought that I should answer him in a way that would help to alleviate that feeling as far as possible. I remarked that he appeared a bit anxious (judging that to explore further at this stage would not be helpful) and told him that sessions normally last for about an hour, but that he was free to leave sooner if he wanted to. I was concerned that Ken might leave at a bad moment, for example in a state of high arousal, but it seemed to be more important to give him control over how long he stayed, in order for him to feel safe.

I gave Ken the relevant information about boundaries, but it didn't look as though he was taking much in. I judged that I would need to take the process slowly, responding to him step by step, as he appeared to be very traumatised by his experience. I asked him how he was and he told me that he was sleeping badly, having nightmares in which he could see the man's face as he attacked him. He was finding it hard to sit still, and could not concentrate on doing anything. He felt as though he were in a daze most of the time. He could not talk to his wife about what was happening to him and he felt guilty because he could tell that she was worried about him. He didn't want to leave the house at all and had found the journey to see me a bit of a nightmare. He had been looking around him for potential trouble all the time, and once he had felt so anxious that he had had to get off the train and wait for the next one. He was bombarded by images of the assault, and could not stop thinking about it. On one level he found it hard to believe that he had actually been hit. His physical injuries had healed, but he did not believe that he would ever get over what had happened to him. He felt really angry with a colleague who had suggested that he should have been able to defend himself.

I asked Ken about previous experiences and he told me that he had been taught to stand up for himself when he was quite young. He said that he felt ashamed about not having defended himself on this occasion.

I tried to reassure Ken that what was happening to him, while very distressing, was quite normal, and that it was likely that he would get better in time and be able to get on with his life again. I could see that he didn't believe me. After forty minutes Ken asked if he could leave. I agreed that he could, but asked if he would arrange to come back, which he agreed to.

I was struck by the strength of Ken's reaction and how paralysed he seemed by what had happened to him. His symptoms suggested that he had post-traumatic stress disorder and everything that I observed about him in the session told me that our pace of work would need to be slow and careful. I was aware that his level of arousal needed to be managed in the sessions in order that he could manage to cope with coming for counselling. It appeared that his belief that he could look after himself in violent situations had been shattered, that he had missed the warning signs and was therefore very vulnerable.

Ken did come for his second session, although he was a little late. I felt relieved that he had returned. My initial assessment of a strong reaction seemed to be confirmed by the fact that little had changed since the first session. He still appeared to be very upset and anxious, fidgeting with his hands all the time as we talked. I repeated that his symptoms were normal but this time I commented that he seemed to find this reassurance difficult to believe. He agreed that he did find it hard to believe that another person might react as he had, and that he could not see how he could ever feel better. He felt completely alone and was sure that even strangers were noticing that he was not normal. He blamed himself for the attack and for not being able to pull himself together – he was sure that his colleagues would think that he was putting it on.

We talked about how he might begin to manage some of his symptoms; for example, I said that it might help him to go out for a short walk every day. He looked doubtful, but agreed to try. Ken again asked to leave the session early, agreeing to come back for a further session.

I had been watching Ken carefully throughout the session. I was very aware of how easily his arousal levels were triggered, and that I needed to ground him sometimes to bring him back into contact with me. I used every way I knew of creating a calm, safe atmosphere throughout the session, sitting in a relaxed position myself, and adopting a calm tone of voice. Ken clearly did not want to discuss the incident in any detail at this stage, and I knew that it was important not to expect this until he was stable enough, and sufficiently well supported, to cope with the anxiety and upset that would no doubt be triggered.

Ken did not turn up for his third session. Feeling concerned about him, I rang him at home the next day. He said that he had not felt well, and agreed to rearrange the session. He came to the next one. His strong reaction was still unchanged, and his symptoms were upsetting him. He said that he was going out for short walks every day but didn't really like doing it, as he felt so vulnerable. Travelling to the sessions once a week was about as much as he could manage for the time being.

From Ken, I got the sense that he did not believe that counselling could help him, or that I could help him. He was coming to see me because he did not know what else to do. In response to this I found myself wondering whether indeed I *could* help him. At times while I was with him I found myself doubting the process. As I thought about my reaction, I realised that this was an indication of how he was, of his fragility. I thought about what might help him and decided that maximising his support might be useful. I also thought about the support that might be helpful to me. I realised that we would need some time to continue to develop our relationship in order to provide a strong enough base for him to undertake specific post-traumatic stress disorder work. In addition, I was aware that his self-criticism showed that he would probably benefit from some work that would help him to feel better about himself.

In the fourth session, we talked in more detail about what was happening to Ken and how I thought we should take things forward. I explained exactly what the next steps would be, and talked more about what post-traumatic stress disorder is. We discussed his fears: that he would not get better, or that he would deteriorate further, eventually 'going mad'. He still thought it was unlikely that anything would make a difference, but was prepared to give it a go. We also looked together at how we could increase his support and I gave him a leaflet to take home for his wife to read, so that she could offer him the support that she wanted to give. I also rang his manager to explain what was happening so that they could give him some time before they began to think about his job.

Following these sessions, I arranged for Ken to have a psychological assessment. He was diagnosed with post-traumatic stress disorder and supportive work was suggested initially followed by Eye Movement Desensitisation and Reprocessing. He continued to come for counselling although he missed appointments at intervals usually saying that he had not felt well enough to come. Eventually we worked using EMDR, which resulted in a decrease in symptoms. He gradually picked up the pieces of his life again, returning to work, albeit in a different job, over a period of time, in a step by step way.

Working with Ken reminded me how important it is to watch a really distressed client carefully and to adjust one's approach in response. I also learned more about my countertransference reaction of feeling de-skilled and how to use it to add to my understanding of and work with my client.

Conclusion

If you take the first letter of each stage of the trauma aftercare model presented in this chapter — Contact, Assessment, Resourcing and Ending – you get the word 'care' which seems to be an appropriate acronym.

The field of trauma counselling is a relatively new one and to work within it is challenging – a continuous learning experience. Being involved in developing the model and in writing this chapter has made me think hard about what impact trauma has on people, and what I do with clients who are traumatised and why. I have come to the conclusion that while I have some knowledge about traumas and their impact, the only traumas I can truly hope to understand are my own. The task of counsellor and client together is to reach for understanding of that incident and its impact on that person. If I am sufficiently attuned to my client they will teach me what I need to know about working with them, and they will know – on some level – what they need to do in order to heal.

Most clients find something positive to take forward from their traumatic experience. In the same way, I learn something from every client I work with, and I find this an enriching experience that adds something to my ability to work with future clients.

Chapter 5

Working with trauma in private practice

Carrie Jess

I am walking down a long corridor. The walls are painted in hospital green. There is carpet on the floor but it clashes with the walls. All along the corridor there are doors, behind them a toilet, bathroom and common room with television. The television is on and several people sit around it but nobody appears to be watching. Other doors lead into bedrooms each with four beds, four bedside tables and four lockable wardrobes. There are peacock blue curtains at the windows. These clash with the walls and the carpet. Further on yet more doors reveal single-bedded rooms with the same peacock blue curtains, the same cold hospital green walls. These rooms offer privacy or isolation depending on the mood of the occupants. All the doors are wide and heavy and fitted with locks, and they all have in them a small pane of one-way glass. Other doors open into cupboards, meeting rooms, an office and one carries the word 'Medication' printed above a large wall-mounted timetable of names. The last door on the corridor is a single-bedded room, it is held open by a blue plastic pedal bin. In the bed lies a tall pale woman. She is so pale and so still it is hard to believe she is not dead. She is wearing a green velvet dressing gown several shades darker than the paint on the walls and it matches perfectly. She looks serene as if she belongs there. She looks as if she has always been there sleeping in the room at the end of the long corridor of doors. She looks like me.

This vivid recurring dream is an extract from a journal kept by Emma[1] during the year following a traumatic incident in which her sister had attempted suicide by jumping under a train. Throughout this time she had quietly come to rely more and more on her journal as a form and source of comfort, support and as a coping strategy in her attempt to make sense of it all. She had more recently begun to realise how she had withdrawn from the world; she kept her thoughts and feelings largely to herself, felt distanced and 'cut off' from her body and many of those around her. Emma was beginning to experience tension headaches which often left her unable to write her journal and it was at this point that she finally decided to take up the suggestion a friend had made at the beginning of the year to see a counsellor. She made an appointment to see a therapist working in general private practice whom she found through personal recommendation. Emma's trauma and grief work over a period of six months forms the background case study for this chapter.

Specialist trauma counselling units, like the one at London Transport discussed in this book, provide for the counselling needs of employees. Individuals outside such a framework may well self-refer into general private practice counselling or therapy unable, or unwilling, at the time to define their symptoms as a post-traumatic stress reaction. Some will seek out an individual practitioner with a known history and/or reputation for working with PTSD or specialist support where it occasionally exists. Emma referred herself to an innovative practitioner from a humanistic integrative training background with an emphasis on working with the body, who had been recommended to her. Those who are variously training as body-centred practitioners will be interested to read how he drew upon his theoretical knowledge toward informing his practice and treatment strategy and might consider adopting some of the concepts and strategies into the general private practice of their work with trauma clients, under appropriate supervision. It is also anticipated that the chapter will interest and further encourage other humanistic/integrative practitioners working in private practice who would not necessarily define themselves as trauma counsellors or their practice as body-centred. Such practitioners may reflect on and consider more actively their own theoretical background, assumptions and practice alongside the specialist trauma work discussed in this book when a trauma client presents. In this way a widening of the scope of dedicated therapists may emerge, some of whom may go on to become specialists in the field and/or become known as practitioners with a particular interest in working with PTSD. We may work differently and come from different theoretical standpoints but our practice can inform and enrich one another's work.

The therapist working with Emma took his approach from what is now a widely held belief that our minds play a fundamental role in how our bodies feel and respond. He believed there is valuable contribution to be had in the understanding and treatment of PTSD from a body-centred perspective.

At the most fundamental level, counsellors and therapists in training, and certainly those of us who have trained in a humanistic/integrative tradition, will perhaps recall how at one stage or another we were taught to be aware of our bodies in the consulting room inasmuch as how and where we sit (in relation to our clients), what messages we give them through our movements and gestures, how we feel on a particular day and how we allowed any such feelings into the consulting room. We were perhaps also taught to look out for these in our clients – their breathing, skin tone, colour, habitual gestures – and even bring them to their attention. Emerald-Jane Turner and Francesca Diebschlag name this process as 'tracking' and discuss it in Chapter 3 (see pp. 81–82). This approach is not specific to private practitioners' work. Thom Spiers also discusses this bodily approach to clients in Chapter 2 and how, through noticing and bringing these qualities to clients' attention, we can begin to make an intimate connection with them and facilitate their work toward expression of felt body experiences (pp. 66–67). On this level, we can say that the therapeutic process involves not only the relationship between therapists' and clients' minds but their bodies too. It is the extent of a practitioner's awareness of this, and how we are trained, not necessarily where we practice, which will determine whether we will choose to work actively with the body in this and other ways and/or with direct touch.

From time to time, from infancy onwards, we all bypass the need or awareness for body contact in different and many ways and we suffer because of this. Bowlby (1969) showed us how an infant's emotional life is affected by the availability or otherwise of touch and implied we needed changes in childrearing whereby mothers respond more fully to their children's needs to be held. This concept has again and again been taken to task not least by feminist contributors. Liss (1991) expanded this concept by stating that a baby does not have the capacity to reach out for the comfort it needs and is dependent on its mother (or mother substitute) to know what she/he needs.

Individual practitioners, like Emma's therapist, who have chosen a training which may involve working directly with the body through touch, will inevitably embrace such theories and include bodywork in their sessions with clients.[2] Others would never refer to themselves as body therapists and will limit or set aside such work. Counsellors and therapists who work with clients presenting after a traumatic event will no doubt, regardless of their own particular theoretical framework, be aware of DSM-IV criteria whereby the conditions their clients present may very well be centred in their bodies and are often psychosomatic in nature.[3] Emma's therapist worked with this recognised mind/body connection toward informing her healing and recovery. He held the belief that to rely wholly on a talking cure would never fully assist her to change how she feels and is in the world.

This position will be further explored later in this chapter which begins with a brief historical overview of Emma's therapist's theoretical influences and goes on to explore the roots and work of some of the contemporary theorists he looked toward. Practical applications, both possible and actual, in the work with Emma will be outlined along with a critique and expansion of some of the limitations of working within this framework. Bodywork training and workshops in the 1960s and 1970s which focused on hands-on practical work with clients with the aim of cathartic release, punctuated by often sketchy theory and arguably inadequate research, left students and participants to draw many of their own theoretical conclusions. There have been many positive changes since then and the reflective style of this chapter is in keeping with that trend.

The therapist's framework of theoretical assumptions: some potential for working with Emma

Trauma has an impact on both body and mind. This is in many ways obvious and widely recognised in the field of contemporary trauma counselling where attention to the body and body processes is now an integral part of the work. This can take place in an organisational counselling setting operating under set criteria, guidelines and/or models or in private practice which by its very nature will provide a less uniform approach and may or may not include these in a defined or specific sense.

From the point of view of therapeutic bodywork, practically all of it has its roots or has grown from the work of Wilhelm Reich whose contribution to psychoanalysis and psychotherapy established the central role the body plays in the theory of personality. Reich believed that emotions held in the body distort the body's structure and impair its function and he published four papers in the 1920s.[4] Releasing these emotions leaves an individual not only feeling better but less susceptible to illness. Much that is written in this book variously supports this theory – such has been Reich's influence. It is well recognised that our body really is the main resource we have for our somatic sense of self, and it can be so easily toppled or overwhelmed through physical trauma. Emma's therapist was mindful of this potential from their initial session together. Encouraging our clients to be in touch, or reconnect, with their body after a traumatic incident is an important early stage in the healing process. This is further elaborated on in Chapter 3.

It was Reich who first posited that he knew the meaning and significance of the body's involuntary responses (our shivers and shakes). Consider here the presenting traumatised client. Reich saw a future where human existence would be free from inhibitions and repressions. To demonstrate this, in 1933 he developed and described in some detail, seven armour segments: rings of tension which divide the body into sections. These segments can be said to relate closely to the Eastern system of chakras, the energy centres of the body. The segments and chakras (the concept of energy existing within the body) is also recognised in some other disciplines, for example, yoga and acupuncture. By the 1950s Reich believed that life energy not only existed but it could be isolated.[5] Although Reich was the first person to link bodywork with psychotherapy he had clearly been influenced by Freud. Both believed that the cause of neurosis is repressed sexual energy. Freud, the 'grandfather' of psychoanalysis, did not necessarily believe in looking at his clients and did not touch them yet Reich, in contrast, would face his clients, make eye contact and sometimes touch them during a therapy session.

The ultimate goal of therapy for Reich was to restore the individual's free natural energy flow. Emma's therapist recognised this would likely be her own goal in therapy. Reich approached the task by working at dissolving the neurotic character structure that restricts us as individuals. Energy, according to him, is restricted by armouring (fixed muscle attitudes), and we must be rid of chronic muscle armouring to allow the release of our repressed emotions until the free flow of energy is re-established in our body.[6] In Chapter 2 Thom Spiers writes of traumatic reactions as a 'failure in the process of energetic expression' and there are other references to working with clients' energy later in this chapter and elsewhere in this book.

Of course, Reich's ideas can only be related to time and place. Yet his theories have since been recognised in different ways and his contemporaries have gone on to contribute to the understanding of character armour (Reich 1933) and psychosomatic tension (that as individuals we possess a character 'type') and have further adapted and expanded his theories in several ways. Some of the schools of thought and forms of psychotherapeutic bodywork which focus on working with trauma and influenced the therapeutic work with Emma will be outlined later in this chapter. Some have specifically applied their approach to working with PTSD; all posit that purely verbal work with clients is limited in facilitating deep change. This does not suggest that 'bodywork' is always 'touch work' or that touch will always form part of the work with a client, simply that it forms the foundation to neo-Reichian psychotherapy and/or a body-centred approach. Emma's therapist's work in private practice was influenced by such ideas and follows a pattern of psychological and somatic integration through regarding and working with the whole person.

In his endeavours to explore further the concept of psychological and somatic integration, Emma's therapist reflected upon the theoretical contributions made in the late 1960s when the roots of two important yet separate elements emerged from the Reichian tradition: Biodynamic Psychology and Bioenergetics. These traditions influenced his work with her and are worth outlining. Other practitioners may look to the roots of their own training tradition and those who followed them for guidance and inspiration in their work with trauma.

Biodynamic Psychology was developed by the Norwegian Reichian analyst Gerda Boyesen in Oslo and brought to London as a psychotherapeutic approach which uses a type of massage to dissolve muscle armour and release blocked energy. Bio meaning life and dynamic meaning force, the psychology of the life force is a biological theory of psychology which concerns itself with the organic link between the body and the psyche. Boyesen trained in Scandanavia and identified libido as a bodily life force which causes psychological symptoms when its flow is impeded. Founding the Gerda Boyesen Centre in Action in 1969, she began to train others in her tradition with the claim that individuals consist of a primary and a secondary personality (Boyeson 1982). The primary personality is in touch with life force whilst the secondary personality is cheated of it. Subsequently, therapeutic work is toward assisting clients to be fully in touch with their own life force, or, in the case of Emma, reconnected with her own life force. Life force, according to Boyesen, flows along vertical and horizontal axes, the ego and the id, a concept which is central to her theory. She is now recognised as one of the most important figures in her profession.[7]

Biodynamic therapists examine the way life force moves through the individual's body and not only look at the disorders created when the life force becomes trapped, say, as a result of developmental wounding (deep trauma) or a more recent traumatic incident, as in the case of Emma, but consider the transformations possible when it is freed. The therapist working with Emma from this position would be seeking to strengthen her independent wellbeing and her capacity for self-regulation by adopting an encouraging and inviting style, often likened to that of a 'midwife', giving her time to explore, feel safe and follow her own rhythms. Her therapist would work with whatever comes up for her. In many ways, this philosophy is similar in style to the four-stage model outlined in Chapter 4 by Alison Dunn. Her chapter is an extremely useful reference point for a practitioner, like Emma's, who is working independently.

Therapeutic breathing work is very important in Biodynamic psychotherapy. Clients aim toward a balanced rhythm of breath whereby their healthy functioning occurs. Working with a trauma client's breathing imbalance will often be a starting point in therapy. If a client's 'in breath' is observed by the therapist to be deeper than their 'out breath', work toward a balance will start here. In general practice, the Biodynamic therapist may also employ a particular style of massage until the underlying repressed emotional patterns in the client are awakened. However, although some of Biodynamic psychotherapy's techniques are in this way more directly physical, the approach does not rely entirely on such work, if at all with some clients. Other techniques are principally more psychological and can be said to fall under three main category headings:

i   Psycho-peristaltic massage, which according to Broadella (1987) is the trademark of Biodynamic therapy
ii   Biodynamic vegetotherapy, which includes body-centred exercises (sometimes referred to as free association through the body) and is often used as a treatment in its own right
iii Organic psychotherapy

Together these form a holistic mind and body approach which can be successfully applied to anyone suffering emotional, physical or mental stress or lacking in spiritual wellbeing. Any feedback the therapist gains through employing the massage comes from the core of the client and assists the practitioner in unlocking the client's pain and suffering, mental, physical, emotional and spiritual. This is because the client's nervous tensions are released (discharged) allowing her/him to move toward balance via a healthy flow of their life energy. In particular, the presenting PTSD client who may have lost touch with the self-regulatory process, or balance, of their breath and an awareness or connection with this and their body may particularly benefit from the body-centred breathing work, as in the case of Emma.

People will often suppress their feelings in order to repress earlier trauma. Recall how Emma entered therapy feeling 'cut off' as a kind of defence against the intensity of her feelings. This concept was taken up in Bio-energetic Analysis by Alexander Lowen who, along with John Pierrakos, built on Reich's analysis of character attitudes and structures.[8] Their work was toward producing an outline of five general patterns of body defence or character types: oral, aggressive, rigid, masochistic and schizoid. These are all extensively laid out by Peirrakos (1991). The character type Emma's therapist felt she most reflected will be looked at later in this chapter. Lowen suggested symptoms of repressed feelings are merely an overt expression of true neurosis and went on to develop many new techniques for somatic intervention (see Lowen 1966, 1971, 1973, 1975a, 1975b and 1982). An outline of all the basic bioenergetic exercises can be found in Lowen (1977).

Crucial to our balance as individuals is how we handle our energy. Therefore, an important aspect of Bioenergetics is working with a client on the balance they maintain as individuals between energy charge and discharge. When our balance is upset through traumatic incident perhaps, as Emma's had been, then symptoms develop (manifesting in our bodies as muscular armouring or chronic muscular tension) which serve to maintain our balance by binding the energy that cannot be discharged. 'A neurotic individual maintains a balance by binding his energy in muscular tensions . . . a healthy individual has no limitations and his energy is not bound in muscular armouring' (Lowen (1975a: 15).

Lowen's Bioenergetics is essentially based on Reich's, in that it describes personality in terms of the energetic processes in our bodies and works with the functional identity of a person's character with his muscular armouring on both psychological and physical levels. It involves the client being vertically grounded.[9] Therapists work with grounding their clients through a series of exercises aimed at enabling the individual to get back together with her/his body to assist the body's enjoyment of life to the fullest possible degee. For example, Emma's therapist might ask her to sit with both feet on the ground throughout the session and encourage her to try to remember to do this on a day-to-day basis as a general 'homework' task.

The use of the concept of ground was Lowen's fundamental departure point from Reich who never used the term or worked actively with it.

Reichian therapy, like the biodynamic work of Boyesen and those who followed her, often works horizontally and requires the client to lie down. It does not necessarily work with her/him holding their ground by sitting, standing or lying down but with feet firmly in contact with the floor. It is here that we can observe a fundamental difference of approach in the European tradition (emanating from Boyesen) and the American tradition traced through the Human Potential Movement and Lowen et al.

Working within a bioenergetic framework with Emma could involve using her own sensory perception or her therapist's awareness of where her body is immobilised (frozen in fear/danger) toward helping her to feel more and express her feelings in life where appropriate. This emphasis on the body includes breathing, moving, feeling, self-expression and sexuality. Emma's therapist might hold her hand (to support her when shaky) or hold her head (if she felt she lacked early support or her therapist observed this) or back her up (quite literally by standing back to back with her). Emma's therapist, if working from this position, might even actually fully hold her while she is learning to reach out for what she wants and needs. She may also be asked to kick, hit out at a cushion or the air, or move her hips. This may facilitate an increase in her energy and deepen breathing, or it may be linked to what is going on in the session. Kicking will often get breathing going as it brings more vitality to the legs. This work may also bring out what Emma needs to kick about, such as deeply felt expressions and any previously suppressed rage, sobbing or deep crying.

Lowen (1991: 34) says this is 'An energetic point of view from which all problems are seen as disturbances in the basic functions of expansion and contraction or as blocks to the flow of excitation in the body.' Emma's therapist could work with her breathing through this concept of contraction and expansion which is perhaps the most basic function and easiest to grasp in this work. 'Contraction and expansion' first and foremost exists in our breathing: when we breathe in (contract) it is inevitable that at some point we must breathe out (expand). Whilst Boyesen also works with these concepts, the Bioenergetic emphasis is on the client's independence, assertiveness and control rather than surrender and acceptance, making use of assertive methods rather than the softer approach of the biodynamic therapies. These are clearly different routes but routes, nonetheless, to the same goal and there is value to be had from the integration of both traditions in trauma work and in general practice. This 'routes to the same goal' viewpoint is supported by Totton and Edmondson (1988). Lowen (1975a) writes of Bioenergetics' firm underpinnings in psychoanalytic and developmental theories. Bioenergetics therapists believe, as many others do, that there is a correlation between the mind and the body and subsequently view their clients as a psychosomatic unity; the things that affect our bodies affect our minds and the things affecting our minds affect our bodies. Consequently, such counsellors will actively work with both.

Further theoretical influences and underpinnings for the work with Emma

It has been mentioned that Biodynamic psychology and Bioenergetics were the two strands which took their main influence from Reich. The two approaches have many similarities but they also have important differences. Emma's therapist considered aspects of both in his formulation and development of an approach to working with her.

Reichian influence on psychotherapy does not begin and end here. His influence can also be seen in many of the schools which emerged from within the Human Potential Movement, for example, certain elements of Gestalt therapy have clearly been influenced by Reich. Indeed Perls, the founder of Gestalt therapy, was very much drawn toward Reichian ideas. 'Anxiety is the experience of breathing difficulty during any blocked excitement . . . it is the experience of trying to get more air into the lungs immobilised by muscular constriction of the thoracic cage . . .' (Perls, Hefferline and Goodman cited in Dytchwald 1986: 128–130). Perls and those who followed him are very much concerned with noticing how clients 'hold' their bodies, their movements and expressions and they work by drawing these to their clients' attention and encouraging them to exaggerate their movements. They would likely never use 'hands-on' touch in a therapy session and rely on an 'outside–in' approach.

Transactional Analysis, Encounter, Alexander Technique, Applied Kinesiology, Polarity Therapy, Rolfing, Feldenkrais, Primal Therapy and Postural Integration also all appreciate there is a connection and a relationship to be found between our mind, our body and our emotions, and work with clients toward the integration and connection of these. These connections are important when considering the presenting trauma client.

Many therapists will pay attention to their client's body. Clients too, notice what is happening in their bodies. Practitioners encourage clients to talk about their bodily sensations and note any changes which occur, and in this way both therapist and client obtain valuable clues to what is going on. This is fairly widely referred to in the chapters of this book. A Gestalt therapist may ask her/his clients to exaggerate a gesture (say, foot tapping) and in this way gain clues regarding what is going on for a client by noticing their own bodily sensations and reactions. Whilst this may be about the countertransference, later referred to in this chapter, it may also be about what the client is unable to express verbally. We can notice and be aware of this when, for instance, a client tells a sad story with a smile on their face and as the therapist we feel sad while hearing it.

Some other integrative body psychotherapists concern themselves with understanding and working with the emotional anatomy of the body: Rosenberg and Rand (1985), Broadella (1987), Kelman (1985a), (1985b), Dytchwald (1986), Van Der Kolk (1994), Rothschild (1995a). This list is by no means exhaustive. Rosenberg and Rand (1985) offer an explanation of Reich's theory and method concerning the energy in the body. They also see the necessity to 'ground' the client in her/his body before counselling can commence and recognise a greater use for the energy of the soul and the self than simply a full orgastic release, as Reich did.[10] Rosenberg and Rand suggest it is our aliveness in the body, our flow of energy, which is our sense of self.

> The self is a non verbal sense of well being, continuity, and identity in the body plus the verbal structure and cognitive process one learns. Our goal in therapy is to find that sense . . . As the body is the vehicle through which we express our being it is important to include it in any process of growth that we choose to follow. The body, self and soul are all manifestations of consciousness. The body is the physical expression, the self is the individual psychological expression, and the soul is the expression of our essence as it merges with the universal consciousness.
>
> (Rosenberg and Rand 1985: 317)

The presenting trauma client will often refer to having lost a sense of themselves or make comments like, 'I don't know who I am anymore' or 'My world has turned upside down'. Broadella (1987) developed a somatic therapy which works toward restoring a client's state of healthy pulsation and along with the authors mentioned above, provide useful reading when considering the trauma client. Broadella distinguishes his work from both Biodynamics and Bioenergetics and suggests it to be the most complete approach of all the body therapies. Rowan and Dryden (1988: 283) go some way to supporting him with the statement that it is 'an expert orientated approach and a well worked out body therapy'. Broadella views our basic life activities as rhythms which give us pleasure so our work with clients must be toward enhancing their contact with their self and with others, a particularly useful concept when considering Emma. This approach posited three fundamental energetic currents flowing in the body (associated with the cellular germ layer, ectoderm, endoderm and mesoderm) which he called Biosynthesis. It brings traditions together which focus on (i) libidinal energy flow (movement through the body, traced through Reich, Boyesen and Lowen's work), (ii) pre-natal experiences: perceptions, thoughts, images and (iii) the mother-infant relationship: a flow of emotional life through the core of the body traced through the Object Relations theorists such as Francis Lake and Melanie Klein. Broadella (1988) offers a clear outline of his theory and suggests his approach toward the integration of life of the individual concerns three streams of libido which differentiate in the early weeks of embryonic life yet the integral functioning of these are 'essential to somatic and psychic health' (Broadella 1987: 156).

Like Boyesen, Broadella suggests we must work with clients in a non-directing way, assisting them to uncover their own inner direction. This is a gentle approach of going with the client and a useful concept when considering the trauma client. Broadella first presented Biosynthesis in 1974 in a lecture at the Tavistock Institute in London. 'This is not a final or fixed set of theories or methods, but a continuous evolving network of concepts and practices drawn from many sources and integrated into a higher level of order' (Broadella 1987: 156). The process of therapeutic growth is more important than the product in Biosynthesis (for example, demanding a client be emotionally expressive implies emotional expression is healthy). This is not the all-important goal, instead it is crucial that the therapist understands the direction the client wishes to move toward and be with that. We do not set goals for clients; we help them to set their own. Here we find yet another approach which places emphasis on the need for breathing work with the aim of softening and loosening a client's muscle tension.

Kelman (1985a) and (1985b), who also works with the bioenergetic concept of 'grounding' in his practice, developed a somatic theory which regards the understanding of muscle tone and tissue pulsation. He founded in 1970 the Centre for Energetic Studies. Dytchwald (1986) also suggests we store our emotions and beliefs in our bodies. Training with Lowen and Pierrakos in the 1970s he developed a comprehensive system of body/mind reading and mapping in his quest to understand the psychosomatic nature of health and disease with the aim of assisting clients' experience of life in a more alive and human way. Like others, Dytchwald (1977) draws upon the work of many different schools: Rolfing, Bioenergetics, Reichian Energetics, Encounter Therapy, massage, Shiatsu, Healing, Feldenkrais, Gestalt Therapy, yoga and more. Emma reported tension headaches and it is well known that as individuals we may have a tendency to overstress our brows and forehead muscles in tension, thereby actually showing any chronic feelings on our faces. Dytchwald suggests that thinking is the greatest contributor to tension and consequently suggests our rationality is held in our forehead muscles. When we tend more toward rationality than spontaneity we can become tense and armoured. Kepner (1987), rather than draw on a variety of approaches, offers us a comparison of just two: Reichian and Gestalt therapies. He sees these as the only two integrated approaches to psychotherapy.

Bessel Van der Kolk suggests that clients who simply talk about how they feel can never really change how they are unless they experience the feelings in their bodies. Talking cannot penetrate until certain tensions in the body have been released. His work with PTSD spans over twenty years and he has written, taught and lectured widely on the subject. Emma's therapist referred to Van der Kolk (1994), Van der Kolk and Van der Hart (1995) and Van der Kolk, McFarlane and Weisaeth (1996). He also referred to Rothschild's suggestion that we often miss out the body when treating trauma and/or neglect the importance of psychological integration. Rothschild is another who has dedicated many years to the body-centred treatment of PTSD and has written extensively and developed a somatic treatment approach to the treatment of trauma (see Rothschild 1994, 1995a, 1995b, 1997a, 1997b, 1998a, 1998b and Rothschild and Jardinaes 1994). Her running exercise technique which involves the client running on the spot (to a safe place decided by the client) is described in a case study (Rothschild 1997a). When her clients feel trapped they can successfully loosen some of the deadness and freezing in their bodies and thereby reduce their anxiety by engaging in this work.

A growing body of literature linked to contemporary practice on working with a body-centred treatment approach to client trauma, some of it from those who work specifically within the field of PTSD, is making contributions to the field. It provided useful background, affirmation and reference points for Emma's therapist when considering his work with her. The European Association of Psychotherapy includes a forum for the (over twenty) body psychotherapy organisations offering practitioner training. Young (1999) offers a detailed outline of its work and body-centred therapy's accreditation and validation is also discussed in her useful article. Let us now look further toward some possible clinical applications from the approaches mentioned in the treatment of Emma.

Theory into practice: working with Emma

The working environment and initial appointment booking procedure found in private practice may well be rather different to that of a specialist trauma unit or one accommodated within a hospital. Emma saw her therapist at a private clinic where several practitioners worked. His room was softly furnished with a variety of seating arrangements – large floor cushions, blankets and a mattress – which lend themselves to his particular style of working. She was able to book her first session directly with him on the telephone and see him the following week when she agreed to an initial contract of six sessions. She was able to mention on the telephone while booking her first session that she wanted to see a therapist because she was having difficulties adjusting after her sister had tried to take her life by jumping under a train. Some trauma units may operate in this way, others might require a referral letter followed by allocation to an available counsellor and a longer waiting period may be necessary before counselling can commence.

Emma used the initial session with her therapist to describe her day-to-day life as that of a single full-time working mother with two teenage children. She made scant reference to the incident. Sensing her need to talk, her therapist allowed the session to continue in this way and sat attentively listening. She told him her parents, two other siblings and a large extended family lived close by and spoke of a previously close and trusted long-term circle of friends. She mentioned she had been primarily prompted to see him at this point in time because of a recurring dream. Her early spoken concerns were mostly about this. When invited to tell the dream she changed the subject. It was several sessions later before she described it to him. Emma's therapist went with this process allowing her at this early stage to go with whatever came up for her. Throughout this and subsequent sessions he made use of the opportunity to observe her posture and movements, how she sat 'rigid', her pattern of shallow breathing and where she held tension in her body. He took note of how she avoided mention of any specific details of the trauma, her independent lifestyle and busy-ness which she described as 'to keep me from dwelling too much but it isn't working'. He paid attention to the tension headaches she reported which, from a body-centred perspective, could indicate a suppression of feelings and thoughts. He did not rule out the possibility of an underlying medical cause and encouraged Emma to see her GP in the first instance to have these checked. It is always advisable to first refer clients on for any physical pains and/or abnormalities so that they can be investigated medically. In Emma's case, her GP had decided they were stress related.

Emma's therapist noted that while she described feeling 'cut off' she had also effectively 'cut herself off' from much of the available support and external resources available to her after the incident and had been relying heavily on her own inner resourcefulness which he recognised had been gradually depleting. She mentioned that she had in the past (before the incident) participated in a fair amount of personal development work undertaken in a group and individual setting. Upon reflection, she described how this had initially seemed a useful resource but she found more and more she was locking herself away and tending to feel worse rather than better. She had initially accepted some support from friends who had congratulated and affirmed her for her swift recovery after the trauma. She described feeling as time passed that she should have recovered by now and felt others' expectations for her to do so as a pressure. She had not yet managed 'inside herself' to come to terms with the 'loss' of her sister, as she once was, or talk about her feelings and find emotional support from her family.

Emma's therapist observed through the telling of her story and other details of her life before the incident that this was a familiar pattern and/or an extension or exaggeration of how she had anyway been living her life. She described to him how she had married as a teenager and had children against parental wishes. Feeling rejected by her family's negative responses to her life choices, she had spent many years coping alone or fiercely independent of them.

Although Emma had shown no signs of PTSD over the years we might consider this rejection as unresolved trauma whereby she carried around the unspoken slogan: 'Nobody's support can be relied upon or trusted, better only trust myself'. In Chapter 2 mention is made of traumatic wounding (pp. 42–45). Emma's coping strategies, characterised by withdrawal and independence, had been adopted to protect herself when she married and had then intensified after the trauma with her sister. Later, with some encouragement and when a basis of trust had been established with her therapist, she was able to re-evaluate this.

Although an important and integral part of the work, Emma's therapist purposefully delayed introducing the taking of a complete case history at the beginning of the sessions, sensing and respecting her need to talk freely and to establish trust and safety between them first. After sessions he would make notes of any information she had given which he may have anyway asked her for during a structured case history, in order to avoid repetition later and aid any future history taking within a natural flow of conversation. However, there is an importance and purpose to case history taking and structured interviews in trauma work and her therapist recognised this (see Chapter 2 on assessment, pp. 37–43). Whilst Emma took the opportunity in these early sessions to talk freely about herself and her life, she also asked her therapist about himself, testing him perhaps and putting him on the spot. 'How can you help me?' she said. She told him she couldn't help herself so couldn't see how anyone else could. He did not challenge her but affirmed her point of view and offered some information about how he thought the work could progress and some brief, open, fact-based information on his professional background. She did not challenge or comment on this, instead she told him she never thought she would be really alright again. He did not probe or challenge this either or encourage her to expand but simply acknowledged empathically what she said. The following session had a different quality to it. Emma had begun to trust her therapist and show a willingness to explore rather than explain her life and process. Emma spoke of perhaps bringing her journal to the sessions which her therapist encouraged.

At this point Emma had seen her therapist for the agreed initial six sessions and they generally reviewed her work so far. She commented that she was beginning to find the sessions helpful and had begun to appreciate them rather than feel she 'ought' to come. She agreed to continue to see her therapist in an open-ended way with regular reviews.

Considerations in this case so far had involved looking at Emma's psychic and somatic responses. These concluded for him that, at her entry into counselling, she suffered a split between body, mind and soul and that her body ego functions were weakened as a result of the trauma. In her dream she was not separate from her sister. She had lost a sense of herself and her body as the basis of her own identity. This was likely due to a number of combined factors which will later be realised in the reading of her story. She had spoken to her therapist of early comparisons to her sister as young children: they looked alike and they had been dressed alike. This had served to fuse their identities so, although contributing factors were connected to her direct experience of the 'loss' of her sister, her condition certainly predated this. Predisposing factors likely included her restrictive upbringing and an absence of male presence (a strict, mostly absent father and a passive mother who waited and obeyed him and encouraged her children to do the same) both of which have had an effect on Emma's development. Messages were given to her which included: 'little girls are sweet and nice, clean and tidy and something to show off', introjects she had 'swallowed' as right and proper information. Precipitating factors took account of her fear of intimacy, impaired self-image and a high accumulation of myths about women. Poor communication in her marriage, guilty feelings about not measuring up not only in her relationship with her husband, who had left with another woman some years previously, but also in her efforts to protect her sister, led Emma to see herself as disgusting, an indication that she had strong mixed feelings about both.

The following sessions commenced with the introduction of some practical 'homework' tasks which were set to encourage Emma to reconnect with her body; in particular her shallow breathing was felt to be limiting her free flow of energy. This involved being outside in the open air, walking in the park and swimming, in fact any activity which involved using her muscles and physical exertion. This was also aimed toward encouraging Emma to experience her body again in her own right. Massage is an excellent way to become comfortable with being touched by another person, in particular being touched in a non-sexual manner is not a usual event in many people's lives, so Emma was encouraged to take relaxing baths and engage in self-massage in the water and observe her diaphragm as it moved with her breathing toward her feeling connected with her body. Her therapist was also able to bring her breathing pattern to her attention, through some deep breathing exercises in the sessions. This form of work can provide preparation through a client's refamiliarisation with her own body toward later bodywork in the session, or may prove useful enough in its own right. It was prescribed for Emma as an aid to improve her circulation and relaxation and to help draw her out of her thinking head by involving her in a whole body experience. Encouraging such sensory awareness may also fulfil a client's need to be touched or held.

Emma's therapist had noticed in the early sessions how she would arrive looking stiff and angry while the telling of her story included a lot of moaning about her life. Again, this may have indicated a holding back of rage. She was certainly angry at her therapist when she initially found the homework difficult and offered some resistance by dismissing it as 'silly' and 'a waste of time'. Yet, when eventually undertaken, this homework served to provide Emma with some degree of self-help in reducing her stress and anxiety levels.

This type of homework can be particularly helpful for clients who report having lost touch with their bodies as Emma had. Often, after trauma, well-meaning people will attempt to hug us or hold us. While for some this may provide comfort, for others it will not. Reflecting that Boyesen posits life energy to be the force which moves us and brings us to life on all levels, physical, mental, emotional and spiritual, the therapist encouraged Emma to energetically engage with herself again, by paying attention to her breathing with deep breathing exercises in the sessions which encouraged both body and mind to become more vitalised, alert and alive. Biodynamic yelling, biting, crying exercises may also have helped. However, her therapist did not suggest these at this stage presumably because Emma eventually managed to undertake and find helpful the homework tasks set for her and progress was being accomplished at a regular pace.

To some extent this work with Emma can be seen as educational, moving toward her being in touch with her own energetic flow and expression, in this instance through the physical work mentioned. Emma was also encouraged to continue to keep her personal journal where she could privately record her sessions, thoughts, feelings, fantasies, dreams and reflections and anything else going on for her through her writing, pictures, photographs and artwork. In this way she was building a kind of scrapbook of her life journey and able to maintain (while expanding creatively) this important resource she had found so helpful over the months since the incident yet at the same time learning not to rely entirely upon it as she had previously done.

Emma began to have more of a sense of her self and her body as she worked and reported back for the first time since she had begun to get really concerned in the time leading up to her sister's suicide attempt. She was now more confidently able to describe how she felt the tension in her neck, her toes, her belly, where previously when asked she had not been able to respond. The body-centred principles of breathing, moving, feeling and self-expression incorporated in her work and the considerable attention to listening and responding to her aimed at building the trust relationship had begun to prove useful tools in the encouragement of her developing self.[11]

During the initial contract of six sessions Emma had offered some resistance which her therapist noted and mostly went along with. They were able to talk about this at the review and Emma was reflective of her therapist's observations and experience of her. After the review, she brought her journal along to a session and read her dream from it. She began to open up and in subsequent sessions to tell him about the incident which she referred to as the 'story'. Again, he was able to listen and give her all the space she needed to do this. A relationship of trust between them had clearly been established. For several more sessions she came along and spoke of the details of the actual incident, her emotional pain and her feelings of guilt.

It has been mentioned that the physical expressions we hold in our bodies – energy, posture, way of moving – are meaningful. When observed as habitual a body-trained therapist acquires valuable information about the client's past experiences. Emma's therapist had been paying particular attention to these in his work with her throughout the sessions and gave thought to the previously mentioned character types, noting that she most reflected the oral type. Kirsch (1991) refers to oral character-type people as those who turn anger and pain in on themselves and are often depressed. Emma held a great deal of tension in her body when she first entered the therapy room. She exhibited a coldness of character and spoke of feeling 'dead', 'cut off', 'empty'. Liss (1991) writes that although in such situations our bodies may ache to be touched we send out messages to others and ourselves to stand clear as the mere thought of being touched is abhorrent to us. Indeed Emma had spoken to her therapist of feeling sick at the mere thought of anyone touching or hugging her. She described feeling frozen and did not want cuddles or sympathy.

Common to so many trauma clients, Emma had been swallowing her feelings since the incident. She had stopped reaching out, anticipating that whatever it was she wanted or needed could never be fully available to her. This coping strategy of 'cutting off' from our feelings in order to 'protect' ourselves from the world is something we learn to do from a very early age as we begin to develop our sense of self: the non-verbal experience we have of wellbeing, identity and continuity. As babies we may cry because we are hungry. If that cry is not immediately responded to we tighten our bodies to keep the pain of abandonment from penetrating too deeply. Sometimes holding in pain and cutting it off before it is even felt is a kind of coping strategy. We feel it in our body and it is vital to our life. Yet when, as a child, our needs are not satisfied in a loving, caring way we may not develop a strong enough sense of our self, for we need to feel comfortable in our bodies in order that a cohesive sense of self can form and we are not left feeling fragmented. This is often described to us in sessions by clients when they tell us they feel 'all over the place' and is typical of trauma clients who describe, like Emma, how they feel cut off from their bodies, feel like stone, or feel nothing.

In this way, Emma, common to us all in varying degrees, had formed a defensive character structure as a chronic result of the clash between her instinctual demands (her 'inside' world) and her outside world which frustrates such demands. Kurtz and Prestera (1982) in a refreshingly straightforward way write of how our bodies actually speak to us and reveal not only the trauma of our past but our present personality. They suggest there is much the trained practitioner can learn from observing a client's posture and body structure and that change in individuals always involves the body.

This is the nature of character armouring which Rosenberg and Rand (1985) refer to as the fixed muscular patterns and emotional responses and belief systems which we hold in our bodies. In this way, we develop an ego strength, or character trait, held in our bodies. We set this up early in our life as a defence system which allows us to hold on to our rationalisations, denials and suppressions in the form of a unique (to us all) muscular pattern which inhibits self-expression through our life. To some extent, on a day-to-day level, this is necessary and serves us all by cutting off pain and difficult feelings. Yet, as a result we are left unaware of our potential, or full potential, for pleasure. Indeed, as Emma had been.

> . . . the affective personality put on an armor, a rigid shell on which the knocks from the outer world as well as the inner demand rebound. This armor makes the individual less sensitive to unpleasure, but it also reduces his libidinal and aggressive mobility, and with that, his capacity for pleasure and achievement.
>
> (Wilhelm Reich, cited in Rosenberg and Rand 1985: 95)

When in a state of repression, for example, when trying to keep an idea or impulse from consciousness, tension or muscle contraction is experienced. In chronic cases this is experienced as armouring, fixed muscle patterns which cannot easily expand. This freezing up of emotions results in deadness as in the case of Emma.[12]

According to the character types outlined by Pierrakos (1991), Emma could be said to exhibit passive feminine aggressive aspects. Her passivity could be seen in her relationship with the world; she appeared to have 'given up hope'. She was feminine in her helplessness, her 'nothing to be done' attitude, and aggressive in her anger and frustration, particularly that she felt abandoned after the incident. She made little eye contact during sessions, often held on to her neck with a cupped hand. Her therapist noticed that her neck was often tinged with pink as she spoke. Pierrakos suggests this clinically denotes held-back anger and hatred. Emma's tendency to stare vacantly for some of the initial sessions then look tearful yet unwilling to talk about what was going on for her except to say 'nobody would be able to help her' was a further indicator toward the oral character type.

Emma's description of her relationship with her own children was one of over indulgence. 'Everyone says I spoil them, but I just want them to have what I didn't,' she frequently told her therapist. Characteristically, oral people do not reach out toward others and are often unable to ask the therapist for help yet nonetheless expect it. A central issue of the oral character is deprivation in childhood. Denial of this displaces the need for mothering and support by placing it on to others. The outline of aspects of the oral character type here acts only as a reference point. Pierrakos (1991: 93) supports this, much to my relief, for his full and comprehensive outline of character types does sit rather uncomfortably. 'The defensive pattern does not define the person, the core does . . . A person in treatment is not a character type or structure of any other label, he/she is a human being whose functioning has gone awry . . .'

Character types are simply overviews and will clearly vary from client to client and as far as Pierrakos (1991) is concerned it is the core of an individual which is unique. Emma's therapist was particularly drawn to this notion of the uniqueness of the core of individuals as working with this can be extremely useful in trauma counselling. It is the primary impulse in our life which comes from our core, our real self. These are impulses which go toward, not against life, and connect to what we need and want for ourselves. Often our secondary reaction, however, can go against us (we do not like others' response to our primary impulse so we react against rather than stay with our primary need). Our positive compromise in life, the final stage here, involves us getting what we need or some of what we need which is related to our primary impulse.

Put simply, Emma's attempts to meet the needs of her primary impulse (her need for someone to help her) brought her into therapy. Her secondary reaction (to her therapist's early attempts to help by suggesting some homework) was to dismiss the idea as 'a waste of time' and was not in touch with her primary impulse (and therefore against rather than for herself). The positive compromise she found (which put her back in touch with her primary impulse) involved her talking to her therapist about her reservations about his suggestions and exploring some of her own thoughts and feelings about the tasks. This was toward not against her 'self' and represented a shift in her as she had been living in her secondary reaction (I need help but nobody can help me, I can't even help myself) for months. Emma had been armouring herself against her past experiences.

There is not the scope in this chapter to further discuss the oral character or any or all of the others which make up the five character types. In any event these can be read about among other sources in Pierrakos (1991). Viewing Emma as a character type gives an example of how to identify and gain insight toward her therapist facilitating his work with her. I would insist that if we look further any one of us will notice particular traits in ourselves of any or all of the characters. However, to assume knowledge and work with a client in a fixed way would bring all manner of moral and ethical concerns to the fore and limit counselling to crudely identifying the type and applying techniques. This is never appropriate.

The process of Emma telling her story took several sessions and the work went beyond her previous explanations of her life and situation. There were sometimes long silences in which she struggled to find the words. Sometimes she was full of irritation, resentment and on the edge of tears. In terms of what had happened to her sister, she said resentfully that 'the writing was on the wall' yet medical and psychiatric referrals had failed to pick it up sufficiently. She had taken an extended break from work since and had become enmeshed in the day-to-day hospital visits, care and rehabilitation of her sister. Apart from extensive brain damage Emma's sister suffered many other physical injuries and broken bones which affected her mobility. Emma recalled spending the first two weeks after the incident sitting next to her sister's hospital bed in the intensive care unit holding her breath, listening to the bleep, bleep, bleep of the life support machine and willing her sister to keep breathing.

The story continued in this way over the weeks as Emma described how she functioned daily in a frozen sort of way. She later returned to the moment the doctors had told her that her sister was not expected to live through the night and how these words had had a physical impact on her body which had immediately become 'like stone' and 'hard and impenetrable'. She had not wanted anyone to touch or hold her at that time and these feelings had remained with her in the year since. This form of story telling can be familiar, whereby clients will move back and forth between events while they piece it all together. Van der Kolk (1996) discusses the many aspects of memory for traumatic events in terms of how the client dissociates and how they process information. We must remember it will likely be the first time they have had the opportunity to fully speak it all out. It certainly was for Emma. Figley (1985) looks at the treatment of PTSD and in Figley (1999) he writes of clients grieving the loss of a loved one who has died in a traumatic way. Such individuals endure both the loss *and* detailed knowledge of the traumatic incident which caused it, as well as subsequently what their loved one went through. Emma's sister did not die, yet her injuries were such that Emma felt she had lost the sister she had known, in effect, she was suffering a bereavement. Her sister had been left brain damaged, did not recognise Emma and even had to learn to speak again. Two train carriages had run over her before the train could stop. She had spent a year in hospital before her discharge, four months of which were on a psychiatric ward. She had broken thirty bones. It was at the point of her sister's transfer to the psychiatric unit that Emma's vivid dream of her daily visits to see her began. Talking about the incident here and there in sketchy format over and again with sympathetic friends had done little except help her to relive the trauma over and over again. In therapy she was able finally to piece it all together for herself, acknowledge that it was real and that it had happened and begin to stop referring to it as the 'story'.

We may recall how, with her therapist's earlier mentioned encouragement, Emma wrote extensively in her journal of these sessions, this time reflecting on her writing and the pictures she was drawing and bringing it along to her sessions. He continued to notice how she sat, her skin tone and colour, her eyes which sometimes focused far away and her breathing. There were sometimes long silences while he simply sat with her. Other times she allowed her grief to surface and she cried. She wrote about appreciating him simply being there. Early therapeutic work with clients is usually around building a trusting relationship before focus on the trauma counselling/therapy can commence, yet this may be an ongoing process throughout the work. Chapter 2 also refers to this (see pp. 35–37). Emma's therapist spent a lot of time listening during sessions and he continued with this patient approach along with gentle encouragement during the 'story telling' period of her therapy. He also looked intently at her (presumably for signs of sympathetic nervous system activation: dilated pupils, pallor in face, increased respiration) so he could keep these to a minimum and not allow her to re-experience the trauma.

Emma eventually reached a point when she was ready to speak of the beginning of the incident. This she did last of all and it was the most difficult for her. She spoke of her fear when her sister had been admitted to a psychiatric hospital as a voluntary patient and had discharged herself the following morning; her guilt that her sister had used the small change Emma had given her for the hospital payphone to buy a one-way tube train ticket to the next station and had gone down on to the platform and jumped in front of the first approaching train; her self-disgust, when she described having felt sure for some weeks that her sister was planning on doing something terrible to herself but was somehow unsuccessful in persuading the doctors of this before they agreed to discharge her; her frozen terror as she drove to the hospital to collect her sister only to arrive too late – she had already left.

Biodynamic massage and other physical reaching out exercises were introduced at this stage to encourage release of Emma's deep sobbing and blocked energy once her tears had begun. Work with her attitudes and responses toward her own body took place in the processing of the work, as there was much information available. This was aimed at maturing both body and ego functions and re-establishing boundaries which had become blurred since the trauma. Initially, this involved separating Emma's energy system from that of her sister (who had recently been discharged from hospital and could barely move unaided) by encouraging highly active physical exercises. There are aimed toward her accepting her body in its own right as a basis of her own identity. Emma's body functions and psychological structure had become arrested along with her sister's at the point of the incident. In her dream she was unable to differentiate between herself and her sister who was lying in the bed. Van der Kolk (1995) looks at clients' intense emotional reactions to PTSD and their disturbed sleep patterns and goes on to say that work in psychotherapy with such clients must be toward them personally integrating (the traumatic incident) so that the various intrusions (in this case Emma's dreams) do not persist.

This later work provoked a deep sobbing and outpouring of blocked emotions followed by several sessions of processing and going over events before and after the incident. After these sessions Emma would walk around the park to really 'ground' herself before driving herself home. It is often useful to suggest to clients they go for a walk straight after a particularly difficult or draining session and sometimes suggest as part of an initial contract with them a safe driving/travelling contract. This might involve arranging with someone to meet them from their session perhaps. Emma had felt there had been little concrete support for her before the incident and slowly began to realise how she had for some time since substantially cut herself off from that which was readily available to her. Part of this emotional closing down centred around her shame. This was a useful time in the therapeutic process. She began to reach out toward available support: she telephoned a friend late one night 'just to talk', and asked another to come and spend the night because she felt a bit low. Lee and Wheeler (1996) make a useful contribution to the therapeutic work of healing shame which is often crucial in the presenting trauma client; consider clients who refer to their guilt as a start point toward recognising the value of such work.

The telling of her early life story had helped Emma to realise how much as a child she had enjoyed being like her sister in looks and personality. She had not given much thought to this in her adult life. As girls they had often been dressed alike and compared to one another in family photographs. She spoke of feeling so much like her sister. This was something she had lost and as her realisations began to come together she allowed herself to cry openly. Telling her history had helped her to feel normal and she spoke of feeling 'less of a freak' and more integrated into society, less outside of it. She wrote about this a lot and then spent a quiet month alone on holiday writing in her journal and reflecting. She made some new friends who knew nothing of her past and this helped her to relax and have some fun times. She arrived back from holiday telling her therapist how much she had enjoyed the break and had even laughed and played. She also spoke of the loneliness she had experienced, especially at night in her room, but saw there was a balance as the next day she was up and about and felt she could be part of her new small circle of friends if she wanted to and she began to feel good about herself again.

Some difficulties arose regarding Emma's extended holiday break as this did not coincide with her therapist's own summer break. It is a good idea to get the trauma client to agree a contract at the commencement of counselling which includes their commitment to complete the therapy. This was not spoken of at the beginning of Emma's therapy. Perhaps Emma's therapist had relied upon her previous therapeutic experience at her entry into therapy with him or perhaps the countertransference of the enormity of the incident meant he did not want to put any additional burden/pressure on her. It can never be enough to rely wholly on such assumptions. Emma challenged her therapist when he labelled her intended break as resistance and a difficult session followed which could have been avoided.

Emma also thought her therapist seemed to stare at her just a little bit too long when she disclosed the incident. This may have been transference. However, her thoughts on this could have provided important feedback to her therapist. Trauma work is sensitive work and we need to simply be with, not intensely with, a client at such times. Chessick (1993) suggests that while empathic listening and understanding form the basis of our understanding of what our clients tell us, listening is a complex multifaceted phenomenon requiring the therapist to have particular qualities, such as maturity, as well as thorough training and personal analysis. My own experience as a psychotherapist and counsellor trainer confirms this. The teaching of listening skills is a complex task as we listen on many levels. Chessick includes a chapter for the teaching of listening to trainee therapists. Kind (1999) looks at the therapist's countertransference reactions when working with a suicidal client and the dynamics of the transference-countertransference relationship. Although Emma was at one remove from this, Kind's contribution is useful when considering this case; in particular, discussing guilt and what any suicidal behaviour actually represents. Despite uncomfortable feelings of what she perceived as her therapist's intense concerns, Emma continued to commit herself to the bi-weekly two hour sessions.[13] We must, however, be aware that some clients may decide not to return at such a sensitive point in their counselling or therapy.

Although there were difficult encounters with her therapist, Emma had over time become far less apprehensive in talking about the incident and/or simply allowing others to know about it. She began less and less to fear being judged or to judge herself. She also began to integrate the fact that although what had happened was an extraordinary event it was ordinary for her. This proved to be a breakthrough in the therapy and took several sessions to accomplish. A balance in therapy between verbal and physical bodywork had taken place over time with breathing, moving and reaching out exercises, self-massage and other homework tasks. There had been plenty of space given over to processing and exploring the work verbally and Emma had brought extracts from her journal, drawings and photographs to the session to work with. She had also initiated some confrontational time in the session quite capably asserting her sense of self and what she needed (a holiday!). In this way, she began to see the trauma as something that had happened not something that was happening. That it had happened to her sister, not to her. That she was separate. Hurting, but separate. Emma's dream became less frequent. She wrote in her journal how she felt she was beginning to reclaim her life again and became more open to accepting social invitations and resumed full-time work. She made a short underground journey with a friend at this point which was difficult for her yet she accomplished it. This was something she had avoided since the incident and her confidence and belief in herself began to return.

Emma had described in her story how she had been nice to the hospital staff, although she felt there had been grounds to take the matter of her sister's early discharge further. She had felt powerless and as a family they had decided not to do this. Her subsequent work in therapy on what kind of reaction she would have received if the family had taken the hospital to task and the rationale for not doing this was helpful. Rothschild and Jardinaes (1994) write of traumatic logic. Bright (1996) writes on powerlessness and looks at strategies to facilitate change and empower clients toward regaining control over their lives after trauma while looking at why and how individuals grieve. It seemed logical at the time to focus the energy and emotional resources they had as a family between them on getting her sister well, not on fighting the authorities. Emma has considered this position and remained with the feeling that it was the best they could do at the time. The family believed they saved themselves a lot of additional pain.

She moved into a place in the sessions where she began to feel angry and let down by her sister. During this final stage of the work Emma reduced contact with her while she raged and became irritable and over-assertive. During earlier sessions, she had described growing up among sisters and they had all been sweet, feminine girls. When there were problems they all sang a song to make it better. The content of what she had shared in the initial sessions began to make sense to her now as she took on an awareness that some of this behaviour was inappropriate (and recognised that she carried some of it into her 'here-and-now' life). A break in this old pattern, for instance taking a more assertive stance with the hospital, would have been useful and appropriate. Emma began to be able to both contain and release emotions more appropriately in the therapy room and slowly began to do so outside in her day-to-day life. These had become stuck in her previously frozen state and facilitated by earlier life patterns and introjects that girls are 'sweetness and light'. Now her emotions began to flow again and she began to lose a sense of the isolation she had felt by having closer contact with her family and friends. It must be noted here with caution that some clients who enter body-centred counselling will make getting rid of their feelings the focus of their therapy hour time and time again, week in, week out, and will actually get nowhere, so the work must be a carefully woven process.

This shift in Emma encouraged her to explore the differences she had experienced with her sister over time. She described having had irregular contact with her as adults, primarily as their lives had taken off in different directions. They had only renewed regular contact in the year preceding her suicide attempt because she was unwell. After the incident their contact had been intense. Now their lives began to assume a separateness again. Emma was 'I' again, the contact between them was less regular, in keeping with her sister's improved recovery and independence. The dream stopped and she decided to end the therapy at this stage.

Her therapist encouraged her to continue until a point where he was taking a long break from work himself. Again, Emma began to feel he simply wanted their endings to coincide so brought it up for discussion in a session where she was encouraged to see it as her resistance. Although it was an uncomfortable time Emma continued for several more sessions but left before her therapist's break. We can view this as appropriate for her and confirmation of the continuing shift in her new behaviour patterns. As an alternative view, we might consider Emma's decision to end her therapy was not being fully respected so this 'early' end represented a turning point for her and was helpful in the restoration of her sense of power and control over her life. She could now talk about the trauma. Her sister jumped under a train. It happened. These days she lives independently, as does her sister. Now, several years on, Emma sees her sister from time to time much as it was before the incident. This is of their choosing, although the experience has changed both their lives.

Some criticisms, ethical considerations and reflections

There will always be specific areas of our training approach and practice we will more readily reflect upon and consider, either because we agree or disagree and/or we view it in some way as controversial. Maintaining regular reflection on all aspects of our work is essential though and is part of an ongoing commitment to upholding good practice in our work with trauma as with any other presenting client.

Body-centred therapists, like some other innovative therapists, look at bodily expressions of character defences and make many of their therapeutic interventions on a somatic level. In this sense although the therapy begins, for all counsellors and therapists, when the client enters the room, for the body-centred practitioner there is an added dimension of observing the body and looking for clues. There is much to consider and reflect upon. However, this emphasis on the body can tend to de-emphasise cognition, which is also part of human functioning. This involves the ways we interpret and evaluate experience and our attitudes and life philosophies. We may dismiss them as intellectualising or label them as the client's resistance, yet there is much value in cognition and it must be fully appreciated. Recall how Emma experienced her therapist as staring at her rather too intently.

Behaviour therapy and psychoanalysis have immense value yet arguably neither is complete in itself. Dryden (1988: 291) suggests 'There is sufficient evidence from the research literature on psychotherapy to show that behavioural interventions have a definite place in any integrated approach to therapy.' The behavioural approach gains in value when it is seen as an expansion of other therapeutic practice and philosophy within an eclectic framework, and it is now increasingly more common for psychotherapists of varying professions and backgrounds to take account of body phenomena and an understanding of body process in therapy. We must surely always be aiming for a balance of approaches not an either/or. If body-centred therapists begin to include specific help for clients in the behavioural domain this would involve the behavioural approach to trauma accepting some body-centred perspectives. I would suggest that there are certain elements of the body-centred approaches which most practitioners either do or can work with although we may sometimes name these differently, so steeped in jargon we have become! Recognising what is relevant in PTSD work is the all-important task presenting the practitioner. This requires skill, confidence and specific analytic, relational and cognitive training in addition to the confidence, skill and training required to work on the body. The extent to which and how we work with it once identified is also paramount. Practitioners who work with PTSD in brief therapy within trauma clinics and hospitals must also question to what extent they can offer counselling with only limited resources. Deeper intrapsychic causes may emerge as a consequence of the removal of surface defences which may require longer-term work and this may be particularly so with body therapy. It is true, these may emerge with or without bodywork, but we need always to be aware of when clients need to be appropriately referred on to a psychotherapist for longer-term work.

Some practitioners will enter a training in the field of trauma work as a specialism (and there are some very short courses indeed) and view their subsequent work in the field as another dimension to an already well-established counselling and/or psychotherapy practice. Often, these practitioners will have several years of training, personal analysis and national accreditation behind them. Clearly this wealth of experience can only be a strength, but let us consider this position. We must be mindful that counsellors working within the specific framework of PTSD will likely experience restrictions on resources, such as the number of sessions they can offer each client. Focus must primarily, in such situations, remain on the presenting client's immediate problem and any temptation to stray into deeper psychotherapeutic work resisted. This can be difficult simply because many practitioners have the experience and skills to do it. Yet such awareness is a strength which along with a strong moral and ethical code of practice and boundaries will act to serve us in continuing to focus the work appropriately. In the case study, Emma entered individual therapy with a practitioner in private practice and paid him bi-weekly until the work was complete (for her), six months later. We must recognise this is only an option open to those who can afford to pay. Neither will all, even if they can afford it, choose this route and nor will it be appropriate and/or necessary.

Body-centred work is often longer term and a full training in almost any of the approaches outlined in this chapter would undoubtedly take upwards of four years and involve the trainee practitioner in personal therapy of the kind she/he intended to practice for the duration of the training. Supervision of bodywork is usually intensive and provided by those who have undergone considerable training in the field themselves. There remains a question of how a hands-on approach to PTSD in a clinical hospital setting could be adequately supervised or resourced, even if it were appropriate, or practitioners adequately trained to facilitate and/or supervise it. The approaches outlined in this chapter all have one major sticking point, they all take time. In the limited staffed and resourced clinical world of trauma treatment, where often counselling is limited to as few as four sessions in which there are specific traumatic issues to resolve, there may be far less scope for bodywork. Yet for the client entering into private practice therapy with the appropriate need and resources of time and finance behind them it can be a sound way forward.

S.M. Johnson suggests

> . . . the theory of each of these newer (Neo-Reichian) approaches is incomplete and unsatisfying and the result of the work done by each is often limited, one sided and even short lived. None really provide a holistic view of what human pathology is all about . . . they provide no owner's manual for mental, emotional and behavioural health and well being.
>
> (Johnson 1985: 4)

Johnson presents his own view of psychotherapy which draws upon many therapeutic schools 'whilst at the same time providing a solid grounding in the principles of characterological development and change' (1985: 4). This is an important consideration when reading the theories of Dytchwald, Broadella and others who claim to borrow from a whole range of theories to complement their approach; inevitably any weaknesses in such theories as well as the strengths will be taken. This is particularly true in the cases of theories and schools which have never been systematically written down in thought-out form in the first place. However there is the beginning of a move from this position and Johnson's comments, whilst worth noting, seem less founded today.

However, in terms of research, Dryden (1988: 292) states: 'innovative therapists could benefit from researching their methods using both research traditions. To date they have been reluctant to do this particularly within the dominant research tradition'. I have found that research into body-centred counselling and psychotherapy, while on the increase, remains arguably thin on the ground. Dryden (1988) goes on to suggest that a dialogue needs to develop between the psychoanalytic, behavioural and cognitive therapists and their innovative colleagues (which include the Neo-Reichian and body-centred therapists) particularly concerning affect, the role of catharsis, social factors in psychotherapy, the importance of the body and the place of spiritual issues in human disturbance. Innovators also have much to learn from the traditionalists. We need a common language which respects our differences, not an increasing number of different therapeutic schools: '. . . if it is true, again as often shown, that the search for the one most effective therapy is a wild goose chase, then an eclectic approach would make the most sense for many therapists' (Dryden 1988: 292).

An integrative approach to therapy and one with a firm and consistent theoretical base which allows for a variety of techniques to be used in any given session is argued for by Thorne (1967) and Rowan and Dryden (1988). Behavioural and cognitive theories with a 'hands-off' body-centred approach which at least considers the principles and theories of the approaches mentioned in this chapter may be all that can be hoped for of the majority of practitioners. I hope reading the case of Emma has gone some way toward encouraging you, the reader, to consider this. If it is to take place then continued attention must be paid to presenting sound theoretical assumptions in psychotherapeutic and academic publications in readable and lay form backed by research.

Mahrer (1985) suggests research in the session itself, rather than that which processes what comes out of therapy sessions, is what is required and in this way we may move toward establishing the type of therapy required. A time may come when a body-centred perspective will be at the forefront of this. It is not enough to rely, on the one hand, on much of the currently available published body-centred theory often so steeped in jargon it alienates the reader and detracts from the serious contribution the work does have to offer, or, on the other hand, on some theorists and trainers who present themselves in person to an audience and do little more than rely on experiential group participation to 'explain' their theories. The validity of body psychotherapy needs to be clearly established. Britain needs to create a national association of body psychotherapy and take it to the umbrella organisation UKCP, suggests Young (1999).

We must also consider the cultural factors which present themselves to us, which is true for all therapeutic approaches. Kepner (1987: 1) writes: 'The world view of psychotherapy, after all, is limited to the world view of the culture in which it is embedded.' It is good practice to remain mindful of this and be constantly critically aware of what we are doing in our work with clients, endeavouring always to facilitate, rather than to lead them.

There are ethical considerations and issues regarding boundaries when the potential for working with a direct 'hands-on' touch approach exists, whether briefly, by holding a client's hand, or longer term, in bodywork exercises and massage treatment. These emerge as deserving of a chapter in their own right and I do little more than cite them for consideration if any touch is involved with a client.

Touching will inevitably exaggerate or complicate the transference-countertransference dynamic and evaluating a client's resistance to touch and respecting it is all important. When considering applying hands-on work in a medical counselling setting practitioners must always err significantly on the side of caution. For recent contributions see Mann (1999) who brings contemporary transference-countertransference views together and writes on the erotic relationship, and Gold (1992) who looks at therapists' personal lives, outside the consulting room, and the possible impact these may have on the client-therapist relationship. Gender issues deserve consideration too. See Schaverien (1995) who looks thoughtfully at female therapist/male client dynamics and usefully explores the transference-countertransference relationship.

Rutter (1991) writes of how easy it is for men in power (doctors, clergy, teachers et al.) to abuse and sexually exploit women. He goes on to suggest that over 90 per cent of sexual exploitation happens between men in power and the women they are caring for. Masson (1988) writes that much regarding the seductive patient has already been written yet very little about the seductive therapist.

It is fairly well accepted that abuse in therapy does occur, although the extent of this may cause differences in opinion, so these major considerations are to be observed when a therapist actually decides to touch a client in the course of treatment. Responsible practitioners will always want to consider their professional 'safety' before proceeding, be aware of their full intention behind any 'hands-on' work, taking any personal issues and reservations to supervision, and be aware of how their client may perceive being touched in a session; a vulnerable client may misunderstand the touch or view it as a prelude to an attempt at seduction of their therapist.

The often sterile working environment in the trauma unit is hardly appropriate for hands-on bodywork, where soft flooring, cushions and gentle lighting would usually provide a more appropriate setting. Clients who come into a hospital setting may well believe touch will form part of the work involved in trauma therapy, however, common sense and experience tells me their expectations are usually more along the lines of a medical examination rather than therapeutic bodywork. I cannot see a time in the immediate future when hands-on bodywork will be routinely used in such a setting. At this point in time I am drawn toward encouraging and noticing and working with the body in indirect ways as outlined in this chapter rather than with direct touch. This should be reserved for those accredited as body practitioners and for those of you who will go on to train fully in this tradition. I would encourage you to view your reservations as a strength rather than a weakness and one which is in contact with the specific nature of trauma counselling. This chapter should be viewed as a contribution to the field in its setting out of simply another way of working. Rely on intuition in any session, backed by training, experience and supervision and a willingness to be consistently open to criticism and learning, as well as to good common sense (see Rothschild 1994). Remember practitioners are human and sometimes will make mistakes.

As a trainee therapist twenty years ago I was always encouraged to view my reservations, whatever they were, as a strength rather than a weakness, particularly if it was in contact with the specific nature of the work I was engaged in. I was further encouraged to rely on my intuition and good sense in any session, backed by training, experience and supervision and a willingness to be constantly and consistently prepared to open myself for criticism and learning, to remember that I am human and will sometimes make mistakes. It is perhaps clear from the reading of the case study that Emma's counsellor made some of those. I now pass these wise words on to you and suggest that other dilemmas will present themselves to you in the form of our value systems. This may even arise for you in the reading of Emma's case. Our values, overt or covert are inevitably present. We may not always fully share our own value system with other practitioners and trainees and it can often be less likely that we will share these with those from different social classes, culture or gender, and we must always be aware of this. It may be that we are not able to reach common agreement on values with our clients, much like the times we have difficulty finding common ground among ourselves in the approaches we bring to the field of healing. Perhaps it is that our clients' values need to change only in as much as they are then enabled to overcome the trauma for which they sought help.

We must be certain that the ideas we are recommending to people are continually subjected to critical scrutiny. Certainly we must avoid passively going along with clients' assumptions and values or expecting them to go along passively with ours. In many ways, choosing to write this chapter forms part of my own willingness to open myself up to scrutiny. To write from a body-centred perspective whilst avoiding jargon presented somewhat of a challenge.

We must further consider that an individual's contact and communication may become fragmented when high energy is contacted during bodywork: they may learn to explode but not pulsate, they may act out but not live in, they may learn to be full of expression but lack integration. Bioenergetic exercises, for example, can get people into deep material very quickly. Many therapists have developed great skills, at times taught by charismatic psychotherapy trainers, which do no more than encourage people to get 'into' their emotions. Their skills end there as they are unable to get their clients to integrate and unify their energies once released. On the other hand, regression in a therapy session into one's early feelings can be used by some clients as a way of fleeing day-to-day problems, suggests Broadella: 'A good therapist with a limited technique will have a good effect on a client in a limited area. Thus, a good verbal therapist may help a client to very important insights yet neglect crucial areas of somatic change' (Broadella 1987: 164).

The encouragement in many body therapies can tend toward cathartic release for its own sake. 'The value of cathartic release is lost if the client is not in emotional contact with the therapist during the releasing' (Rosenberg and Rand 1985: 95). It is this contact which provides the healing factor, grounds the experience and makes it real. Expressive release often does make the client feel better immediately afterwards but it does not last and many people, sadly, get 'hooked' on 'venting' emotions without any deeper awareness. 'The armour is softened only temporarily and reforms when the client goes out into the world again' (Rosenberg and Rand 1985: 97). The underlying cause of the armour has not been touched. As therapists we need to be able to connect the emotional experience to the bodily one. Broadella (1987: 165) writes: 'invading therapists penetrate the client. They become not a therapist, but the rapist.' As practitioners we must never use pressuring body techniques to force a response and overide the client's resistances. This can be especially likely if the impression is given by the therapist that an emotional response indicates a healthy individual. Clients need their responses and their boundaries respected. Cathartic release is always useless and potentially dangerous when the client isn't emotionally touched.

In conclusion

Each of us has our own unique path toward our potential for happiness or fulfilment. We shall all pursue our own unique ways of getting there. As clients, it is what each individual wants or seeks for themselves that is important. As practitioners, we learn over the passage of time in training and practice that whilst we adhere to codes of ethics and practice and whilst we may follow guidelines and models for treatment there is no one way to do counselling or therapy. Whether the focus be trauma work or any other issue, what needs to exist from a practitioner and client perspective is the freedom to explore creatively the myriad ways we have as individuals for developing our full potential.

The pressure on Emma to hold life together intensified when her sister jumped under that train. In particular she found herself surrounded by close friends who said little, perhaps through their own shock and embarrassment or for fear of saying the wrong thing. Her immediate response was to close down and try her best to look and act 'normal' from the outside. Her own particular set of circumstances eventually led her into private practice therapy. I believe this worked in supporting her on her way to reaching what at best could only ever be a positive compromise in the Reichian sense and this amounted to a step toward successful therapy on her terms. Indeed, she was fortunate to have had the time and money to undertake the process. The final completion came when she eventually began to reach out again toward caring, sharing relationships with friends and family. Yet her increasing capacity for self-assertion and increased levels of energy, improved physical health and self-esteem, along with her greater ability to cope with her depression, were most observable. Emma, on the other hand, spoke of her improved sleep patterns, her breathing and energy levels, small areas of pleasure in her life and some connection with her body again. Perhaps most significantly, she spoke of feeling alive once more.

There is no intended recipe for trauma treatment in this chapter, it is simply one practitioner's perspective of one of his cases. May the reading of it inspire you to go forward with your own.

Notes

1 The client's name and personal details have been changed and altered to protect confidentiality. She read and agreed this chapter.
2 Reference is made to those who trained in and specifically extended Reich's work theoretically rather than others who identify as body therapists/workers and may or may not include themselves in this category and/or provide specific training in the field. See Institute of Biodynamic Psychology and Psychotherapy. http://www.users.dircon.co.uk/-ipp/index.htm
3 The DSM-IV diagnostic criteria for post-traumatic stress disorder is reproduced in Chapter 2.
4 Reich's published papers on psychoanalysis and sexology in the 1920s were: *The Function of the Orgasm* (1927); *Dialectical Materialism and Psychoanalysis* (1928); *The Mass Psychology of Fascism* (1933); *Character Analysis* (1933).
5 According to Reich, life energy could be isolated in the form of vesicles, which he called bions and stored in accumulators 'orgone boxes', a word he invented derived from orgastic and organism. Reich also believed it was possible to cure patients of cancer and other diseases by placing them inside these boxes. See http://inventors.miningco.com/science/inventors/library/weekly/aa03149/.htm
6 Reich pointed out that the structure of society is reflected in the character structure of its individual members. The notion that as individuals we all possess a character structure is later discussed in this chapter.
7 See Southwell (1988) for an excellent outline of Gerda Boyesen's method.
8 Alexander Lowen was in therapy with Reich and studied with him from 1940–45.
9 Grounding is the present containment of energy in the body. A person who is not grounded may have all their physical energy in their head. We might refer to such people as 'spaced out' or 'not in touch with reality'.
10 An orgastic release is a total body release which may or may not include orgasm i.e. a genital release.
11 The potential for hands-on touch work, which should never be engaged in without prior consent (in writing) from the client and appropriate training and supervision, had been purposefully reserved until, perhaps, later in the therapeutic process. A Biodynamic approach might take the route of actively working with a client's posture even from the very first session; this involves exercises in which the client stands grounded in the room and is observed by the therapist. At this stage there is no direct touch by the therapist although the work may sooner or later include this.
12 Tension or muscle contraction can take the form of character types. The body is divided into seven body segments. Different theorists who work directly with the body through touch will approach the task of working with these in different

ways. Rosenberg and Rand (1985) suggest starting with the neck, throat, mouth and shoulders first. Others, including Gerda Boyesen, work in no particular order and will start where a client's tension is perceived to be held.

13 Such an arrangement of therapy sessions is usual with this form of work as it allows time for any bodywork undertaken to be processed. However many, if not most, practitioners from a humanistic/integrative background may offer the traditional weekly one-hour session or the more contemporary fifty-minute therapeutic hour.

Chapter 6

Trauma and spirituality

Jeremy Woodcock

This chapter seeks to guide readers who may be unfamiliar with religious and spiritual ideas through fascinating but complex territory. To ease understanding some quite complex ideas are presented in a factual way, although the deeper issues are also indicated. It is hoped that those who wish to continue reading will follow up the references in the text, which provide a rich bibliographical resource.

Introduction

Many survivors emerge from traumatic events with a sense of existential change, which for some only really makes sense within a religious or spiritual framework. The chapter maps out why this happens and how the therapist can work with those experiences. It begins by offering a psychological understanding of how a sense of connection to the transcendent can emerge out of trauma. It then summarises the beliefs and practice about trauma, suffering and change from the standpoint of several religious traditions. The chapter then goes on to consider how the therapist can maintain his or her capacity for reflective practice, despite the innate pressures of working with trauma, that can make good use of their client's experience and enable them to work across boundaries of spiritual and cultural difference.

Western psychological models and spiritual experience

Western culture tends to presume that individual development proceeds along a path in which autonomy and choice increase as we get older. These beliefs are neatly summarised by Maslow's hierarchy of needs, in which the summit of expectations is 'self actualisation' (Maslow 1972). This is a teleological model of change, which assumes that things get better in life. In the protected West these ideas have a powerful validity because society is also seen as moving in the same direction of improvement and rationalisation. We are fascinated by developments in technology and medicine that appear to be pushing the frontiers of human life toward greater control over our own destinies. Even religious life in the West supports these beliefs. Natural disasters, war and traumatic accidents challenge those expectations.

Trauma and existential and spiritual change

The experience of extreme events is known to challenge the meaning of life. Personal recollection (Bettelheim 1986; Levi 1988), clinical practice (Frankl 1963) and the small amount of research in this area attest to this (Carli 1987; Eisenbruch 1991; Agger 1992; Gorst-Unsworth et al. 1993). Survivors are reported to re-evaluate the meaning of life in existential or spiritual terms either actually during or in the aftermath of experiences. Many record long-term changes in belief with a sense that survival involves a deeper grasp of the significance of life. Thus, despite profoundly horrible experiences, a sense of innate spiritual survival often remains intact. This may be true even when overwhelming grief, profound depression and despair afflicts survivors. What these findings suggests is that a sense of the patient's spiritual life can indicate to the therapist deeper life-giving resources within them, which can make psychotherapy a worthwhile task in the face of profoundly shattering experiences. It is when their sense of spiritual wholeness is shattered that the psychotherapist may intuitively feel that his or her patients are most at risk. Ultimately, this means that the therapist who can get in touch with patients' spiritual resources, which can be understood in quite a secular way, may be in a better position to offer treatment.

A model of trauma, attachment and the transcendent

Over recent years attachment theory has developed a compelling theoretical and empirical basis for understanding how children develop their internal working models of relationships with themselves and others. In a nutshell, various strands of attachment theory explain how parents transmit their own internalised relationship schemas to their children. Understanding good attachment can help us to appreciate changes that occur when things go wrong. Thus clinical experience with both adults and children who have endured extreme events very often reveals that their attachments are disintegrated by such events. This is not only caused by the secondary impact of momentous life changes on relationships but also quite directly by the way in which extreme events interfere with the actual attachment nexus itself. In fact, an understanding of attachment theory can throw light on what happens in the actual traumatic moment itself. It can also explain the role that the 'transitional space' can play as the wellspring of creative and spiritual experience that can lead to reintegration of the self (Winnicott 1971).

Attachment theory goes to the heart of how extreme events are internalised and how traumatogenic symptoms are set in motion

The attachment theorist Mary Main (1991) has done a considerable amount of research into how parents transmit their attachment styles to their offspring. Her findings suggest that very young children are unable to be 'metacognitive'. In other words, they are unable to get 'meta' to their cognitive processes. This means they cannot transcend and therefore think about their own thinking. It follows that they are also unable to transcend and thereby think about their feelings. This means that they experience the world in an almost purely subjective and non-reflective way. To use Main's language, because young children cannot be metacognitive they are unable to 'dual code' things. For instance, they understand things, relationships and events as being one particular way. For instance, an aunt cannot be simultaneously auntie and daddy's sister. Sometime however between the age of three and four children do begin to gradually develop the ability to dual code and thus to be able to take different perspectives on things.

Optimal attachment emerges out of the mother's and father's[1] responsive attunement to the infant's needs. In responding to her child's needs for attachment the mother replays out the qualities created in her through her own experience of attachment to her own mother, mediated of course through her life experiences and maturation processes. In the attachment process each child's development is facilitated if they experience relationships with their key attachment figures that are emotionally congruent and cognitively coherent. In other words they develop to their best potential where there is a good fit between the cognitive and emotional world. It therefore follows that parents with coherent explanations of their childhood attachments, gained through direct experience or through reflection or psychotherapy, are more likely to attune to their children's needs for proximity and thereby provide an experience of attachment that fits for their child. To summarise, a child develops emotional and cognitive coherence from the parent's responsively modulated attunement to its needs.

It is conjectured that the process of attunement between parent and child creates a zone between them described by Winnicott as the transitional space in which symbolic interaction such as play springs forth (Winnicott 1971). The transitional space forms the crux of the creative nexus. It is the cognitive and emotional space in which thoughts and feelings brought into consciousness through metacognitive action are processed and modulated.

---

1 From hereon I will stick to using the singular term mother – true perhaps in most cases but without necessarily any implied gender bias.

How extreme events interfere with attachment processes: adults' internal working models of attachment and the transitional space

During extreme events adults report being 'lost' in the moment and being unable to process what is happening to them cognitively and emotionally. This is because extreme events overwhelm their ability to be reflective and therefore to internalise events in a meaningful way. What in fact occurs is that they lose the ability to be metacognitive to the extreme events, consequently there is a loss of the ability to dual code what is happening. As a result, extreme events are internalised as concrete Gestalts. These are then sometimes re-experienced as intrusive 'iconic' images and physical sensations of the original experience. These concretised sensations represent successive attempts by the physical and psychological self to recreate and metabolise extreme events. However, they are likely to be too far beyond the scope of a person's cognitive or emotional range to be easily accommodated. Simultaneously symptoms of avoidance emerge because the self does not wish to and perhaps cannot consciously recall the event because it challenges the basis of their earlier psychic development and as such represents an unsurpassable problem of assimilation. On top of all this what is felt as particularly devastating is the person's sense that they are absolutely alone with the experience. As a result, adults feel devastatingly parent-less. They experience the sensation that no one can attune themselves to what has happened to them. This is experienced as a terrifying existential loneliness (Woodcock 2000).

The 'concretisation' of psychic and social processes caused by extreme events is the opposite of the creative symbolising experience that arises in the transitional space or 'third area'. This contrast throws into focus the central task of trauma therapy, which is to provide a basis on which extreme events can be symbolised cognitively and emotionally and thereby assimilated. It makes sense of why practices in psychotherapy and play and arts therapies, which promote symbolic realisation and so enable alternative views to arise, are likely to enable healing. Furthermore, it explains why indigenous healing practices are effective because they bring into play similar creative and symbolising functions (Englund 1998).

Spirituality, creativity and the transitional space

As we have seen, the transitional space is the zone that develops between mother and child as each attunes responsively to the communications of the other. As those who have closely observed mothers and their infants will recognise, attunement is a process that has both an obvious and an extremely subtle register. The mother will respond to subtle cues such as pitch of breathing, rhythm of limb movements, quality of cry and fleeting facial expressions in the infant. Equally, the infant will respond to the mother's repertoire. Subtle responses from the mother, such as a sharp intake of breath, will warn an infant of danger, or a change in her tone of voice will indicate approbation or pleasure. The transitional space is therefore highly complex and consists of layers of intimate verbal and non-verbal communication interacting with the whole of one's socially and culturally given way of being in the world. The transitional space develops as the baby responds and learns symbolic communication. The creative, symbolic aspects of communication spring out of the transitional space because its many layers simply invite creative and symbolic communication. For instance, the baby learns that the frown is both literally about and symbolic of approbation; likewise the smile is literally about and symbolic of pleasure. In the transitional space the baby also learns to be creative and to play with the symbols of communication. For instance a child learns the pleasure of literally and symbolically disappearing from sight by hiding himself behind a cloth. It learns that humour arises when one symbol is replaced with another by accident or deliberately.

Playfulness and symbolic communication are therefore at the heart of the transitional space. They are the key aspects of being metacognitive, which, as we have seen, is at the heart of self-consciousness, and the ability to be reflexive, or to take a view of oneself. Thus the transitional space encompasses consciousness from the undifferentiated oceanic self that is literally submerged in itself, through to the highly differentiated consciousness that makes subtle and highly self-conscious use of symbolic communication.

A definition of how the transcendent emerges

Human beings' sense of the transcendent emerges in the same way. The transcendent is a key notion in the chapter and it will help to carefully define the term. The transcendent has two aspects. One is the sense of the transcendent as something that is subjectively experienced as numinous, sublime, out of this world, excelling humankind and therefore elusive and beyond our consciousness to fully grasp. This sense of the transcendent coincides with the transitional space, which is similarly numinous and oceanic at one pole. The second aspect of the transcendent is its differentiated state. This is somewhat of a contradiction in terms but constitutes the attempt by humankind to name and define the transcendent. This fits with the second pole of the transitional space in which symbols and metaphors are made use of to grasp the sense of things. Thus there are symbols that are both self-referential insofar as they point to themselves and say 'I am a symbol' but at the same time they symbolically grasp the sense of the whole of a thing, a situation or sensation. The symbol of the Christian cross is a good example of this. Another would be of statues of the Buddha in meditation. Often symbols are synthetic in the way they pull together the cognitive, emotional and bodily sensations of a thing. For instance, when someone draws their finger across their throat we not only grasp the meaning of what they are 'saying', we also have a sensation of it too.

Religious ritual makes use of the richness of the symbolic communication offered by the transitional space. For instance, the Christian rituals of Holy Week enact the passion of Jesus Christ, his journey to Jerusalem, the last supper with his disciples, his trial, torture, death, burial and resurrection. Christians immerse themselves into the story during the week and participate in rituals such as the enactment of Christ's washing of his disciples' feet on Maundy Thursday, in which the priest washes the feet of twelve members of the congregation. The ritual is replete with symbolism. As people participate they enter a transitional space which has numinous, oceanic and timeless qualities, indicated by the rituals which both point back through the ages to a specific point in history and also play out the universal and timeless qualities of the passion narrative. Similar qualities are found in many religious rituals. Another instance is the Muslim Haj or pilgrimage to Mecca, in which pilgrims celebrate and commemorate the Abrahamic origins of Islam, central to which is their faith in 'Allah, the One true God'.

Religious ritual provides believers with opportunities to dual code life itself because it gives the sense of being able to look at life events from a perspective that is removed from everyday life. Key aspects of belief are also dual coded merely by virtue of their elusive, symbolic quality. Meaning cannot be tied down and constantly remakes itself, depending on all sorts of social, cultural and historical factors, not least one's own changing perceptions of self because of one's position in the lifecycle. In this way, religious ritual and symbolism makes good use of the transitional space and as such can introduce creativity and movement into stuck psychic processes.

Thinking about transcendence within a sociological, psychological and theological framework

Religion occupies the interface between society, the inner world and the transcendent. One of the questions this chapter therefore raises is how to conduct a conversation about religion which is salient but also makes sense in the often competing realms of sociology and psychology, and without causing the sort of confusion or offence that will alienate a client. In what follows an argument is made for a respectful and engaged way of thinking that complies with both a rigorous scientific and religious frame of reference. It follows the outlines of Wittgenstein's thought, which posited that different disciplines and ways of life use language in different ways, each with their own internal intelligibility (Pears 1971). The sociologist Peter Winch argued that, if this is so, then this relativism means that we shall be unable to conduct meaningful conversations across the boundaries of disciplines (Winch 1958). For instance, the scientist's concept of real cannot be carried into the religious domain. When a scientist says, 'This rock is from an asteroid that passed close to Earth 600,000 years ago,' he is referring to an objectively verifiable fact. Whereas when a religious believer refers to the fact that 'Jesus rose from the dead and ascended into heaven forty days later,' this is not a fact that is objectively verifiable, it is a belief held in faith. It can be seen that the two categories of reality do not coincide nor can the two truth statements, although relatively true, be related to each other. It has been argued that the lack of objective proof of religion literally makes nonsense of its claims (Ayer 1936). However, the work of Kuhn (1970) throws a different light on both the claims of science and religion and subsequent scientific discourse has tended to confirm the liberating value of his thinking. Kuhn argued that scientific thought also advances by way of imaginative discourse and metaphorical thinking and if this is so it is therefore difficult to really draw a hard and fast distinction between scientific thought and the symbolic thought of religion.[2] This allows for a pluralism of thought and the possibility that discourse in one domain can be understood symbolically in one as it is in the other. If this is so, the sociology of religion, insights from psychology and from theology or religious belief can be related to one another and a sensible dialogue continued. This is roughly the method of this chapter. Language and matters of truth are held to be metaphorical and the metaphors from one domain, say psychology, help us in understanding the metaphors in another, for instance spirituality.

The sociological approach used is borrowed from the work of Durkheim (1915). This suggests that religious experience is the transfiguration of social forces into the supernatural realm. This means that the Gods will tend to take on the character and preoccupations of the societies that worship them. Of course, the argument can be used to insist on the primacy of society as the force that creates religion. However, while recognising that as a possibility, the chapter follows the pluralistic notion outlined above that allows for the revelation of revealed religion and thus the inspired application of wise minds to the problems of living and religious answers to those issues. This thinking is taken further using the secular thought of Steiner (1989) pushed in a direction sympathetic to religion. Clearly then, no one definition of spirituality will ever suffice. However the secular notion of transcendent experience developed by Steiner is very compelling because it can appeal either to those with openly religious or those with humanistic values. Steiner argues that transcendence is an innate human experience of the sense of the other, the universal and the beyond, which may be conjured

2 I am grateful to Aylward Shorter (1975) for the outline of this argument.

by aesthetic experience, such as music, poetry or performance – be it theatre, politics[3] or ritual. Of course, Steiner's contentions emerge from sophisticated notions that 'God is dead' in the sense that twenty-first-century humankind has come of age and has no need for the comforts of religion. Theologians have also argued this point, notably Dietrich Bonhoeffer, a pastor and theologian in the Confessing Church in Germany during the 1930s and 1940s. He wrote from prison, before the Nazis eventually executed him: 'So our coming of age forces us to a true recognition of our situation *vis à vis* God. God is teaching us that we must live as men who can get along very well without him. The God who is with us is the God who forsakes us. The God who makes us live in this world without using him as a working hypothesis is the God before whom we are ever standing . . . God allows himself to be edged out of this world and on to the cross. God is weak and powerless in the world, and that is exactly the way, the only way, in which he can be with us to help us' (Bonhoeffer 1959: 122). Interestingly, the thought of Bonhoeffer at that time reflects that of Isaac Luria, the Jewish mystic referred to below (see p. 175), who wrote during the period of savage persecution of the Jews in Spain and Portugal in the sixteenth century. Luria conceived that in the act of creation God had withdrawn from the world.

To summarise, as this section has outlined, the approach of this chapter will be to value difference in all fields of knowledge without resorting to logical absurdity or reductionism.

Beliefs about suffering and change in various religious traditions

Theodicy

Every religion attempts some sort of theodicy, which is a formal way of trying to explain the problem of evil. Typically, a theodicy is an attempt to understand what justice is and why the innocent suffer. For survivors of trauma theodicy emerges as a demand for an answer to a most personal existential question: 'Why me?' None of the major religions have an easy answer to such a complex and far-ranging issue but all offer some sort of coping mechanism, usually based on an ongoing dialogue between the believer and their faith. For instance, the Hindu doctrine of karma may appear to offer a simple solution to its adherents, but in fact the doctrine has subtle and intricate inner workings. Questions of fate, self-

---

3 Politics of the universal, not nationalism, xenophobia or party politics. By definition transcendence implies a universifiable experience. One thinks of Bateson's essay *Pathologies of Epistemology* (1972).

determination and free will come in. Ultimately, as in the Biblical story of Job, what emerges is a sense that life in a created world demands that one lives with a respect for tension between duty, endurance and a knowledge of one's place in the world, despite the desire for self-determination. Each religion is therefore full of stories which take up that theme, for instance, the passion of Christ, stories of Christian and Muslim martyrs, lives of the saints, struggles between gods and man as in the *Mahabharata*. Each of these offers an exemplary way of how to live in a created world. Ultimately, each of these stories or revelations does not provide an answer in a cut-and-dried formula but an example that can be dwelt on and interiorised.

Interiority

Each of the vignettes on world religions that follow will emphasise the interiority of the faiths described. The admittedly difficult, aggressive tendencies found among them will not be dwelt on. The reason for this is because connection is sought between faith as a source of solace – 'the heart of a heartless world' – and the interior space opened up by trauma. What is undoubtedly true for those so inclined from any of these traditions, is that prayer, contemplation, meditation and other mystical practices will open up an interior space. If prayer is taken as an example it can be seen to be a personal dialogue between the self and another. Whether one believes in God or not, the simple act of carrying on this reflective dialogue can be understood as enabling the believer to stand outside the self and by so doing to open up a metacognitive space. Typical themes that run through prayer life, especially in the traumatised and bereaved, are those of sin, guilt, anger, desire for revenge, forgiveness. The role of the counsellor or psychotherapist is to wonder if the religious language of the client/patient and the beliefs and emotions they augur are helpful. The counsellor who shares the religious faith may be able to suggest other religious themes for reflection. The counsellor or psychotherapist who is sympathetic to their beliefs but does not share the heritage will have to use their own framework for thinking and use a collaborative approach to elicit other themes and to wonder if these may be helpful.

Buddhism

Buddhism is perhaps most easily understood as having a contemplative core. The story of the Buddha exemplifies the Buddhist approach to suffering, although suffering is really a rather a poor translation of *dukka*, which means unsatisfactoriness or the realisation that one cannot hang on to life, nothing is perfect, things change, we grow old, we die, things decay. Gautama Buddha was an Indian prince raised in the splendour and protection of his father's palace. At the age of twenty-one, despite his father's entreaties, he left the palace and encountered the misery of life in the outside world for the first time. He dedicated himself to understanding how one could be released from the endless cycle of *dukka* that made up life in the world. He made use of the self-discipline and meditation practices of yoga current at the time. According to legend he eventually meditated for a whole night under the Bo tree with massive commitment and concentration. This led to his enlightenment by which he saw the inner meaning of *dukka* and how mankind can be released from it (Snelling 1987).

Gautama Buddha began teaching others how to achieve 'Buddhahood' which literally means arriving at enlightenment. This entails overcoming the dualism of mind that compels the desire to grasp at things and constantly harasses us to go beyond our limitations (Watts 1957). Buddhism understands that the world of things, at which we grasp, is illusory. Rather than really being solid, as we might think, the world of things is made up and conditioned by an infinitesimal number of facets or *dharmas*. It is only through meditation that the adherent is able to penetrate the double meaning of dharmas. As the Heart Sutra states they are both essentially full and also essentially empty. One way to illustrate this seeming paradox is to think about an electric fan. If it rotates really fast it appears as if the blades are a solid object. This is how most people view the world, as if phenomena are quite solid. However, the seeming 'solid wheel' of the fan is made up of separate blades, which are like the separate *dharmas* that underlie reality. Furthermore, the Buddhist also realises that these *dharmas* too are essentially empty and it is the movement of his own mind, constantly vibrating in action, as it were, and desperately wanting to grasp reality that gives the illusion of reality (Sangharakshiva 1987).

According to Buddhism, suffering emerges because the unenlightened constantly desire. Desire isn't just the gross act of wanting something but is also caused by the self-conscious mind that is constantly busy reflecting on itself, categorising and defining things and experience and imposing an order on the world rather than just being at one with it. The enlightened Buddha mind is not confined to the head but is immanent in the body and immanent in the world; it is still, like the centre of a whirlpool. The unenlightened mind, however, is always divided and always on the move, like the spokes of a wheel in motion. Meditation practise enables the adherent to move closer to the still centre of the wheel and from that vantage point to realise that suffering is an illusion. The bare bones of this understanding might lead one to think that Buddhism takes a harsh view of humankind as being caught up in the illusions of desire and suffering. On the contrary, Buddhism is at best a very compassionate religion that fully understands the nature of humankind to be so ensnared (Merton 1968). Enlightenment allows one to step out of the cycle of reincarnation, that is the cycle of life, suffering and death, which causes the unenlightened to be reborn. Many fully enlightened Buddhas however become Bodhisattvas, that is they choose to re-enter the cycle of reincarnation in order to lead others to enlightenment.

Buddhism spread through Northern India into the Far East. Different traditions emerged. In India and the Far East Mahayana Buddhism developed a distinctive philosophy of enlightenment and a moral and social framework. In China Buddhism was influenced by Taoism and emerged in a distinctive format that became Chan Buddhism, which migrated into Japan as Zen Buddhism. Zen, particularly as it has become translated in the West, emphasises the centrality of Zazen or sitting meditation as a way of enlightenment. It has little to say about ethics or society. There is some emphasis that most people will practise meditation alongside the continuation of their everyday life. Allied to that is an understanding that the practitioner will have a respect for all life, which will eventually emerge from an interior knowledge of suffering and release through enlightenment (Kapleau 1989). Huineng, the sixth patriarch involved in the transmission of Buddhism into its distinctively Zen format, described the process of enlightenment as 'seeing into one's own nature' (Suzuki 1996: 74). In similar terms, Suzuki, the great twentieth-century translator of Zen for the West described enlightenment in similar terms as like 'coming home and quietly resting' (Suzuki 1996). The message that comes through is one of a deeply held self-acceptance and compassion for the self, which emerges from the tumultuous struggle for enlightenment.

Judaism

Few would dispute that persecution and suffering form an essential element in the history of the Jews (Cooper 1988). This is played out each year in the festival of the Passover, which consist of family and community enactments of their collective suffering and the role of faith and divine agency in their deliverance from captivity in Egypt. During the Passover supper the story is read from the Haggadah, a liturgical text that links the festival to historical and contemporary themes of suffering, deliverance and belief in God's purpose for the faithful. Later in the calendar year the three weeks of mourning refer back to the destruction of the first and second temples and encapsulate all the suffering that has occurred since that time. The month before Rosh Hoshanah or the New Year is a time of repentance. This is immediately followed by ten days of penitence which culminate with Yom Kippur or the Day of Atonement. On that day everyone fasts, penitents seek forgiveness from those in the community they have wronged. The services are solemn and cathartic. The intensity of the day amplifies the belief that atonement will be granted for sins that are genuinely repented (Unterman 1981). The festivals also emphasise that the response to suffering is primarily a collective rather than an individual event.

Communal life is so central to Judaism that the idea of a purely separate self and the notion of self-determination are very problematic. For instance, if a Jew were in a state of spiritual doubt, they wouldn't go to a rabbi because of their belief that what the individual may think is less important than that of the community. Instead there is a strong belief that one understands by doing and that doing is done in community. In this respect prayers are always about 'we' rather than about individual needs. They believe however that in each individual there is an inclination to both good and evil but by extension it is life in community that will ameliorate the inclination toward evil. The emphasis on communal life means that suffering is seen as a communal event rather than an individual thing. One particularly noteworthy response to suffering has been the tradition within Judaism of complaints against and debates with God. The book of Job perhaps exemplifies this. Job was an apparently righteous man who was struck down by terrible suffering. In the book itself there is no apparent single answer to why he should have suffered. In the end the answer is less important than his own attitude, which was to remain faithful to God. Such debates have been part of Jewish life and they continue, not least in relation to the Holocaust. Needless to say, the debate with God about suffering in Job and down through the millennia has always been understood in collective terms.

Normative Judaism is enshrined in the Halachah, which is the code of practice developed over millennia from the Mosaic books of law that developed into the Talmud. The Hassidic tradition represents something of a departure although aspects of their beliefs are now firmly embedded in Orthodox Judaism. Their tradition is of interest because it really began as a form of protest among the marginalised as a response to suffering. They made use of the mystic text of the Kabbalah and their beliefs developed through a series of charismatic leaders, among them Isaac Luria, who pressed the notion of God's contraction and withdrawal from the world in the act of creation. This perhaps fitted the sense of catastrophe in his times, which coincided with the persecution and expulsion of the Jews from Spain and Portugal in the sixteenth century. Nevertheless, although God was absent from the world the creative process was initiated by the projection of divine light into the cosmos. The vessels on earth were unable to contain the holy brilliance of the light and shattered into shards. Luria believed it was man's task to continue the act of creation through good works. If properly and mystically intended, acts of good faith will cause the shards of light to be reunited. Cosmic unity will then ensue, heralding the dawn of the messianic age (Heschel 1973). During eras of intense suffering these beliefs sustained the heart of many communities and provided something of an explanation for evil. While taking up aspects of Hassidic beliefs, Orthodox Judaism remains rather aloof not least because of its suspicion about charismatic leaders, which probably began even before the advent of Christianity (Vermes 1973).

Christianity

Jesus' passion, by which is meant his commitment to his message that through faith humankind can have a relationship with God, personified by Jesus himself, as like a child with a father, led to his trial and death, and, so followers believe, his resurrection (Schillebeeckx 1979). The passion is enacted in the culmination of the liturgical calendar during the week of Easter each year. Eastertide begins with the forty-day period of fasting and prayer known as Lent, which commences on Ash Wednesday. In the Ash Wednesday service each communicant is marked on the forehead with ashes, made from the remains of the palms from the previous year. In the old liturgy the priest intoned the words, 'Remember oh man that from ashes you have come and to ashes you will return.' Palm Sunday itself marks the beginning of the Holy Week. The congregation process into church carrying palms and singing 'Hosannah'. The service enacts Jesus' triumphant entry into Jerusalem on a donkey after his three years of ministry. It sets the scene for the passion narrative that unfolds in the week ahead. This progresses on Thursday evening with the feast of the Last Supper, in which a priest symbolically representing Jesus, washes the feet of twelve of the congregation, who represent the twelve disciples. There follows an all-night vigil, which acts out Jesus' invitation to his disciples to pray with him in the Garden of Gethsemane as he waited to be arrested. This is followed on Good Friday morning with the Stations of the Cross, in which believers follow the narrative of Jesus' trial, torture, death and burial by way of a series of fourteen icons or other symbols set on the walls of the church. The Good Friday service that follows in the afternoon is a solemn service, with no celebration of the Eucharist, in which Jesus' death is symbolised by the stripping of the altar. The Easter vigil, usually on Saturday evening, concludes the cycle of services in Holy Week. Most vigils start outside the church with a brazier being lit with the symbolic flame of Jesus' resurrection. The flame is then passed to each member of the congregation who joins a candlelit procession into the unlit church. The service then opens into a magnificent liturgy that celebrates salvation history. The services of Holy Week are very evocative. They enable Christians to identify their personal or community vulnerabilities and sufferings with the exemplary life of Jesus.

Christianity became a powerful political force after the conversion of the Emperor Constantine in the third century CE. Nevertheless, a strong, learned, pietistic and mystical tradition flourished. In various ways Christian mysticism sought for an imaginative union with God, primarily through an interior identification with Jesus' predicament, who took on man's separation and distance from God through his incarnation into humanity. This posits that in essence humanity suffers because of sinfulness that has led to a separation from God. By following Christ's example however and by God's grace and infinite mercy and by one's loving commitment to others, revealed through a passion for justice and compassion toward others and also by contemplative and mystical prayer, humanity can bridge the gap and have a relationship with God.

Protestant forms of Christianity eschewed the efforts of contemplative prayer in favour of a belief that one achieves union with Jesus Christ, as the Son of the Father, by an act of faith. Identification with suffering remains current in their practices but more emphasis is placed on the outward signs of grace such as public morality and wellbeing. Getting on in the world is often held as a significant manifestation of having a good relationship with God. Deep pietism is also part of Protestantism, often characterised by simplicity of lifestyle, simple prayerful worship and withdrawal from the world, which is viewed as sinful.

Christians tend to emphasise the need for endurance in the face of suffering and an expectation that suffering is part of the natural order because of humankind's fall from grace. Identification is made with the passion and the persecution of the early church and the martyrs throughout its history. There is also a generally held belief that purification of the self emerges in the face of suffering.

Islam

Western antagonism to Islam has represented the religion in popular culture as rigid, authoritarian, rule-bound and fundamentalist. Islamic culture, characterised by traditional Sharia law and the states that make use of it, have been viewed with suspicion and distaste. The demonisation of Islam has of course overlooked the richness of the religion and the loyalty of its estimated one thousand million adherents across the world, roughly a fifth of the human race (Ruthven 1984). In fact Islam has a very rich internal world, which is enormously supportive to those of its followers who suffer misfortune. The better-known core of the religion is the five pillars of Islam. These are: belief in the one God, Allah, who has no intermediary, whose prophet was Muhammad; the tradition of prayer five times a day; the requirement to fast during the holy month of Ramadan; to give alms; and to make the haj or pilgimage to Mecca, the holiest shrine of the faith, at least once during one's lifetime. These are the outward expressions of a faith that is rooted in the dynamic interrelationship of Quran, community and tradition (Guillaume 1956).

The holy text of the Quran is of central importance and is understood as the expression of Allah. To Western critics the text has seemed jumbled, repetitive, contradictory and wooden. However, in Arabic the text comes alive and has an allusive, poetic character rich in symbolic beauty. It is considered a sacred duty for Muslims to internalise the Quran. The isomorphic character of the text enables this to happen for those without the means to learn the whole, because having learned part, one is in a sense in command of the character of the whole. The central message of Islam is that the religion mirrors and illuminates the natural world, and that, together, religion and the natural world are the expression of Allah. Similarly Sharia law, which literally means 'the river that runs toward life', reflects the inextricable and dynamic link between the way things should be in the natural world order and the purpose and will of Allah. Central to the religion is the emphasis on the community of the faithful as a living expression of the truth rather than the rationalism of the religious text. The five pillars of Islam unite the community.

Muslims do not believe that simple rational explanations can determine why the apparently innocent suffer, only faith can enable understanding about suffering to emerge. As always they emphasise the importance of the community of the faithful. Thus, their attitude to suffering is summarised in the saying that it is 'Better to live for sixty years under an unjust Iman than for one night of anarchy.' By anarchy is meant what it would be like to live outside the community of believers and thereby outside the rule of Allah's will as expressed through Sharia law. Strength therefore comes from blind faith in Allah and acceptance of his will in all matters, good and bad. Muslims believe that humankind has limited knowledge of the future and of the unseen and that the reasons for all actions that lead either to affliction or happiness are part of God's mercy. The Quran specifically mentions in the Sura Bagara that, 'On no soul does God place a burden greater than he can bear.' They therefore believe that it is a spiritual duty to accept any burden that befalls them, because they believe that Allah first gives mercy along with the misfortune. It is therefore with Allah's knowledge and will that misfortune occurs and that affliction is a test of faith in Him. It is only by turning to Him and through acceptance of the burden of suffering that it actually becomes bearable, that by His mercy and grace good actually emerges out of affliction.

This brief sketch cannot do justice to the real richness of beliefs or the subtle differences that lie between the Sunni and Shia traditions in Islam. The differences however can be summarised by the suggestion that the problem of evil and the question of suffering is central to Shia. Their community has seemingly always been the more restless and radical and uncompromising in the interpretation of how matters of faith relate to the realities of politics and governance. In the first century of Islam, Hussain, the nephew of the prophet and later Ali, the grandson of the prophet, challenged the orthodox and more conservative rule of the caliphs. Both were massacred. The events are memorialised in Shia countries with passion plays in which the suffering of the painful martyrdoms provide an outward expression and resolution of the suffering of the faithful in general.

By contrast with the seemingly questing and restless Shia, the Sunni tradition is settled and autochthonous – literally rooted in the concrete realities of adherents' lives, which it seeks to make sacred through detailed observance of Sharia law. This often gives the superficial impression that the Sunni tradition is more conservative, more likely to stress orthodoxy and less spiritually inclined. In fact the Sunni tradition is deeply spiritual. At its heart it sees the potential for each moment to be ritualised as a reflection of religious purpose, even the most mundane such as eating or defacating.

Another significant section of Islam are the Sufis who represent the mystical tradition in Islamic culture. They developed and kept alive the interior meaning of the religion. Ultimately, Sufism is not concerned with suffering per se but with mystical union with God, from which we all originate and by this transcend suffering.

Suspicion, misunderstanding and the demonisation of Islam has meant that the pietistic qualities of the faith have been overlooked in the West. Yet, as the foregoing suggests, Islam provides a powerful way of comprehending and enduring suffering. Its beliefs articulate the link between faith and experiences in a very direct way. For instance, in a group for survivors of torture one man said, 'When people are tortured it makes them better people. They turn away from materialism and are kinder to people. Even though it hurts, torture changes people. I have met many people of whom this is so.' Another husband and wife whose family like many in their Shi'ite community had endured intense suffering said, 'We Shia are like ants walking on glass, we must make no sound.' By this he meant that to suffer is to be expected, it is the way of life in the world and understanding and through faith and community one conforms to the experience without complaint.

Inner and outer worlds

One of the aesthetic beauties of religious life is the way that the inner world and outer worlds are linked in an isomorphic way, so that patterns of belief, inner convictions and feeling states are expressed outwardly in ritual and symbols. In this way, symbols and ritual provide a way of exteriorising beliefs and feelings. Each religion, no matter how plain and pietistic, will have a set of formal rituals and symbols and every community of believers will develop ritual elaborations. These may be local practices or they may be accepted across the religion as a whole. For instance, in the Roman Catholic Church saints' days are very often marked by processions around the locality with a model of the saint carried on a bier. However, each locality will have its particular practices relating to this. For instance, at St Marie de la Mer on the south coast of France, a Virgin Mary is carried on a bier around the town and then taken out to sea in a fishing boat, thereby conferring prayers for the safety and prosperity of the fishing fleet. Rituals and symbols also provide a way of interiorising beliefs. For instance, many of the Hindu temples of Tamil Nadu in South India are richly carved with scenes from the lives of the Gods. These allow believers to relate the relationships and struggles of the Gods to their own life events. Alternatively, the carvings may allow devotees to take themselves beyond the limitations of their circumstances. Beautiful frescos painted in small cells in the outer wall of the Kailasanathar Temple of Shiva at Kanchipuram in Tamil Nadu, South India, depict more intimate scenes of the life of Shiva and the cycle of creation. These would have allowed *sadhus*, or holy men, to meditate and to internalise at a conceptual and emotional level the whole of creation and at a subtle and transcendent level their place in the scheme of things.

In the same way that communities will elaborate symbols so will believers also elaborate personal associations around ritual and symbols. Believers may have a favourite icon, or a ritual or a passage from the scriptures that is most meaningful to them. Ritual and symbols open up the metacognitive space. In so doing they provide a richer internal world in which the believer can process events. This can be so even if the rituals or symbols do not directly relate to their circumstances or trauma. Needless to say, if they do, then the efficacy of the symbolic area may be enhanced. The ease with which the believer can move between the actual and symbolic can facilitate psychotherapy. Insofar as symbols mediate the inner world and the external, or social world, so can language itself be understood as both a mediator of the internal world and an accommodation with the external social world that enables both to interact in a meaningful way. So conversation can be richly symbolic and make good use of metaphor, with the unique facility that metaphor has in the words of Cox and Theilgard (1981) to effect the 'instantaneous fusion of two separated realms of experience.'

It must always be remembered that religions have often externalised beliefs about living in a created world in terms of demands for social justice. This is true for Taoism, Judaism, Christianity and Islam. In this context one should make the connection that trauma is all too often linked to issues of social justice. It is no accident that it is the poor, the marginalised, those without a voice who very often bear the brunt of the traumas that we witness in the modern world. Therefore, taking up the religious call for social justice has a resonance within a counselling or psychotherapy relationship that takes spirituality seriously. Ultimately, spirituality is about living well in this world.

Responding to the psychological complications of trauma

Several of the complications of trauma relate to the withdrawal of the sufferer from life around them. As we have seen, trauma imbues the sufferer with a sense of existential loneliness and interferes with their capacity to relate to their own internal self and thereby to have empathy with others. It also undermines basic trust. Because of these three factors the sufferer may withdraw into themselves, finding the company of others unrewarding and even threatening. In these circumstances religious life can offer a trap for the unwary because one of the themes of all traditions is the virtue of withdrawal and contemplation in order to deepen spiritual experience. What the psychotherapist has to determine is whether the withdrawal has an ultimately positive element or whether it has a pathological character. As a rule, one could say that withdrawal with a genuinely spiritual character will enable the person to relate better to others and will also deepen their empathy. This is because what occurs in religious withdrawal is an identification with the universals of human existence, which promotes self-awareness and empathy. However, a pathological withdrawal will leave the sufferer in a non-empathic situation, withdrawn because they are struggling both to relate to their own inner world and hence to others. Withdrawal can also be caused by the melancholia associated with mourning. In both instances, the psychotherapist or counsellor needs to have an awareness of the object relations of the sufferer. By this is meant to what and how are they relating consciously and unconsciously in their internal world? Do they have a depleted or distorted sense of self and others that will not self-correct over time? Or are their inner objects attenuated but basically intact? Careful judgement is required. Enquires about how the sufferer relates to himself and his thoughts about others in the withdrawn state will throw light on how healthy the withdrawal is.

Another complication is to wonder what happens to anger. Most religious systems of the contemplative sort tend to eschew or sublimate anger. It is doubtful if this is psychologically healthy as a long-term strategy. After trauma anger may be so great as to seem dangerous. Because of the deadly and, in fantasy, uncontained quality of the anger it may be repressed or denied as a way of being managed. What is most important, however, is that anger is not ignored by the psychotherapist. Fortunately, religions do have stories of righteous anger that can be used as ways to express and vent this anger. These can be used to provide a permissive stance toward anger and rage that can enable the emotions to be expressed openly in a contained way that will facilitate their exploration and integration.

Even at times when anger is acknowledged, religious belief allied to cultural practices can leave believers in a bind. For instance, a Muslim Tamil woman from Sri Lanka, had alcohol forced down her throat and was then gang raped by paramilitary police. She could not tell her husband about what had happened because of shame. She feared her infant daughters would not be able to marry in years to come because of shame. She also could not bear to have a sexual relationship with her husband and could not explain to him why, although he was not naïve as to the possible reasons. She felt her body was disgusting and no longer her own. She had the impulse to hurl herself under an underground train not only because she felt that life was shameful and pointless but, to use her words, 'So this body can be crushed and broken.' Her strong religious beliefs just about kept her from suicide but they also meant that she regarded rape as so shameful that her life was ruined. Work with her entailed acknowledging her positive religious beliefs, which strengthened her and working cognitively and emotionally to reduce the sting of the intrusive memories. This was achieved within the confines of a confiding counselling relationship, in which her basic trust was re-established. Then gradually we reframed where the blame and shame lay for what had been inflicted on her. Thus it was only when the counselling relationship was very secure and had made some gains, which supported the general value of her core beliefs, that the woman could allow her beliefs about shame to be reconsidered. This was done on the basis that religious beliefs do not impose absolutes, and that especially in unusual circumstances religion always offers a compassionate way out. First of all she had to believe again that her life had value, despite the shameful event inflicted on her. It was the counselling relationship that demonstrated that she was of value, which was at the core of a successful outcome. This shows how beliefs always operate within the context of relationships. It is only when they get detached from relationships and real dilemmas of human experience that beliefs become oppressive.

The last complicating factor covered here is the problem of narcissism, which often becomes evident after trauma. What may occur is that the person becomes preoccupied with the wounds to themselves to the exclusion of empathy with others' situations. The loss of basic trust makes narcissism more likely and more complex because the sufferer will not have an internal framework for deriving real comfort and satisfaction from others. Narcissism is difficult to treat because the sufferer lives in a pretty closed system in which the real self is undernourished and only the narcissistic part may be allowed to flourish. Insofar as other exists it is usually solely to provide the split off narcissistic part with satisfaction. In the case of the traumatised with narcissistic wounds, that usually means attention is demanded for the wounded part of the self, to the exclusion of the rest of the sufferer and also the mental health of others. If narcissism gets transfixed on to religious objects the psychotherapist may find it a struggle to redirect the sufferer who may counter with the imperatives of religion, thus placing the sufferer in a doubly closed system, that of religion and narcissism. One of the keys to treating narcissism is to offer oneself as a person to whom the sufferer can relate the whole of their personality, not just the split off part. This means reaching out to the healthy aspects of the personality which may normally be hidden from view. Also it requires acute observation as to what is part of the narcissistic system and what is part of the healthy functioning system. When psychotherapy offers this degree of care, differentiation of feeling states and sensitivity to object relations and

meaning, people may make a choice to turn toward life that finds satisfaction in others, what Symington (1993) refers to as 'turning toward the
lifegiver'.

Reflexivity, psychotherapy and spiritual practice

The dilemma for the reflective practitioner who has a spiritual practice is
how to make legitimate use of that knowledge and experience. For instance,
I have a colleague who sees exactly the same sort of families as I. She has
the same success and failure rate. Although many families have strong
religious beliefs she never talks about those issues with families. Although
tolerant of religious belief in clients she is allergic to it in other settings,
having been brought up in the 1930s by leftish-feminist-rationalist parents.
Other colleagues are from Muslim cultural backgrounds, but reject the
belief system. Other staff are Christian, but believers in a private pietistic
tradition, which believes that religion is a private affair and not for discussion unless raised by the family. However, the majority of the individuals and families we see in the clinic where I work are strong believers in
a variety of religious traditions. They live and breathe their beliefs and
make sense of the world through the frameworks they provide. But they
tend to keep their beliefs quiet because they do not trust that Western-
trained psychotherapists working in a Western institution will have very
much understanding or sympathy for them.

However, as supervisor and a reflective practitioner I believe that
spiritual practice can lead to transformation and greater freedom. Indeed, I
believe that spiritual practice can sustain and transform people who have
been through extreme events and conversely, that extreme events, as noted
by Frankl (1963) and by Gorst-Unsworth and Goldenberg (1998) represent
an opportunity for personal and spiritual transformation. This belief does
not seek to minimise the overwhelming losses or the acute painfulness of
people's experiences and the ongoing stress of living with forced change.
However, it notes that the awfulness of life situations can be held in
dialectical tension with belief and that by making use of family beliefs in
psychotherapy, transformation and healing can occur. This leads me to
encourage the rationalist-secular and private-pietistic colleagues who are
working with religious individuals and families to make use of the resources
of family beliefs and practices in their psychotherapy practice.

Religious belief as reframe

Systemic therapists are familiar with the notion of 'reframing', whereby a
negative idea is connoted in a positive way by the therapist, in such a way
that new light is thrown on a situation and beliefs are challenged and may be
shifted. It can be argued that religious beliefs are full of reframes. For

example, take the scandalous death of Christ, which Christians say demonstrates Christ's victory over the power of sin and death because of their belief in his resurrection. Such powerful reframes are the familiar stuff of religious faith and believers are often very quick to understand a reframe that may be offered as food for thought, which can challenge and extend their personal beliefs. For instance, a Muslim woman from Rwanda who had endured the full horrors of the genocide including the 'disappearance' of her husband and two of her five young children, was about to be reunited with her children. This wasn't easy because of the way that separation had changed them all and particularly because her eldest son who had been a sweet lad of ten when they were separated was now a young man of sixteen. She experienced him as a potential sexual threat to herself and her two daughters because of her history of sexual abuse as a child, serial rape during the genocide and sexual exploitation by a priest who had helped her to escape. Some of our work focused on enabling her to express and manage her fears and fantasies and to cope with being reunited with her children. Just prior to the family's reunion she was in a state of acute anxiety and despair and wondered why had all these terrible things happened to her? Why should she have to face more difficulty? Why had she not been killed with the others? She was a woman of strong beliefs and I said to her, 'At these moments when we have little hope, often God gives us the gift of hope. It is of course a gift, which we are free to refuse.' This was a subtle reframe, which invited her to believe that the fragment of hope that sustained her was a gift, which should not be refused. This actually amplified the meaningfulness of her hope and it shaped her ability to cope. It allowed her to look at her dilemmas with different eyes: those of a survivor with some measure of choice over her internal world and the way it shaped her ability to cope.

Often parables and religious stories hinge on a reframe that makes one see the world as if through the eyes of the spiritually enlightened. Take this story about St Francis of Assisi. Toward the end of his life, he was travelling with Brother Leo to each of the recently established Franciscan monasteries. As they trod the road to the next monastery St Francis wondered aloud, 'What would you consider to be perfect happiness, Brother Leo?' Leo replied, 'To be able to preach with such eloquence that all unbelievers came to Christianity and we were able to establish Franciscan houses throughout the known world.' 'No, Brother Leo,' St Francis replied, 'I would not think that perfect happiness.' So Leo tried again and again, mulling the question over as their journey passed. Eventually, with their destination in sight he begged St Francis to provide an answer, to which the saint replied, 'It would be to arrive at our destination, footsore and hungry, knock at the door and have the night watchman (who knew them well) shout 'Go away beggars' and throw us out. Then to knock again and have the watchman beat us back with a stave and shout 'Thieves, miscreants, go away before I have you jailed' and then lock the door against us for the night. Perfect happiness would be to be able to accept that with perfect equanimity'.[4] Grasping the point of such a reframe can leave the listener viewing the world as if through a different set of spectacles.

Different beliefs, different lenses

The use of different lenses is widely appreciated as being pretty essential to good reflective counselling practice (Liddle 1991). This is a necessary approach when encouraging colleagues to make use of religious beliefs. This is because the history of religion from the Western experience is a story of religious belief as an overarching perspective and a controlling ideology and as such a singular lens through which all other phenomena should be perceived (Foucault 1986). For instance, one can think of Galileo's battle with the authorities of the Catholic Church. Conversely, the history of secular rationalism is a history of the replacement of religion by rational thought. Interestingly, secularism as a development rather than replacing one controlling ideology (religion) with another (rationalism) ultimately introduced different perspectives and the notion of plurality. This allows different belief systems to live alongside each other and may be thought of as the sociological corollary of the systemic notion of different lenses. Despite the implied openness of this to other belief systems, psychotherapy has tended to share the common scientific heritage of Western rationalism. As a result it has been rather rejectionist of spirituality, seeing it, for instance, in Freud's terms as a form of inferior rationality. Consequently, religious objects such as God and revered prophets and leaders are seen as vehicles for projected wishes (Freud 1927). In these terms, religion tends to be understood as a defensive system against the sometimes unbearable reality of life.

Some guidelines for reflective practice

This chapter has taken the approach of respecting the plurality of domains of thought without being reductionistic and this approach is also followed when thinking about guidelines for reflective practice. In working with people who are different it is obviously important to respect their cultural difference and to work with empathy, which means trying to see the world through their eyes. When one has never encountered a person from a particular culture before it is important that a two-way dialogue is encouraged. This begins with the psychotherapist trying to find out as much as possible about the client's culture and to dwell on that knowledge in a reflective way. The psychotherapist can then approach the work as an

4 Teisho with Roshi Gen-un-ken/Fr. Ama Samy S.J. during session at De Tiltenberg, Netherlands, November 2000.

outsider, but with some understanding, which will usually be appreciated by the client. Therapists can also make use of curiosity to explore the areas of difference. For instance, over the years I have developed a knowledge of Islamic beliefs and cultural practices. This was particularly helpful on an occasion when I worked with a very observant Muslim family. The family consisted of father, mother and six daughters who ranged in age from six to eighteen. From the outset of the initial session the father took the lead and spoke on behalf of the family. I showed him respect and sought to understand family relationships from his perspective for the first part of the session, despite the fact that I felt that the mother and daughters had important things to say about the things that had brought them into therapy. These included the anxiety in the family about the life-threatening illness of the second to youngest daughter and the way this threatened family relationships in a way that resonated with an earlier episode of political persecution that they had experienced as deeply traumatic. Once I felt that the family had the measure of my respect for their traditions, I then asked the father for permission to speak to his wife and daughters. I highlighted our cultural differences, by saying something like, 'As you know, in my culture men and women are permitted to speak to each other in a range of different circumstances from your culture. For instance, men and women may even talk to each other when they are strangers. But now that we have got to know each other a little, I wonder if I could speak to your wife and daughters, not as a stranger but as someone with an outside view who may find things that are helpful?' We then had a very revealing dialogue, which didn't have to work against the resistance that I might have encountered if I had plunged straight in at the beginning of the session and cut across the father. Despite using the language of culture and difference I didn't assume that the family was a cultural stereotype but invited them to enter into conversation with me from their individual perspectives within the context of the family. I wondered if her serious illness gave the second to youngest daughter a more privileged position and how this showed itself in family relationships? I wondered what were the effects on the eldest daughter and the youngest girl, whose privileged positions the second to youngest daughter had seemingly usurped? I wondered if their religion and culture have any wisdom to shed on this situation? The daughters' answers conveyed their beliefs in the need for patience and forbearance in the face of suffering and the rightfully privileged position that is occupied by one who suffers. At the same time they were able to express their chagrin at how events had upset the natural order in the family. These facets of family life were expressed as a collective dilemma, not an individualised discourse about how one daughter had displaced another, although there was a truth in that understanding too. Thus there were many mutually interacting layers involved in understanding what was going on in the family: culture, religious belief, the family as a system, individual feelings and desires.

In all encounters with clients from other cultures it is also important to hold in mind the history of the relationship between the client's country of origin and one's own. The client is in a less powerful position than the psychotherapist and often the psychotherapist represents a country with a colonial past, therefore it is wise to notice if one is playing out the residue of that history. In the cases where there has been a colonial history I wonder aloud with the client how we each relate to it. Does the history give us some sort of common thread or might it alienate because they feel that the West was responsible for the impoverishment of their country. This sort of enquiry is not just politeness or good technique, it is also salient to the suffering that people from other countries endure. Many suffer from extreme events and loss because of the consequences of war caused by post-colonial political dynamics.

It is also important to have both confidence and scepticism in the efficacy of spiritual transformation. This chapter has leant toward confidence. Necessarily it is good if such confidence is developed within the therapeutic relationship with believers, so that emotional empathy can work alongside the intellectual scepticism that a psychotherapy training develops in one. Private scepticism is helpful because it leads to a state of mind in which things are properly evaluated. This is useful because one's own balance between confidence and scepticism can attune one to the layers of enthusiasm and doubt that are often found in believers. The sections above have outlined some areas where religious belief can create big difficulties for the client. There are others. For instance, some people feel persecuted and damaged by a religious upbringing forced on them by family and community. Reflective practice should be alert to these. Not least it should also be vigilant to the problems of idealisation and flight into health.

We have also seen how religion, spirituality and creativity are related. Religious life opens up an interior dialogue that can be ultimately healing. There are limits to the psychotherapist's work and good use of sympathetic priests, imams and other spiritual leaders should be encouraged. For instance, a psychotherapist can work with the guilty feelings of a patient, but he cannot offer a rite of forgiveness that may allow a person a final transfiguration and expiation of their guilt. Similarly, if a priest offers a rite of forgiveness but the client is still preoccupied with guilt, then continuing psychotherapy may be helpful.

It is also important that the psychotherapist does not fear fundamentalism. Fundamentalism tends to be a pejorative term. However, one person's fundamentalism is another's cherished belief. Understood carefully of course, fundamentalism is a rejection of plurality. It is rare to find people where this is entirely the case. Furthermore, psychotherapy works through the relationship with the client. If fundamentalism is encountered and cannot be worked with intellectually it is advisable for the psychotherapist to eschew religious dialogue and to concentrate on making the emotional relationship. In other words, making an empathic attachment to the client in which emotional themes can be worked through. The religious frame can then be used later within the relationship as another mode of exploration and healing.

Conclusion

At the heart of this chapter is the understanding that extreme events can cause a diminishment in the creative inner life of individuals. This theme has been developed alongside an understanding of how religious belief can help people overcome trauma and suffering simply because religious belief is at best a very creative act. After all, other than the creation of life itself, what could be more creative than faith? The chapter has sought to encourage practitioners to collaborate with their clients in order to reach a creative understanding of how their beliefs may sustain them in the face of suffering. It has shown that the very demonstration of respect for beliefs can release the potential of those beliefs to provide enlightenment and support. Finally, religion has a long history of understanding the dilemmas of life, central to which is the problem of suffering. Practitioners are encouraged to understand what they have to offer both to themselves and their clients.

Chapter 7

Trauma and the therapist

Hattie Berger

The nature of the trauma relationship

The process of writing this chapter reflects the essence of my experience as a trauma counsellor. I have had moments of clarity and sure-footedness swiftly followed by ambivalence and self-doubt. At times I have felt certain of what I am doing and then discovered I am lost in the process again and no longer on firm ground. In describing and separating aspects of the experience for the therapist, I have been struck by how often personal dynamics merge and overlap with those of the client. There is a way in which things connect in the trauma counselling relationship that often cannot be explained and does not fit neatly with theoretical explanations.

The therapist witnesses the rawness and senselessness of traumatic wounding. This witnessing more often engages our vulnerability than our knowledge, our own fears and grief, our sense of mortality and morbidity, the humility and humiliation in human suffering. We are open to absorbing profound loss, hurt and mistrust from our clients but also to the stimulation of these human states present in us all.

Paradox is inherent to the therapist's experience (Hycner 1993) and makes the work challenging and daunting. The effective therapist involves herself[1] deeply with her client's experiencing and yet keeps enough back to hold distress without getting lost in it, a particularly difficult balance when faced with the overwhelm resulting from trauma. The therapist needs to 'know' about trauma – the symptoms and how they manifest, something of the stages of integration and change – and yet be open to meeting her client as an individual whose experience and way of being she knows nothing about. Perhaps his[2] journey to recovery and her own experiences along the

---

1 I have chosen the female gender to represent the therapist or counsellor, but of course the material is relevant to both men and women.
2 Likewise, I have chosen the male gender to represent the client, although the material is relevant to both sexes.

way do not resemble learned theory. Both the objective knowledge and the subjective experience are essential yet 'both tear at each other for dominance' (Hycner 1993: 13). The trauma therapist is pragmatic and skilled in her work with her client and yet feels helpless as her client struggles with the existential crisis engendered by the traumatic experience. The therapist attunes to 'being' rather than 'doing' and struggles with the incumbent insecurity. She needs to be able to sit with the uncertainty of not knowing and yet know when explanation or technique might help. The therapist may find herself with oscillating and contradictory feelings in relation to her client. Sometimes she feels powerless or overwhelmed in sessions, at other times punitive and distant towards her client. Feelings can be polarised, emerge suddenly and change from session to session or even within a session. These ideas are explored later in the chapter in terms of transference and countertransference.

Therapists have a power conferred by their clients, as the experts who are going to resolve their pain. The therapist is not recently traumatised like her client and therefore may not be as immediately vulnerable. She may know something about the symptoms and patterns of trauma unlike her client and has experience of being with people. She has a cognitive grasp that may be missing for her client at that time. Yet whilst it is not a relationship of equals, if it is to help, then neither is it a relationship based on the expertise and 'knowing' of the therapist. In its essence trauma counselling must be a meeting of two people engaged in a delicate relationship. It is this relationship and its shifting struggles over time: doing versus being, control meeting vulnerability, uncertainty challenging knowledge, that provides the growth for both client and therapist.

This chapter explores the dynamics of trauma counselling focusing largely on the experience for the therapist. The themes explored may apply to all trauma counselling, both short- and long-term, and to any counselling relationship where the client has had some traumatic experience either recently or in the past. My experience is rooted in short- and medium-term work for an organisation where the client has suffered one or more recent traumatic experiences. This necessarily flavours my approach.

The dynamics of the therapeutic relationship

Countertransference and transference

Used here countertransference, a psychoanalytic term (Freud 1912; Slatker 1987; Clarkson 1995), describes the emotions, physical sensations, thoughts and images that the therapist feels towards the client during the course of counselling. Countertransference can be in response to the client's transference or in reaction to the client's experience, or it can be subjective resulting from the therapist's own character structure or history. The term also encompasses the universal human reactions to this kind of suffering.

Transference refers to the complex of reactions that a client experiences in relation to, or projects on to, the therapist in the course of therapy (Freud 1915; Clarkson 1995). These feelings or reactions may be replaying the dynamics of a previous relationship or situation from childhood. In trauma counselling countertransference and transference reactions can be linked directly to the traumatic event representing dynamics of the victim's and perpetrator's experience (Wilson and Lindy 1994; Clarkson 1995).

Countertransference reactions are present in all counselling relationships but how much attention is paid to them varies greatly. It will depend firstly on the theoretical approach held by the therapist. Working psychodynamically these aspects may be the keystone of the work. From a person-centred perspective, however, transference–countertransference dynamics may not be defined or worked with explicitly. The duration of counselling is another factor. If counselling is limited, dynamics may only be explored if they seem to be impacting directly on the resolution of the trauma. In long-term work more room can be given to therapist's and client's experience of each other. The stage of the counselling relationship is further defining: the counsellor may choose to hold hunches about her reactions at the beginning to allow trust to be established in order to sustain exploration. Awareness and willingness in the counsellor will shape how much she notices and what she then does will vary with her personality, experience, with different clients and at different times in her life. Her response will also depend on how she feels about PTSD and trauma and her own experiences and beliefs.

The setting the therapist works in becomes defining, in regard to the degree of trauma counselling undertaken, for example. Similarly this defines how much time is made available for reflection between seeing clients and the support available from colleagues and supervisors. Where counselling takes place in or for an organisation, both the client and the therapist carry the cultural dynamics and expectations of the organisation and bring them, often unconsciously, into the work. The company's attitude to traumatisation, to vulnerability and psychological help will impact on the nature of the working relationship. For example, is the expectation that counselling will provide a speedy return to work?

One counsellor's experience included working for a large transport organisation counselling train drivers who are witness to suicides or accidents whilst they are driving. It is a predominantly male and somewhat macho environment where having your first 'one under' is known as 'joining the club'. The standard refrain from manager to driver is: 'I had a couple when I was a driver – ten years ago we never had PTSD, we just got on with the job.' The focus at work is managing sickness absence so the manager's first concern with the driver is how long he or she will be away from work. The same refrain and question are offered to the counsellor.

The client arrives for counselling trying to contain and minimise his feelings (perhaps unconsciously) and the counsellor colludes with this (unconsciously relieved). She is struggling with a dual role of professional (and personal) commitment to her client, and the competing needs of the organisation in which counselling is expected to reduce sickness absence.

If the nature of the client's experience was overwhelming, the counsellor may find herself feeling more intense emotions herself. Or she may notice she feels nothing despite hearing a horrible account or witnessing great distress in her client. The gender of the therapist and client will also shape their relationship (Stoller 1968; Mitchell 1974), as will the therapist's attitude or perception of the trauma described and how the client perceives the therapist. All are unique and form a complex interweaving, as particular to the time of counselling and the nature of the incident as to the therapist and the client. Without the room to explore these ideas in detail here, they are offered as points of reflection within individual practice.

Conceptualising the counselling relationship is an essential part of the process but no easy task. Reactions often have no linear pattern, progression is unpredictable and the dynamics are not necessarily stage-specific. This reflects the nature of traumatic overwhelm and distress. Sometimes several contradictory themes occur within one counselling relationship, at other times a therapist is not aware of any particular reaction. I think it is unhelpful to assume transference 'is there somewhere'. The therapist then subtly impinges her/his own agenda on the process, failing to value the client's here-and-now experiencing. Watching and noticing and, critically, *observing one's own responses and feelings* will give the therapist the clues needed to their own and to some of the client's experience. In other words focusing on the therapist's experience of the client is as supportive of the counselling process as the client's experience. This demands a phenomenological approach to the counselling, working with what *is*, in both therapist and client. Consequently the focus of this chapter is largely the therapist's responses.

The counsellor is likely to experience reactions at some stage in the counselling process. What matters is that therapeutic and supervisory space are created to allow for and expect 'forbidden feelings' (Wilson and Lindy 1994: 14). These include arousal, voyeurism, disgust and horror. They may be 'forbidden' in terms of feeling inappropriate given what the client has been through (for instance arousal and voyeurism) or feel forbidden given the role of the counsellor: 'I should be able to hear this without feeling horrified.' The feelings that follow may then be guilt and shame.

Broadly speaking, countertransference is experienced on a plane polarised by over-identification with the client or the client's material and avoidance of contact with the client's material (Wilson and Lindy 1994: 15). The following is by no means an exhaustive description of countertransference dynamics and, although these dynamics apply to all trauma work, the complexity of long-term work with survivors of sustained trauma is not explored in depth here. In exploring four common themes, the possible transference that may invoke it, the qualities in the therapist that may contribute and the other factors cultural and contextual that may be shaping the therapist's response are described. Reading these descriptions too rigidly will limit the work and dulls the therapist's intuitive response to her client. These ideas are intended to contribute to conceptualising the client's and therapist's experiencing.

Countertransference: over-identification

Somatic responses

The therapist finds herself with physical reactions in sessions or in anticipation of sessions. She might notice feeling physically sick, her heart rate increasing, perhaps some generalised anxiety or fear. She might feel an overwhelming desire to get up, leave the session, or at the very least move. She may notice involuntary shifting in her seat. This can happen as the client describes material (or indeed in anticipation of what the client may describe). Physical symptoms may be felt by the therapist before there is any indication of trauma material and can be an indication of some experience of trauma for the client that is undisclosed. One counsellor experienced an unexplained 'blinding' headache in two successive sessions with the same client. The client later revealed his fear of the headaches he had been experiencing since the event and of his poor eyesight that he felt had made him more vulnerable during the assault. The countertransference may express itself in certain sensations, such as dread. The therapist secretly hopes her client will cancel the session or not turn up.

The therapist's somatic resonance may be mirroring the client's feelings at the time of traumatisation or his fears around coming for counselling. The therapist often experiences resonance when the client is dissociated from these feelings himself. Somatic resonance can be an indication of current stress in the therapist or tapping into her own wounds. There is often an extraordinary synchronicity present in trauma counselling when the client works with a counsellor with similar personal issues. Very often somatic resonance is about the therapist's fears of not being enough, unable to contain the horror or relieve the client's pain. The longing in clients who are traumatised to be freed of their anxiety, to feel back in control, is intense. More often this desire is communicated non-verbally, through projective identification. Projective identification (Gomez 1997) is felt by the therapist as her own anxiety, dread or physical feelings when it is in fact a transference on to the therapist of feelings the client is not able to communicate or bear for themselves. Longing may also be expressed verbally through 'why' questions, a fixation with how things were before the incident or asking the therapist directly for ways of getting through this. The awareness of these feelings allows her to choose to contain the feeling for the client temporarily or to gently help the client take it back as his own to integrate the experience.

Rescue responses

The longing to rescue and make better is dormant in most therapists and is particularly awakened by the longing to be rescued experienced by trauma clients. Herman (1992) understands this in terms of the powerful parent/child dynamic evoked in trauma counselling. The experience of overwhelm from trauma reduces the client to a dependent child emotionally, looking for rescue and nurture from the therapist/parent.

This can show behaviourally with the therapist blurring boundaries. She finds herself booking additional sessions because her client 'needs the support'. Or she finds herself holding on to the client's material excessively between sessions, thinking about how she might work with him. The therapist may simply find herself feeling very merged with her client, experiencing difficulty separating out where she begins and ends. She understands her client intuitively, is drawn to protect and can feel similarities in the way they experience things. This can be a reflection of the counsellor's own developmental wounds, created when, as a child, the counsellor was the emotional caretaker of one of her parents. Behaviourally it may demonstrate in the desire to advocate (Herman 1992) on behalf of the client, taking on the fight with authorities and managers (in the workplace) rather than empowering the client to do this for themselves. When trauma sessions regularly have a pragmatic and organising theme it can indicate the 'social worker' response in the therapist.

If the over-identification described above persists without awareness it can leave the therapist with an intense feeling of helplessness, not knowing how to be with her client. Ultimately she feels de-skilled: she doesn't know enough or have enough experience to be doing this kind of work. Left unnoticed and unchecked the therapist fails to support her client or herself. It is the fastest route to burnout explored later in this chapter.

The cognitive or visual component of this countertransference may be clear images of the traumatic material, particularly where there is physical violation or injury. It can feel intense, as though these images are intruding into the therapist and violating her in the way her client has felt violated. She may feel aroused by images, wanting to know more details or feeling sexually stimulated by the violence described leading to a voyeuristic attunement with the perpetrator, or indeed reflecting the client's experience at the time of the incident. The following case study is intended as an illustration of some of the countertransference dynamics just described in practice. All case study material has been disguised to protect the identity of the client.

Bill attended counselling having been assaulted by a member of the public at work. He had previously been assaulted at work and had attended counselling with the same counsellor but he had patched himself up and returned to work within a few sessions. This time he was very distressed and he struggled to contain his overwhelm. The inability to control his feelings frightened him. His therapist was a few weeks' pregnant at the time counselling began. As sessions progressed the therapist noticed herself feeling unsettled before sessions, carrying a generalised anxiety into the room. She could feel a strong need to do something for this client, to help him try to contain his distress. However, she doubted her ability to be there for the client, believing this might be because she was pregnant. Her thoughts outside of sessions regularly turned to this client, particularly his distress as he described the trauma.

Exploration of Bill's childhood experiences revealed trauma at the hands of a violent alcoholic father. The extent of the trauma was profound. Bill had survived this in part through dissociation from his feelings at the time of his father's violence and through watching closely his father's behaviour. The counsellor became aware that this was partly how Bill had managed to recover from the first assault. In this latest assault an alcoholic man had swung at him from behind. He hadn't seen the assault coming and had been unable to protect himself. This took the lid off his deep fear and traumatisation from childhood. Dissociation was no longer working. The therapist was tuning into a level of overwhelm in the client that went far beyond the recent trauma. She could feel the full force of his childhood experience as it swept over him.

With an awareness of some of the reasons for the client's over-whelm as well as her own, the therapist was able to stay with his experiencing and resist the urge in the client to put things back together. A couple of sessions later the client revealed his longing for his mother's support in childhood which had been effectively absent and how he wished he could have talked with her. In this way part of the therapist's experience was further explained. She was playing the role his mother had played — caring yet somehow distant and uninvolved. She was also picking up on his mother transference and feeling it blend with her own anxieties about becoming a mother. The transference was parental but explicitly linked with the client's experience of trauma in childhood. His childhood experiences were so psychologically shaping that recovery clearly demanded long-term work. This example demonstrates the complex interweaving of therapist and client material displaying the synchronicity in client's and counsellor's lives.

Countertransference: avoidance

The other type of reaction the therapist notices in herself takes the form of avoidance of the client's material (Wilson and Lindy 1994). Broadly this can take the form of a focus on analysing (managing the intensity of feeling by avoiding feelings), or of minimising the depth of contact either with the client or their material.

Analytic responses

As part of establishing the working relationship, therapists often need to explain the symptoms of trauma to their clients. This can be hugely relieving for clients: to hear that what they are experiencing is a human reaction, and a normal way of managing distress. However, the intensity of working with traumatic reactions can be overwhelming for both client and counsellor. Therapists sometimes manage the intensity of their own anxieties by focusing on the symptoms of trauma in addition to taking an analytic approach to the work, or by unconsciously helping the client to collude in the avoidance of his experiencing. The therapist manages the uncertainty of involvement through objective focus rather than in subjective experiencing with the client. This may be illustrated with a case example.

Paul, a train driver, was coming to terms with an accident in which a man fell under his train. This was the first such incident the driver had experienced in his ten years' driving. During the initial session he was sweating and highly anxious. The therapist could feel his anxiety and found herself sitting rigidly in her seat as he talked, trying to contain the feelings. Though the incident was explored in some detail the therapist noticed after several sessions that both herself and the client were taking a problem-solving approach to reducing Paul's symptoms and returning him to driving. The client would set himself goals to achieve in between sessions and the therapist was working cognitively with him, focusing on understanding his reactions and managing them. Over the sessions he could clearly measure his improvement. They were able to measure the trauma symptom reduction together and the therapy seemed to be progressing in a very linear fashion. Yet this felt a bit too 'neat', a fact which engaged the counsellor's curiosity.

She was not entirely surprised when Paul's anxiety returned full force when for the first time since the accident he rode on the front of a train (accompanying the driver). Deeper exploration of Paul's experiencing showed that he had learned to manage and control his feelings, had experienced bouts of anxiety in the past and had a deep-rooted fear of failure resulting from painful childhood experiences. Paul had unresolved grief which he managed by building a wall around himself and avoiding intimate relationships. The therapist felt she had unconsciously been responding to the need in the client to rationalise and manage his feelings.

On further reflection the therapist realised it had been a relief for her to be working with a traumatised client who wasn't 'swimming around in a mass of feelings'. It appeared her work with him would be contained, it seemed to have a clear, short-term focus following a standard model for trauma reaction. She was thus going to be able to manage the company's needs by delivering a driver back to the workplace quickly and with his symptoms diminished. The therapist had been unconsciously carrying her longing for a 'straightforward piece of work' and the pressure to prove the counselling team's worth into the dynamics of the counselling. Of course her client, as part of the workplace, carried the same pressures: 'I should be over this by now – it should only take a few weeks shouldn't it?' was Paul's persistent question. Therapist and client were responding to these contextual dynamics and individual pressures and avoiding the deeper confusion of both their experiences in the work.

Dissociative responses

One therapist found images of broad open landscapes and ravines appearing in his head periodically in sessions as the client described two near fatal motorcycle crashes. These had occurred in mountainous countryside in the United States and the therapist's initial feeling was that the images were triggered by the client's descriptions. Reflecting outside of the session, the therapist realised he didn't feel particularly emotionally engaged with the client. There was a sense of space in the room and distance between them. In this case the counsellor was picking up the client's dissociation from the trauma. He wasn't able to feel much because his client wasn't feeling very much either. The images he visualised symbolised the distance between them and the client's lack of connection with his experience or with his counsellor.

Behaviourally, signs of dissociation can show in a counsellor forgetting that a client is waiting or double booking a client. I found this happened a few times with a traumatised client – enough for me to decide it was not coincidence. As well as experiencing some dissociation, a potent part of this man's experience was feeling he had no place in the world and of not being taken seriously at the time of the assault – by the police, the hospital or his place of work. Besides the assault he had a history of feeling victimised and denied equal treatment. My trouble remembering sessions mirrored his experience of himself as invisible and reinforced his experience of victimisation.

Minimisation

The therapist may notice herself exhibiting some form of denial or mini-misation of the client's experience. This perhaps shows in not believing what the client describes or doubting the level of traumatisation. The therapist may unwittingly lean towards a different focus for the counselling, perhaps the client's relationship or work-related issues. Clients who are difficult to reach through being very defended can provoke this reaction in the therapist but it is often about the therapist too. The level of emotional engagement required feels too much, or the counsellor is feeling pressured for time in short-term work. It can sometimes be a joint unconscious effort by client and therapist to avoid the incident because it feels too frightening. This client or his experience may be re-stimulating traumatic material for the counsellor. One therapist experienced a deep relief when her client talked about leaving work as a result of being assaulted. This was a reflection of feeling under pressure to resolve this trauma quickly and have the client return to work and was unconsciously easier to focus on than the traumatic material itself, and the long-term existential questions it had evoked in the client.

Victim, persecutor and rescuer

Just as transference and countertransference can represent parent/ child relationships, in trauma counselling (particularly for issues such as assault or torture), the dynamics can reflect the experience of victim and persecutor. Into this mix comes the rescuer perhaps in the form of the therapist's fantasised role, or the client's projected longing (Herman 1992).

Denial of the client's experience or distress described above can reflect the therapist's identification with the perpetrator. From the client's experience, 'protracted involvement with the perpetrator alters the client's relational style so that she not only fears repeated victimisation but also seems unable to protect herself from it, or even appears to invite it' (Herman 1992: 138). In working with a client who experienced an assault at work and subsequent further harassment from male colleagues in the workplace, I experienced this dynamic. I felt impatient and irritated with my client's helplessness and focused on practical ways to deal with the harassers. Her long-standing experience as a victim and her consequent 'learned helplessness' projected itself in a longing to be rescued. The intensity of this need felt too much for me and I felt punitive, pushing her away psychologically (mirroring her physical assault). Her victimisation stimulated my own fears around sexual intimidation and helplessness. The subsequent guilt I felt was in not meeting my client's distress and a sense of myself as an unhelpful therapist reflecting both our helplessness and anguish and the difficulty of working with this material. More clearly understood through supervision, I could find ways both to support myself and become available to my client.

Sometimes the counsellor experiences more than one point of the victim, persecutor and rescuer triangle in the course of a client's therapy. I emerged from my first counselling session with Oya with the strongest desire to 'advocate' I had ever experienced for a client. He was traumatised by an assault but he also had a long history of experiences at work in which he felt harassed and racially discriminated against and these seemed to be at the root of his troubles. Undoubtedly I was picking up his longing for me to do something, to resolve the trauma symptoms and take action with the organisation. It tapped into my struggle with the limitations and dual nature of my role at work, my perceived power as a white counsellor and my 'white guilt' in not taking enough action to combat racism within the organisation (Ridley 1995). In staying with these struggles, I noticed as sessions progressed an increasing tendency in me to offer directional suggestions and question my client's approach to his problems. This tendency would emerge suddenly. I now felt persecutory and then proceeded to oscillate between the desire to help and rescue and a punitive approach. Oya's experience of victimisation was so profound that I was playing alternately rescuer and persecutor. This was his experience with most people in his life, reinforcing his powerlessness. Working directly with my countertransference experiences over time helped Oya internalise awareness of his own states.

Witness guilt

When a counsellor is witnessing the distress but has not been part of the traumatic experience herself she is prone to 'witness guilt' (Herman 1992). This is sometimes triggered in the counsellor when it parallels survivor guilt in the traumatised client. The counsellor sometimes feels witness guilt when the client projects doubt that the therapist can manage the material or that the therapist won't understand, not having suffered too. The client's desire to answer the question 'why me?' triggers the counsellor's guilt that it wasn't her. Unidentified it results in the therapist feeling disempowered – that she couldn't possibly know enough. Sometimes witness guilt manifests in the counsellor feeling she doesn't have enough traumatic experience of her own to entitle her to do this work.

With a fair proportion of trauma counselling taking place in or for organisations and many traumatic incidents occurring in the workplace it is essential not to underestimate the impact of organisational culture on the trauma counselling relationship (even when the counselling is taking place independently).

Counsellors working in or for organisations can feel witness guilt. They are not exposed to the risk of trauma as are their clients. Witness guilt can emerge because the therapist is part of a system that failed to protect the client. This is a very common theme in workplace counselling where trauma is a risk in the job. The underlying statement from the client might be: 'Work has done this to me – you are a part of work.' It might show in being dismissive of counselling and a resistance to engage. Anger may show directly towards the therapist but it is more likely to be disguised (particularly if the client's character structure makes anger unacceptable). The therapist may feel the anger instead or feel that nothing she can do or say seems sufficient to support her client.

Therapists working in private practice may be less susceptible to witness guilt and more likely to feel echoes of the victim, rescuer and persecutor triangle because of the intensity of this type of work and the isolation that accompanies both the client's experience and the practice of private therapy. In this setting, bearing witness and the pressure to hold and contain relies on one person, rather than a team. The disconnection experienced by the client can be intensely mirrored in the therapist working alone, sometimes even the sense of contamination that may be part of the client's experience can be felt by the therapist if she works in her own home. Thus the need for a network of support and containment is essential as described later in this chapter.

Other organisational factors

One client's first contact with her manager following a traumatic incident was to be told: 'Nobody else is reacting to this incident except you.' No account was taken of the fact that this client had discovered the badly mutilated, dead body of a young man. She had received no preparation for what she would witness and she was the sole witness for the company. In addition the young man who died was of a similar age to her own son, provoking her maternal anguish. Neither of these factors were considered at work, compounding the client's experience of victimisation and damaging the necessary bonds between staff for effective recovery in the workplace. Her manager's anger was in part displaced guilt and anxiety (this had happened on his shift). He was also managing a high sickness absence amongst his staff. The need to manage these pressures for himself resulted in minimisation of the client's experience. The session is no longer just the therapist and client working with a traumatic experience. It is a three-way relationship involving the manager, with therapist and client struggling with their roles as employees within the organisation.

> Whether the traumatic event occurs when travelling to or from employment or as a result of performing within the scope of duty of the job, work trauma is resolved differently than that experienced privately and personally as an outside-work event. The context of work, that is virtually all aspects of the organisation, acts to change and intensify the character of the traumatic experience, as well as providing the venue in which the survivor seeks to understand and resolve the traumatic event. Stated somewhat metaphorically, the trauma that occurs at the workplace creates a ripple effect and its wave possesses the power to generate countertransference reactions in fellow workers.
>
> (Wilson and Lindy 1994: 353)

This includes the counsellors, who can feel a similar sense of isolation, battling against the odds and disconnection from the rest of the workplace. It is necessary for the counsellors within an organisation to ensure connections on a positive and nurturing level are maintained with the organisation.

If it is not simply the relationship between therapist and client that is needed to recover from trauma but those with managers and colleagues, then developing awareness of trauma is key for the other supporting roles. Yet counsellors working within organisations often find they are expected to play a mediating or bridging role between the company and the client. They are working with both the individual and cultural dynamics, dealing simultaneously with a traumatic incident and poor working relationships. The pressures and conflicting demands can be intense leading to overwhelm or cut off in the countertransference. Developing relationships with the company independent to individual client cases and feeding back to the organisation ways of improving support can help the counsellor take an active role within the company separate from the knotty dynamics of individual cases.

For counsellors in private practice, it might be about ensuring a balance in their work which includes some teaching or non-trauma work to balance the intensity of trauma counselling. On the other hand, taking an active role in organisations working at the preventative and political level may help to rebalance the impact of the therapeutic work. Certainly having an experienced and well-trained supervisor, to hold the therapist in her work, provides the support those working in organisations may get from colleagues.

Occasionally employees use traumatic experiences as levers against management (through taking time off for example) for other unresolved workplace difficulties. The therapist needs to distinguish where the client's experience is genuine. With an increasing move towards compensation and litigation for trauma in all areas, some clients engage in trauma counselling for these purposes. I am not denying the need for litigation or the real impact of trauma. However, occasionally a therapist meets a client who describes all the symptoms of PTSD but the actual distress is not witnessed or felt by the counsellor. Whilst this might be an indication of the therapist's countertransference or of dissociation it might more simply reflect the needs of the client. This needs to be acknowledged as a further contextual dynamic of trauma counselling today and is explored further in Chapter 4 (see p. 121).

Countertransference dynamics can reflect the cultural ethos of an organisation. London Underground, for example, is a company that has long felt 'under fire' from a critical public and is regularly used as a political football. It is not surprising therefore that a somewhat military language has developed within the company. Staff are described as 'front line' and as 'troops'. Front line staff have 'points of safety' within stations and the company devises 'operations' to 'target' improvement. In some ways the counselling service becomes the military hospital where the shell-shocked and wounded are sent. Clients will displace their feelings of betrayal by the company on to the counsellor. The counsellor may find herself dealing with dynamics of war in the form of 'allies and enemies' (Wilson and Lindy 1994: 360). The therapist may be idealised as an ally by the client, preventing her from feeling she can successfully challenge the client when necessary. Or she is seen as part of the officer ranks, encouraging the client back to the 'front line', leaving him feeling betrayed. The therapist searches for neutral territory, symbolised by retreating from full engagement with the client. Rarely does the counsellor experience a comfortable balancing of the needs of her client and those of the company for whom she works. Managers are suddenly left without key members of their troops, feel exposed and vulnerable and look for someone to blame.

As a counsellor it is worth thinking about the setting in which one works and how this flavours the contact between therapist and client, including the private practice setting.

Cultural difference and trauma

Aside from the cultural transference and countertransference relevant for all counselling, ethnicity plays a significant part in the trauma counselling process. In addition traumatic experiences can have, or be perceived to have, a racist element.

Where the client's experience may have led to a deep mistrust of the counsellor's ethnicity, it is important to explore these aspects before attempting to work with the traumatic material. For example, an African man was assaulted by three African-Caribbean youths. His entire experience of the police and the hospital was of being dismissed, ignored or of assumptions being made about his experience. It was important for his African-Caribbean counsellor to talk with him about how he felt meeting her and to acknowledge the potential for racism within black culture. This ensured both were engaged and minimised the chance of his experience being repeated in the counselling.

Western civilisation is fundamentally individualistic in nature. Most non-Western cultures are collectivist. The ambivalence with which clients live of staying with traditional beliefs and behaviours and/or adapting to Western ones may play out in the therapy. The very idea of counselling, for example, with its focus on an individual's experience can feel quite alien to a client. Culturally there may not be much emphasis on feelings and yet the focus of most counselling is on expression of these. The experience of isolation and disconnection and the process of recovery can therefore be very different and reflective of living and working in majority white culture. It is essential in working with clients of a different ethnicity that therapists are able to think about the many different ways to benefit their clients in recovery. Participation in local community activities, for example rituals and religious activities, may be more helpful than individual counselling, or at the very least part of the process of healing.

Exploring cultural difference is not necessarily key to the initial stage of trauma counselling unless cultural issues feature as part of the client's immediate or traumatic experience (for example a white counsellor working with a black client who has been raped by a white man). The depth of distress caused by trauma can supersede cultural difference in the first instance. Most clients long to be met with in their distress and find huge comfort from someone knowing something about how they feel and providing a safe space to talk. Their immediate concern may not be the cultural differences between themselves and the therapist so much as the need to be heard and believed. The key is the therapist's willingness to support, explore and understand the individual's story as it includes ethnicity. Otherwise there is a potential risk of unintentional racism through an overt focus on cultural difference, or 'colour consciousness' (Ridley 1995: 68). For deeper exploration of cultural issues see Ridley's (1995) chapter on trauma and transformation.

Difficulties for beginning practitioners

In identifying those challenges which can be acutely felt by the beginning practitioner working with trauma I am aware of how often these themes recur at times even for the most experienced trauma counsellor. This reflects the struggle of staying with distressing material and being compassionate and aware of our own vulnerability and suffering.

Trauma counselling, like any approach which is recognised as 'specialised', can feel quite daunting at first. One of the ways the therapist manages anxiety and feels competent is through applying structures and frameworks to the work, perhaps using psychometric tests and symptom checklists, specialised trauma counselling techniques or taking a very structured approach to the counselling. This may well be a necessary or required part of the work but in the process counsellors often forget or dismiss their traditional tools. Becoming consumed with what one should do or say can override the meeting between two people that is the essence of all counselling. The counsellor may need to remind herself about approaching the work person-to-person and to feel assured or reassured in the importance of being with her client above *doing* something with her client. In addition to focusing attention on the client's experience, some examples of the skills required are: being with the client without trying to 'fix' them, acknowledging the distress or sadness in oneself as counsellor and sitting with silence or with grief in oneself and/or client as it emerges. In putting aside person-to-person relating the beginning practitioner can be more prone to overwhelm or cut off from her clients.

A counsellor early in her practice emerged from a session feeling anxious about what she should be doing to help her client. She found herself reading books, reviewing models for working with trauma and planning the next session, which she took to supervision. Her supervisor identified her fears, worked with her own fear of overwhelm and encouraged her to trust her intuition as she usually would with her clients. The supervisor identified the counsellor's need to do something as reflective of the client's longing to be freed from pain and to make the distress more manageable.

One therapist describes the essence of trauma counselling as 'showing up, shutting up, tuning in and getting what's going on' (St Just 1999). Roughly translated this involves being present, listening and noticing, intuiting and sensing and working in the here and now with the detail of the client's experiencing. This is an equally important process for the therapist to apply to herself and in reflection on her work. Although stated simply, it is a more challenging approach than any technique for working with traumatised clients.

Trauma reactions in clients are not always profound. Some individuals recover quickly from very distressing experiences for any number of reasons, individual and contextual. Some clients patch themselves up, surviving through avoidance, some will need to work through the experience and some have very little reaction. As a beginning practitioner it can be harder to recognise and respect individuals' very different ways of coping. In my experience many people will patch up, particularly if this matches their way of coping developmentally. It is often after a subsequent traumatic experience or when something else distressing occurs that their feelings re-emerge and demand some attention. It is then that they engage in counselling. An example from my early practice may illustrate this.

Malcolm attended counselling with me following a train suicide. I approached our first few sessions with building trust and normalising his symptoms. I had recently learned the technique for resolving trauma known as Traumatic Incident Reduction (TIR) (see Chapter 4 for an explanation of this approach). It seemed that it would be effective in helping Malcolm face and integrate his experience. He was obliging in the preparation sessions, yet he didn't seem quite involved. I didn't expect him to be enthusiastic about the process but there was very little anxiety and I put this and the disengagement down to some dissociation from his experience. On the session planned to run TIR my client informed me he had returned to driving trains. I was surprised. However, in exploring this, it transpired that Malcolm hadn't wanted to do TIR but felt he ought to because I had recommended it. We both laughed. I was coming from the perspective that all traumas are best and most quickly resolved through practical techniques and felt temporarily secure in this 'expert' role. Initially I felt I was failing by not taking him through a recovery procedure. But he was recovering in his own way. Even if it was some form of avoidance or suppression of the trauma, I needed to respect his way of coping. Anything else would have been failing Malcolm therapeutically. I had been ignoring the essential coping of my client, which was a stronger basis for our therapeutic work and arguably more valuable to my client. It taught me to respect the mystery of individual coping and pay closer attention to the client's experience to guide me.

Support for the therapist

Therapist self-care

If we are drawn to psychotherapeutic work because of our own wounds, as well as altruism, this is perhaps particularly so with trauma counselling. The work engages us at our deepest and most wounded level. Many of the techniques and approaches which structure the work (such as Eye Movement Desensitisation and Reprocessing (EMDR), TIR and Critical Incident Debriefing) foster denial of the therapist's wounds through the focus on technique rather than relationship. The longing to heal and be healed is most ardent in trauma counselling and evokes the rescuer in the therapist.

We may be drawn to trauma work having some experience of trauma ourselves. This can allow the therapist to make a profound connection with clients and she can use this to help her empathise with her client. The therapist who has not experienced trauma will nevertheless bring her own developmental wounds to the work. It is easy for trauma work to encapsulate subtly the split whereby the counsellor sees herself as untraumatised and the client as needy. The therapist can ignore the subtleties of how her own experience is reawakened, robbing the counselling relationship of depth or leading towards compassion fatigue (Figley 1995). This is particularly true in short-term work and for counsellors with large caseloads, as the time for reflection is necessarily limited.

There are good reasons for limiting the amount of trauma work one undertakes as by its very nature it grinds down the counsellor and can erode her sense of wellbeing, her ability to trust in the world and relationships, and her basic faith in humanity (Herman 1992). The 'Lone Ranger' persona describes a rescuing pattern that can develop in counsellors. The lone counsellor takes on the 'bad guys single-handedly for the good of the client' (Munroe et al. 1995: 221). This can be psychological or literal in terms of advocacy and over-involvement and is as common in practitioners working in or for an organisation as for those in private practice. Whilst the counsellor is outwardly strong and challenging she is unwittingly modelling a 'traumatised world view' of disconnection and isolation.

These effects cannot always be avoided, they are literally a part of the work. However they do need to be identified, acknowledged as the therapist's own and managed appropriately for safe and effective therapy. To counteract these tendencies it is essential that the therapist works closely with others or meets with others to share her experiencing but also that she focuses on her own reactions to the therapeutic process. This needs to be actively fostered by those working in private practice.

Self-care is effected in numerous ways. Danieli (1994: 384) identifies a three-stage model. First, recognise one's feelings and develop awareness of somatic signals of distress. This requires time. Time for reflection, time to allow depth of feeling to emerge and time to name accurately what is being felt. With a large caseload and in short-term work this often doesn't happen. Furthermore the counsellor is often unaware that she absorbs traumatic material unwitting of its impact.

Second, self-care is about containing one's reactions, trusting that feelings have a beginning, a middle and an end and allowing this flow. This requires honesty and acceptance of ourselves as human beings with our own needs and vulnerability. A willingness to recognise and use one's 'limitations' as they serve the counselling process is essential to this work, in order to create connection and to stay tuned to the client as the ultimate source of his own recovery. Humanity is vulnerability and it is this commonality within the relationship that fosters reconnection (Herman 1992). The success of counselling is also dependent on the counsellor's ability to stay in contact with her own unknowing, limited self.

Third, self-care is time to heal and grow. Danieli (1994: 385) expresses this as 'realising that nothing will ever be the same'. This is often a key stage of the client's process and is also true when the therapist is confronted with a profound level of personal suffering. Therapists themselves must take time to heal when feeling wounded (sourcing support, taking breaks, using annual leave or taking regular time off and managing client load in terms of numbers and intensity, for example). It is essential to grow through pursuit of non-therapy-related pleasures and provide oneself with 'avocational avenues for creative and relaxing self-expression in order to regenerate energies' (Danieli 1994: 385).

Trauma counselling is weighty. One supervisor suggests a trauma client to be equivalent to two general clients. Because the work is challenging the therapist must make time to have fun. This can be surprisingly difficult as it is often easier for counsellors to resonate with another's suffering than to feel delight in their own lives. Whilst this is appropriate in the session, outside the session this resonance fails to support the therapist: '. . . feeling free to have fun and joy is not a frivolity in this field but a necessity without which one cannot fulfil one's professional obligations, one's professional contract' (Danieli 1994: 385). The use of humour is essential as a resource, a means of connection with life and of disconnection from the pain of trauma (Yassen 1995). It is vital that therapists maintain links with humour for themselves, outside of sessions, and thus model in a non-direct way reconnection for the client. This is often experienced in 'gallows humour' amongst trauma counsellors. There is an absurdity to some trauma situations which helps us temporarily to manage our distress and fears of mortality.

Trauma counsellors, like all therapists, do not cure people. The resolution for trauma is ultimately how the client is able to transform their experience and suffering into a source for their own growth in life: '. . . the three most common narcissistic snares in therapists are the aspirations to heal all, know all and love all' (Herman 1992: 143). First, this work is driven by the fact that only the client can heal and only as much as they are able. Second, as therapists we rarely 'know' very much (that we can be sure of) and, third, our feelings can be negative and unloving (particularly when our clients are stuck or victimised). This work is shaped by humility, the need to respect that at times there are greater forces at work in our lives.

The means of self-care are first, self-supervision (Casement 1990; Hawkins and Shohet 1989); second, to live consciously and relate to and through our own wounds and longings as they emerge in the work; and, third, to meet our own needs outside of all things therapeutic and outside of the client's process. There are many helpful books that focus on self-reflection and balancing therapeutic work (see Kornfield 1994; Rainer 1980; Horton 1997; Rowe 1995). In this way trauma counselling becomes a channel for the therapist's own growth as well as the client's.

Supervision and other support

> Therapists who work with traumatised people require an ongoing support system to deal with these intense reactions. Just as no survivor can recover alone, no therapist can work with trauma alone.
>
> (Herman 1992: 141)

Supportive, regular, ongoing supervision is an essential part of trauma work for the emotional support of the therapist, a space to unload and to be with distress safely, as much as it is a focus on the dynamics of the therapeutic relationship.

Experiences in supervision often reflect features of traumatic stress. It is not uncommon for a therapist to experience symptoms of dissociation or avoidance: feeling confused, phased and unable to think clearly in describing client work. The therapist may feel flat, tired or yawn (or the supervisor notices she feels tired and flat). She may notice she doesn't feel much at all. A therapist explored in supervision her lack of emotional response as a client described being stabbed. She realised she had a great fear of being stabbed herself and dissociated to protect herself. Conversely, managing overwhelm can show in an obsessive focus on particular details of the client's story and an inability to conceptualise the whole. The therapist may feel the client's feelings, over-identifying, wanting something to be done and looking to the supervisor for answers. These factors are likely to be reflections of both the client's experience and the therapist's coping strategies.

The intensity of helplessness felt by the therapist sometimes reflects in lack of engagement in supervision. The fear of exposing our own sense of overwhelm or of facing the limitations of what we can do for the client can put us off using supervision, opting instead for 'the easy ways out of blaming others – clients, peers, the organisation, "society" or oneself'

(Hawkins and Shohet 1989: 4). Or the therapist remains content with analysing symptom reduction and measures of social functioning. This can be pertinent to work within organisations, where large caseloads and the conflicting dynamics and roles can divert the therapist from the relationship with her client.

Being part of a trauma network with different counsellors using different methods and approaches or engaging in group supervision are both sources of support for therapists. Competition often emerges in these group processes. In the trauma field this reflects the pressure to demonstrate containment of the client's distress and manage the horror of some stories. Common themes can be the sharing of gory stories, competition over caseloads and presence at the worst disasters. These are the natural (if grandiose) coping mechanisms we use to face the enormity of human suffering. They become unhelpful if they perpetuate denial of our own vulnerability. In private practice, the opposite may occur: the therapist becomes increasingly burdened and vulnerable from exposure to the material, has nowhere to offload it, and doubts her ability to cope with this kind of work.

Secondary traumatisation and burnout

'Secondary traumatic stress' (STS) and 'compassion stress' (Figley 1995) are terms given to the experiences a therapist may have in the course of her work which bear a notable similarity to trauma symptoms. In a similar way when working with a bereaved client, the therapist may feel her own grief triggered and, providing she can modulate it, is able to empathise more closely with her client. As with countertransference reactions, it is not that compassion stress can be avoided or prevented – some impact is a natural byproduct of engagement – but the symptoms need to become conscious to the counsellor and supported effectively. In this way it can contribute to and feed the process rather than damage the relationship and the therapist.

Compassion stress can show in the therapist staying attuned to clients' affect long after the sessions. This will happen occasionally when doing intensive work, or with a client in great distress, but when it is happening regularly it is a warning sign. The therapist finds she is feeling depressed or sad and is not able to identify anything in her own life contributing to it. She might notice that images of clients' material recur when she is at home or memories of clients' experience are triggered by another person's talk (intrusive thoughts and flashbacks). As the stress builds the therapist finds herself unable to remember much about sessions, or has difficulty staying focused within them (concentration). She stops making notes after sessions which would otherwise help contain and offload the material. The therapist may notice an increased irritability with colleagues, friends and family or with clients (arousal). Eventually she becomes more isolated in her work, not really sharing much in supervision or with her colleagues. She feels increasingly disconnected from friends and family or they experience her as such whilst she remains unaware of it. She no longer wishes to socialise much, experiencing intense self-consciousness and anxiety and perhaps taking sanctuary at home (withdrawal). When she is out she feels wary of who is around her and fearful of being out at night (hypervigilance). Her sleep is disturbed: it is increasingly difficult to get to sleep, turning over cases in her head, and her dreams express generalised anxiety and fears (arousal). She wakes early feeling exhausted. Her diet becomes poor, relying on coffee for stimulation and before sessions she experiences dread or nausea and doubts her ability to contain material in sessions. Eventually she begins taking time off work or finding reasons not to take on new trauma clients.

Unsupported, these symptoms will lead to compassion fatigue and then burnout: 'a state of physical, emotional and mental exhaustion caused by long term involvement in emotionally demanding situations' (Figley 1995: 11). Secondary traumatic stress disorder (STSD) on the other hand can emerge suddenly, like PTSD, provoked by a particular incident, session or at a certain point in the therapist's life. In many ways STSD is more likely to occur in those working with the immediate aftermath of trauma situations such as natural disaster, rescue and war. But a build-up of compassion stress is likely to occur in anyone working regularly with traumatised people. STSD and compassion fatigue need to be distinguished from natural stress symptoms which build up in all therapeutic work. Though they may share some features, STSD and compassion fatigue are clearly delineated states (Figley 1995).

Beginning practitioners can be prone to these syndromes, particularly if they are not moderating the amount of trauma that they work with, taking necessary supervision, sharing the anxieties and distress with colleagues and being compassionate towards themselves in terms of their limitations. It is necessary to build up this kind of work gradually in order to protect oneself against burnout and remain available to one's clients.

As yet there is little recognition of secondary traumatisation (Figley 1995: 6). This can be attributed to the trauma field being relatively young. I think it also reflects the need in helping professionals to appear as strong containers of this material. Some trauma approaches assume the therapist's ability to model strength, manage overwhelm and constitute the wise and nurturing parent who can contain the child's distress. The need to demonstrate this containment is often in direct proportion to the depth of traumatisation in the client. Whilst faith and confidence in the counsellor and process are the beginnings of reconnection for the client, these factors can sometimes lead to a denial of the impact of trauma on the therapist.

Essentially the focus must be prevention of compassion fatigue, rather than cure. Primary, secondary and tertiary approaches to containing trauma help those working in this field (Yassen 1995). A primary way in which a counsellor can counteract the helplessness engendered by traumatised clients is to contribute to the process of prevention separately from their casework. For example, in some organisations the counselling team may contribute to policies and training for minimising trauma in the workplace. Feedback to management on ways in which they can limit the effects of trauma through support of employees becomes the secondary tier. The tertiary structure is the provision of counselling. A practitioner working alone may provide these through support of causes for the prevention of trauma (primary), developing a network of support to define and refine their trauma work (secondary) and ensuring a focus on self-support as the tertiary level. It is the breadth of the structure which contains and supports the therapist in her work, creating a 'holding environment' (Danieli 1994).

It is essential that the counselling process is structured to contain the work. This structure is defined by developing a clear contract including type of treatment offered, boundaries such as length and duration of counselling, suitable supervision and limits to caseload (both in private practice and organisations). One therapist likened trauma work to a wave where the wave is at its peak between therapist and client and then ripples out and diminishes in impact as it is shared with colleagues and supervisors. The management of trauma impact is always both environmental and individual (Yassen 1995).

A counsellor working in an organisation had a particular ability to resonate with the feelings of her clients. Her countertransference reactions when working with trauma fell into the category of over-involvement and enmeshment. Aspects in her personal life included playing a very nurturing and responsive role with her own mother when growing up. She was providing trauma counselling, seeing up to six clients a day and after a number of months started to suffer burnout. Four years on her memories of that time have been enough to prevent her wanting to work with trauma again. The environmental factor that contributed to this state in the therapist was an absence of clear boundaries for the provision of counselling within the company, including supervision and limits to caseload. The unidentified 'rescuer' dynamic – present in those most vulnerable to the contagion of trauma (Figley 1995: 6) – was the individual characteristic contributing.

Professional training is a further container to working with trauma. I think this is about developing an approach to trauma which supports the whole person of both client and therapist, and which recognises traumatic wounds as part of life and self-development. The techniques and training available tend to separate traumatic events from the whole person's experiencing, sometimes leading to a dislocated experience for therapist and client. Further training for the private practice therapist can therefore be one means of widening her support network. The wider the net to contain the existential fear and shame provoked by these experiences, the more successfully we can all integrate traumatic wounds both individually and socially.

Conclusion

Writing about trauma for the therapist deadens feelings somewhat. Writing can neither fully capture the struggle and complexity of two people's engagement, nor the counsellor's day-to-day being with herself and her clients. Writing by its nature needs to separate and distinguish, label and define, and this necessarily limits description of the experience for the counsellor. In conclusion I am brought back to the less easily defined aspects of this work that express its essence. Ultimately trauma counselling is about our humanity – less often about what we offer of our strength and understanding and more of our daily struggle with vulnerability, loss, confusion and doubt. Paradoxically it is in these – our 'limitations' and our ongoing attempts to be compassionate with ourselves and our own wounds – that as counsellors we offer our clients the support to reconnect after traumatic wounding.

Chapter 8

A brief history of trauma

Thom Spiers and Guy Harrington

From Dunkirk to Dunblane, the Great Fire of London to the fire at King's Cross, history has shown that in the aftermath of wars, disasters and awful experiences, some people display a number of physiological and psychological symptoms. Despite these symptoms having been identified as far back as 850 BC (Scott and Stradling 1998: 6), medical and social opinion has taken nearly three millennia to acknowledge the existence of the disorder we now readily refer to as post-traumatic stress.

It is not unusual for ancient knowledge to be lost only to be rediscovered many centuries later. The story of trauma is one of enlightenment and forgetfulness. It is an account of knowledge gained and lost time and time again, and a history characterised by criticism and denial. Even now there are those who question the legitimacy of PTSD, people who view it as a contemporary phenomenon, a product of a victim culture and weakness of character.

As therapists and counsellors we seek to understand the nature of a problem by recognising its existence, considering its origins and seeking a solution. The approach outlined in this book is an appropriate beginning for a practitioner seeking to understand the nature and treatment of trauma.

The term 'trauma' comes from the ancient Greek word meaning to 'wound' or to 'pierce'. It was used in reference to soldiers who had suffered wounds or injury resulting from the piercing of armour. The soldier's defences, designed to protect him from death, had been overpowered. This overwhelming of physical defences provides a useful parallel when considering psychological trauma. As we have seen, people's response to traumatic incidents can be understood as an overwhelming of their psychological defences. When discussed in the context of the mind this crushing of defences and the related symptoms is often considered to be a recent phenomenon.

For the diagnostic criteria for PTSD to be credible they must describe the reality of human experience and not simply be a contemporary creation. Compelling evidence of the emotional impact of traumatic events is available in pre-psychological history. The great literature of the past delivers in poetry and narrative a convincing account of post-traumatic reaction.

Shakespeare, writing in 1594, describes poetically in *Henry IV, Part II* the symptoms of PTSD in Lady Percy's sympathetic enquiry of her troubled husband:

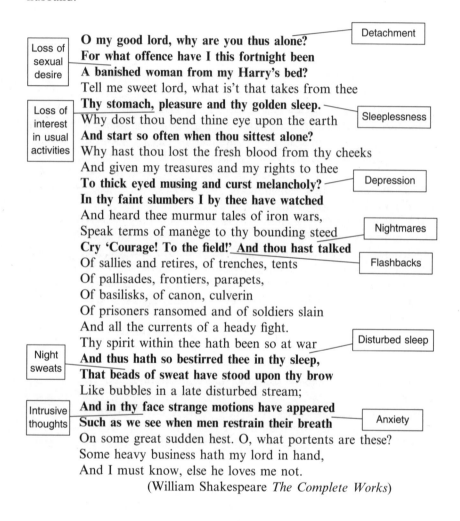

O my good lord, why are you thus alone? — Detachment
Loss of sexual desire — **For what offence have I this fortnight been / A banished woman from my Harry's bed?**
Tell me sweet lord, what is't that takes from thee
Loss of interest in usual activities — **Thy stomach, pleasure and thy golden sleep.** — Sleeplessness
Why dost thou bend thine eye upon the earth
And start so often when thou sittest alone?
Why hast thou lost the fresh blood from thy cheeks
And given my treasures and my rights to thee
To thick eyed musing and curst melancholy? — Depression
In thy faint slumbers I by thee have watched
And heard thee murmur tales of iron wars,
Speak terms of manège to thy bounding steed — Nightmares
Cry 'Courage! To the field!' And thou hast talked — Flashbacks
Of sallies and retires, of trenches, tents
Of pallisades, frontiers, parapets,
Of basilisks, of canon, culverin
Of prisoners ransomed and of soldiers slain
And all the currents of a heady fight.
Thy spirit within thee hath been so at war — Disturbed sleep
Night sweats — **And thus hath so bestirred thee in thy sleep, / That beads of sweat have stood upon thy brow**
Like bubbles in a late disturbed stream;
Intrusive thoughts — **And in thy face strange motions have appeared / Such as we see when men restrain their breath** — Anxiety
On some great sudden hest. O, what portents are these?
Some heavy business hath my lord in hand,
And I must know, else he loves me not.

(William Shakespeare *The Complete Works*)

Likewise Samuel Pepys famously recorded his own post-traumatic reaction (Daly 1983: 64–8). Pepys, his family and community were exposed to the Great Fire of London, which destroyed huge swathes of the city. Comparable with modern-day catastrophes Pepys diarised his own and others' responses to the disaster. During and immediately after the fire he describes his hyperarousal (p. 65) mentioning often being frightened by or noticing new chimney fires. He narrates a clear account of his disturbed sleep (p. 66) and his work is dotted with references to nightmares: 'Much terrified in the night nowadays with dreams of fire and falling houses' and, months later: 'I cannot sleep anight without great terrors of fire.' Pepys also reported feeling detached from others and irritable and, having been a man who enjoyed good food and good company, felt both evaded him in the weeks and months that followed the fire. His is a clear account of what could be described as a fairly typical post-traumatic reaction.

These anecdotal observations began to assume greater substance in the second half of the nineteenth century. Although historical evidence clearly demonstrates the existence of psychological elements in the reaction to trauma, studies at this time were undertaken by physicians who sought to discover the physical basis of the individual's distress. It is important to note that the science of the mind was then in its infancy. There was no clear conceptual framework by which to understand psychological distress which meant that 'health' could only be considered in terms of bodily function.

The nineteenth-century scientific community sought to bring rational understanding to the physical world. In the field of medicine the discovery of new conditions and related cures was considered to be the pinnacle of achievement. This rich tradition of pioneering work was a motivation for great discoveries. However, there were also negative consequences. The competitive nature of scientific exploration led to the creation of a considerable number of conditions, all recording the same symptomatology. The lack of collaboration meant that previous observations were either forgotten or deliberately ignored as physicians desperately attempted to establish a name for themselves. This attitude was best summarised by the American psychoanalyst Abraham Kardiner writing in 1947:

> It is a deplorable fact that each investigator who undertakes to study these conditions considers it his sacred obligation to start from scratch and work at the problem as if no one had ever done anything with it before.
>
> (Kardiner and Spiegel 1947)

In 1866 a physician named Erichsen (Rick et al. 1998: 7) described a condition which he termed 'Railway Spine'. He had noticed that some individuals displayed certain symptoms after having been involved in accidents, including fatigue and weakness, intestinal distress, irritability and insomnia. He held that this condition was due to concussion of the spine resulting in a weakening of the nerves. The psychological aspects of the reaction were considered to result from hypochondriasis. Symptoms such as sweating, increased heart rate and headaches he believed to be a result of the imagined sufferings of physical illness. The attribution of symptoms as being a product of physical injury and psychological weakness became a recurrent theme as the understanding of trauma evolved.

In the 1880s Charcot, a French neurologist, catalogued the symptoms of hysteria (Herman 1992: 11). His aim was to find a reasoned and scientific explanation for the symptoms experienced by the women he was treating at the Salpetrière, a Parisian sanatorium. He described women appearing to enter a trance-like state. He postulated that the reason for this might be psychological in nature because it could be reproduced and alleviated with the use of hypnosis. His explanation for this dissociative state was that it was induced by being exposed to an unbearable experience. He called this condition 'Choc Nerveux' or nervous shock. Charcot had identified that people who were overwhelmed by awful experiences could suffer a strong psychological reaction. This was a major step forward in accepting that people's reactions to traumatic events were genuine.

Charcot's work came to the attention of two doctors, both of whom were deeply impressed with his ideas: Sigmund Freud and Joseph Breuer. After visiting him in 1885, Freud embraced much of Charcot's work on hysteria which then led to some of the most significant work examining psychological responses to trauma, Breuer and Freud's 'Study on Hysteria' (1893–1895). Their evidence suggested that trauma was a precursor to the symptoms of hysteria including disassociation. They also noticed that by engaging with their patients and by encouraging them to retell their experience their symptoms began to disappear.

In 1896 Freud published *The Aetiology of Hysteria*, a collection of eighteen case studies, all of which were women. He discovered through talking to them that all had experienced underlying childhood trauma.

> I therefore put forward the thesis that at the bottom of every case of hysteria there are one or more occurrences of premature sexual experience, occurrences which belong to the earliest years of childhood, but which can be reproduced through the work of psychoanalysis in spite of the intervening decades.
>
> (Freud 1955 Vol. 3: 203)

This was a shocking revelation and, given the prevalence of hysteria, it was not well received. The political and social climate was not conducive to the support of such claims and in the face of great opposition Freud retracted his theory. The extent of his *volte face* can be seen in his own writing:

> I was at last obliged to recognise that these scenes of seduction had never taken place, and that they were only fantasies which my patients had made up.
>
> (Freud 1925 Vol. 20: 34)

Having recanted his theory about childhood sexual abuse, Freud began to study fantasy, which in effect became a 'dissociative' study. Avoiding the horror of reality he created a more acceptable story concerning repressed infantile sexuality and the Oedipus complex. The previous link between trauma and the symptoms of hysteria now gave way to an explanation centred on intrapsychic fantasy.

The unfortunate consequence of Freud downplaying the external event resulted in the focus for many years being on the weakness of individual character. This is still promoted by some schools of thought and has been one of the biggest obstacles in the development of an effective treatment for trauma.

Freud returned to the subject of trauma in his work following World War I. He now appeared to acknowledge once again the existence of an external stressor causing symptoms. In his analyses of Freud's *Introductory Letters on Psychoanalysis* (1917) Wilson (1995) suggests that implicit in the text is an identification of the core PTSD symptoms some seventy years before they were detailed in DSM-III. These include such symptoms as revivification of the event, intrusion and arousal.

In ignorance of Freud's and others' work, the response to the symptoms demonstrated by soldiers during World War I, symptoms that had never before been present in such numbers, was to cite a physical cause. In 1919 Mott defined the term 'shell shock' as the direct damage to the cortex of the brain by carbon monoxide and flying shrapnel (Mott 1919). This explanation did not account for those soldiers who developed shell shock but had not experienced physical trauma. The response to this threat to the heroic ideal of the combat soldier was harsh. Individual sufferers were described as 'moral invalids' (Leri 1919: 118) and were treated by being ignored. One of the most prominent proponents of this approach was a British psychiatrist, Lewis Yelland, who supported treatment that amounted to no more than the naming and shaming of veterans (Herman 1992: 21).

In spite of this traditional view a more progressive approach was simultaneously developing which acknowledged the existence of a psychological explanation. W.H.R. Rivers is identified by Herman (1992) as being one of the most influential of the 'enlightened' psychotherapists. In his treatment of the war poet Siegfried Sassoon he advocated a treatment of writing and speaking about the experience. Even today this can be a rare experience for veteran survivors from the world of military machismo. As in Freud's initial work a key part of the treatment seemed to be the quality of the relationship that was established between client and therapist.

Although there were fewer casualties, World War II created a resurgence of interest in trauma. Two American psychiatrists, Appel and Beebe, restated the external nature of trauma, concluding from their observations that 200–240 days in combat would be enough to affect any soldier: 'There is no such thing as "getting used to combat". Each moment of combat imposes a strain so great that men will break down in direct relation to the intensity and duration of their exposure. Thus psychiatric casualties are as inevitable as gunshot and shrapnel wounds in warfare.' (Appel and Beebe 1946: 1470).

This seemingly sympathetic approach was born more from pragmatism than compassion. The motivation was to try to rehabilitate soldiers as quickly as possible so that they could be returned to combat. In contrast Abraham Kardiner was troubled by the severity of soldiers' distress and worked to develop a successful treatment for the psychological response to a traumatic event. His work included the use of hypnosis and drug therapy to induce altered states of consciousness and enable memories to be recovered. Although this was highly successful he warned that catharsis alone would not provide sufficient resolution and that there needed to be a cognitive shift leading to a conscious integration of the experience as well as an emotional and physiological discharge.

War once again proved to be the catalyst for further significant study in the field in the 1970s, at the height of the Vietnam conflict. It was the returning veterans themselves who highlighted the distress experienced by so many soldiers when exposed to stress and combat. Now at last there seemed to be an irrefutable link between post-trauma stress and exposure to combat. This link was confirmed by a five-volume study by Egendorf et al., *Legacies of Vietnam* (1981). When confronted with protests from veterans and the emerging evidence of causal links, the American Administration was forced to fund research. This political response resulted in the inclusion of a diagnosis of post-traumatic stress disorder in the *Diagnostic and Statistical Manual of Mental Disorders* (third edition) published in 1980. It detailed twelve symptoms providing for the first time diagnostic criteria which covered three categories: re-experiencing, numbing and other miscellaneous symptoms. To fulfil the diagnostic criteria, an individual had to display four symptoms from across the three categories. The entry in DSM-III acknowledged the importance of the stressor: 'a recognisable stressor which would evoke significant symptoms of distress in almost anyone', thus delineating traumatic stress from situations which occur in everyday life. The diagnosis was further refined in later editions of the DSM in 1987 and 1994, the details of which are discussed in Chapter 2 on assessment.

Vietnam veterans were not the only movement to force trauma to the top of the psychological agenda. During the same period women's movements began to demand a change in traditional perceptions and the feminist movement placed women's issues and experience firmly on the political map. It was identified that large numbers of women had been victims of sexual and domestic violence. The idea of the existence of traumatic stressors other than combat began to emerge. At first these were identified as specific reactions such as rape trauma syndrome and battered women syndrome but 'It became clear that the psychological syndrome seen in survivors of rape, domestic battery and incest was essentially the same as the syndrome seen in the survivors of war' (Herman 1992: 31).

It is clear that the emergence of PTSD has seen a struggle between physiological and psychological explanations for the symptoms produced by traumatic events. In the nineteenth century Railway Spine and Soldier's Heart represented the physiological school, while Charcot and Freud developed increasingly psychologically focused ideas such as nervous shock. In the early twentieth century Kardiner's work essentially merged the two explanations when he described traumatic neurosis.

Today our understanding of effective treatment for trauma recognises a combination of elements: creating safety for the individual, revisiting the traumatic event, experiencing emotional and physiological discharge and cognitive integration of the experience. We recognise both physical and psychological elements in treatment interventions designed to meet the needs of individual clients.

Another recurring historical theme is the conflict between identifying an internal or external cause. These respective viewpoints of course determine whether trauma is seen as a character weakness or as a natural consequence of being overwhelmed by particular events. Our current understanding developed from both standpoints suggest that the severity of a traumatic response may be affected by an individual's pre-existing psychological constitution and, again, this view suggests that treatment needs to be matched to the individual. Throughout, the main success in treatment has not been due to technique but to the establishment of a successful relationship with the client.

It is clear that whilst trauma studies proliferated at times due to war, disaster and technological advance, when the movements supporting investigation collapsed or there was a change in political direction the knowledge of the impact of trauma was lost.

Nietzsche's (Hall 1996: 179) idea of eternal recurrence would suggest that history is a chronicle of the rediscovery of truths already known rather than a record of civilisation's linear advance. Optimistic periods of discovery are matched by times of disillusionment. This allows an understanding of how, although trauma would appear to be new to our age, it actually has a significant history.

Time has allowed an awareness of this process. Despite the tremendous progress made in the latter half of the twentieth century perhaps we are once again moving towards a period of disillusionment. What was once seen as a courageous breaking of taboos, as self-empowerment and truth-telling, is now often derided as a manifestation of the victim culture where everyone wants something for nothing. This warrants particular attention because it has been the absence of a supportive political environment or the stark opposition of the prevailing *zeitgeist* which caused previous knowledge and understanding of trauma to be lost.

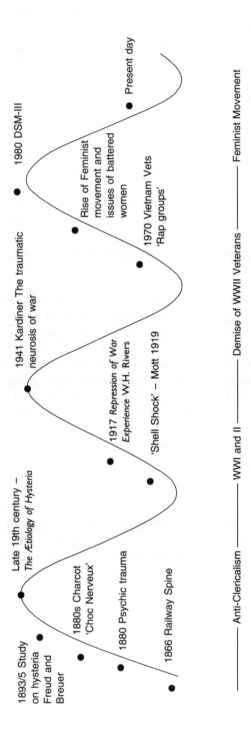

Figure 8.1 A diagrammatic history of trauma

From the front lines of military conflict and law enforcement to the everyday pressures of work and home stress has become the byword of our time; but now people have had enough of counselling and aromatherapy: instead of trying to fight stress they're learning to love it – and thrive on it . . .

(Elaine Showalter, *Guardian*, Tuesday 23 June 1998)

In the above article Showalter reveals much of what we are talking about. There is the familiar backlash against the acceptance of trauma which results in obvious attempts to trivialise its effects and once again casts aspersions on the victim. It is the individual who is blamed and attacked. Despite a significant body of work researching the causes and effects of trauma ignorance still prevails and a deliberate blurring of the distinction between stress and PTSD occurs. In its depiction of counselling and charlatanism, this article highlights the creeping amnesia in regard to the impact of trauma.

Faced with a negative prevailing mood psychotherapy has retreated, recanted and conformed until a new political movement has emerged to permit a re-presenting of its truth. Taking a position on psychological trauma which places the alleviation of individual suffering above all else, is to take an increasingly political stance. This is especially true when the prevailing culture is focused on commercial value, uncertainty about the worth of counselling and has developed a progressively litigious bent. It is not that the care of the individual is a superior or a more noble end, simply a different one and it is this divergent position of critique or variance with the norm that has often been missing during the forfeited periods of trauma's history. This is the challenge for trauma counselling: to hold to the truth of what is known of people's experience and to allow change and growth in this knowledge.

Judith Lewis Herman (1992: 1) says that we the bystanders must take sides when we bear witness to human distress, that moral neutrality is unacceptable in the face of human suffering caused by accident or by others. She dares us to look, to listen and not be silent in our response to trauma.

May I never look the other way
And if I do may I have the courage to look back

(Thom Spiers)

Appendix 1

Name: _____ Date: _____

Instructions: Below is a list of difficulties people sometimes have after stressful life events. Please read each item and then indicate how distressing each difficulty has been for you DURING THE PAST SEVEN DAYS with respect to _____, how much were you distressed or bothered by these difficulties?

	Not at all	A little bit	Moderately	Quite a bit	Extremely
1. Any reminder brought back feelings about it.	0	1	2	3	4
2. I had trouble staying asleep.	0	1	2	3	4
3. Other things kept making me think about it.	0	1	2	3	4
4. I felt irritable and angry.	0	1	2	3	4
5. I avoided letting myself get upset when I thought about it or was reminded about it.	0	1	2	3	4
6. I thought about it when I didn't mean to.	0	1	2	3	4
7. I felt as if it hadn't happened or wasn't real.	0	1	2	3	4
8. I stayed away from reminders about it.	0	1	2	3	4
9. Pictures about it popped into my mind.	0	1	2	3	4
10. I was jumpy and easily startled.	0	1	2	3	4
11. I tried not to think about it.	0	1	2	3	4
12. I was aware that I still had a lot of feelings about it, but I didn't deal with them.	0	1	2	3	4
13. My feelings about it were kind of numb.	0	1	2	3	4
14. I found myself acting or feeling like I was back at that time.	0	1	2	3	4
15. I had trouble falling asleep.	0	1	2	3	4
16. I had waves of strong feelings about it.	0	1	2	3	4
17. I tried to remove it from my memory.	0	1	2	3	4
18. I had trouble concentrating.	0	1	2	3	4
19. Reminders of it caused me to have physical reactions, such as sweating, trouble breathing, nausea, or a pounding heart.	0	1	2	3	4
20. I had dreams about it.	0	1	2	3	4
21. I felt watchful and on-guard.	0	1	2	3	4
22. I tried not to talk about it.	0	1	2	3	4

A☐   I☐   H☐

Appendix 2

The purpose of this assessment is to collect information that will assist the counsellor in assessing the current impact of the trauma on the client, and the likelihood of the client's developing PTSD, and the implications for their work. This will enable the counsellor to develop a treatment plan that is aimed at the individual – their symptoms, their life and using their own resources for coping.

The assessment interview is also an opportunity to give the client advice and information about PTSD, and to begin to develop a working alliance based on collaboration and empowerment.

The questions are intended to form the basis for exploration and the counsellor may wish to expand on some areas as appropriate or to get the information less formally.

CLIENT DETAILS

CLIENT NAME:

DATE:

CLIENT ADDRESS:

CLIENT TELEPHONE NUMBER:

GP NAME & ADDRESS:

GP TELEPHONE NUMBER:

COUNSELLOR'S NAME:

CHANGE IN WORKING STATUS SINCE REFERRAL:

REPORTS TO BE ADDRESSED TO:

COUNSELLING AND TRAUMA SERVICE
Trauma Assessment Form

The Incident

In this section, the counsellor will be looking for factors that may indicate the likelihood of the client's developing PTSD. This will include factors about the event itself (eg. threat to life, intentional harm), the client's cognitive and affective reactions to the incident, in particular shame and anger, and the immediate reactions of others (eg. support, blame, etc.).

1.   Tell me about your day prior to the incident:

... ...
... ...
... ...
... ...
... ...
... ...
... ...
... ...
... ...
... ...

2.   Can you give me a brief account of what has happened to you – there will be time to talk about this in more detail later:

... ...
... ...
... ...
... ...
... ...
... ...
... ...
... ...
... ...

3.   What happened immediately afterwards?

... ...
... ...
... ...
... ...
... ...
... ...
... ...
... ...
... ...
... ...

Impact of Trauma – Symptoms

In this section counsellors will be looking for evidence of symptoms of post-trauma stress, of three types: avoidance, intrusive imagery and hyperarousal. It is extremely important to normalise the client's symptomatic reaction, and counsellors can give advice on what to do and what not to do in terms of coping with the symptoms.

4. How are you sleeping?

....
....
....
....

5. Have there been any changes in your eating patterns?

....
....
....
....

6. Has there been any impact on your relationships with others?

....
....
....
....
....

7. Are you able to go out and about as you would usually? (E.g. to follow leisure and social activities, job etc. Try to ascertain what these hobbies/leisure activities are.)

....
....
....
....
....

8. Have you had any thoughts or feelings of wanting to harm yourself since the incident? (If so, check for details, etc.)

....
....
....
....
....

9. How have you been feeling since the incident?

....
....
....
....
....

Current Life Situation

In this section counsellors will be looking to ascertain the client's life situation, both immediately before the trauma and in the past (e.g. history of depression, child abuse). Are there any pre-existing problems that may have an impact? What resources does the client have for support, etc.? Are there any factors that will need to be taken into account when planning a treatment strategy?

10.   Can you tell me a little about your family and friends?

....
....
....
....
....
....

11.   How did you feel about your current job before this happened? (Prompt for information on relationships with colleagues/managers.)

....
....
....
....
....

12.   Have you ever sought help for any psychological or emotional problems? If so, what was the outcome?

....
....
....
....

13.   Prior to this incident, have you had problems with recurring headaches, stomach aches or other illnesses?

....
....
....
....

14.   Are you taking any medication currently, or undergoing any medical treatment?

....
....
....
....

15. Have you taken prescribed medication or undergone medical treatment previously?

....
....
....
....

16. Have you ever had counselling before? If so who with, where, when, and for how long?

....
....
....
....

17. Have you ever considered or attempted suicide? (If so, get details.)

....
....
....
....
....

18. Please tell me about your use of drugs and alcohol? Is this different since the incident took place?

....
....
....
....
....

19. Do you have any worries or other problems currently?

....
....
....
....
....

Previous Trauma

In this section counsellors will be looking to identify previous traumatic reactions and whether they have a current impact.

20. Have you witnessed any traumatic incidents previously? (E.g. violent crime, accidents or death.)

... ...
... ...
... ...
... ...
... ...

21. Have you been the victim of any criminal activity?

... ...
... ...
... ...
... ...

22. Have there been any deaths that have affected you?

... ...
... ...
... ...
... ...
... ...

23. Have you been involved in any illegal activity?

... ...
... ...
... ...
... ...

24. Have you had any serious accidents?

... ...
... ...
... ...
... ...

25. Have there been any losses that have affected you? (E.g. relationships, jobs, property.)

... ...
... ...
... ...
... ...

26.   How are you feeling now?

Bibliography

Chapter 1

Appel, J.N. and Beebe, G.W. (1920) Preventative Psychiatry: An Epidemiological Approach, *Journal of the American Medical Association* 131: 1468–71.

Caldwell, C. (1997) *Getting in Touch*, Wheaton, IC: Quest Books.

Cooper, D.E. (1990) *Existentialism: A Reconstruction*, London: Blackwell.

Frankl, V.E. (1959) *Man's Search for Meaning*, New York: Washington Square Press.

Freud, S. (1964) *New Introductory Lectures on Psychoanalysis*, Vol. 2 Penguin Freud Library, London: Penguin.

Goleman, D. (1996) *Emotional Intelligence: Why it can Matter More than IQ*, London: Bloomsbury.

Hall, C. (1979) *A Primer of Freudian Psychology*, New York: Mentor.

Hayes, N. (1994) *Foundations of Psychology*, New York: Routledge.

Herman, J.L. (1992) *Trauma and Recovery*, London: Basic Books.

Hillman, J. (1965) *Suicide and the Soul*, Woodstock, USA: Spring Publications Inc.

Hodgkinson, P.E. and Stewart, M. (1991) *Coping with Catastrophe*, London: Routledge.

Jacobs, M. (1985) *The Presenting Past*, Buckingham: Open University Press.

—— (1988) *Psychodynamic Counselling in Action*, London: Sage.

Johansen, G. and Kurtz, R. (1991) *Grace Unfolding: Psychotherapy in the Spirit of the Tao De Ching*, New York: Bell Tower.

Joseph, S., Williams, R. and Yule, W. (1997) *Understanding Post-Traumatic Stress. A Psychosocial Perspective on P.T.S.D. and Treatment*, Chichester: Wiley.

Khan, M. (1991) *Between Therapist and Client*, New York: Freeman & Company.

Levine, P. (1997) *Waking the Tiger*, Berkley, CA: North Atlantic Books.

Lifton, R.J. (1993) *International Handbook of Traumatic Stress Syndromes*, New York: Plenum Press.

Oxford University Press (1998) *New Oxford Dictionary*, Oxford: Cameron Press.

Parkes, C. Murray (1972) *Bereavement: Studies of Grief in Adult Life*, London: Pelican Books.

Sandler, J. with Freud, A. (1985) *The Analysis of Defense: The Ego and the Mechanism of Defense Revisited*, New York: International Universities Press.

Sainsbury, M.J. (1986) *Key to Psychiatry*, Chichester: Social Science Press.

Scott, M.J. and Stradling, S.G. (1992) *Counselling for Post-Traumatic Stress Disorder*, London: Sage.

Spinelli, E. (1994) *Demystifying Therapy*, London: Constable.

Watson, J.B. and Stradling, S.G. (1920) Conditioned Emotional Reactions, *Journal of Experimental Psychology* 3: 1–14.

Worden, J.N. (1983) *Grief Counselling and Grief Therapy*, London: Routledge.

Yalom I.D. (1980) *Existential Psychotherapy*, New York: Basic Books.

Yates, W.B. (1995) *Collected Poems*, London: Picador.

Chapter 2

Box, S. (1971) *Deviance, Reality and Society*, London: Holt Rinehart and Winston.

Campo, R. (1997) *The Poetry of Healing*, London: W.W. Norton.

Carlson, E.B. (1997) *Trauma Assessments: A Clinician's Guide*, New York: Guilford Press.

Early, E. (1993) *The Ravens Return, The Influence of Psychological Trauma on Individuals and Culture*, Wilmette, IL: Chiron Publications.

Freud, S. (1926) *Inhibitions, Symptoms and Anxiety*, Standard Edition, Vol. 20, London: Hogarth Press.

Freud, S. (1984) *On Metapsychology – The Theory of Psychoanalysis*, London: Pelican Books.

Gendlin, E. (1996) *Focusing-orientated Psychotherapy*, New York: Guilford Press.

Herman, J.L. (1992) *Trauma and Recovery*, London: Basic Books.

Hodgkinson, P.E. and Stewart, M. (1991) *Coping with Catastrophe*, London: Routledge.

Jacobs, M. (1985) *The Presenting Past*, Buckingham: Open University Press.

Johansen, G. and Kurtz, R. (1991) *Grace Unfolding: Psychotherapy in the Spirit of the Tao De Ching*, New York: Bell Tower.

Johnson, S. (1985) *Characterological Transformation – The Hardwork Miracle*, New York: W.W. Norton & Co.

Kurtz, R. (1990) *Body Centred Psychotherapy – The Hakomi Method*, Mendocino, CA: Life Rhythm.

Levine, P. (1997) *Waking the Tiger*, Berkley, CA: North Atlantic Books.

Littlewood, R. and Lipsedge, M. (1989) *Aliens and Alienists – Ethnic Minorities and Psychiatry*, London: Routledge.

Ogden, P. (1997) Hakomi Integrative Somatics, in C. Caldwell, *Getting In Touch*, Wheaton, IL: Quest Books.

Ogden, P. (1999) *Lecture on Developmental and Traumatic Wounds*, Ireland: Theosophical Publishing.

Rick, J. (1998) *Workplace Trauma and Its Management: A Review of the Literature*. London: Health and Safety Executive.

Rowan, J. and Dryden, W. (1988) *Innovative Therapy in Britain*, Buckingham: Open University Press.

Sainsbury, M.J. (1986) *Key to Psychiatry*, Chichester: Social Science Press.

Salzberger-Wittenberg, I. (1970) *Psycho-Analytic Insight and Relationships, A Kleinian Approach*, London: Routledge.

TACT (2000) *Tact Matters*, No. 16, March.

Thoits, P.A. (1982) Conceptual, Methodological and Theoretical Problems in Studying Social Support as a Buffer Against Life Stress, *Journal Of Health and Social Behaviour* 23: 145–59.

Van der Kolk, B. (1998) Video-recording of presentation at United States Association of Body Psychotherapy.

Washburn, M. (1994) *Transpersonal Psychology in Psychoanalytic Perspective*, New York: State University of New York Press.

Weiss, D.S. (1993) Assessment, Methodology and Research Strategies, in *The International Handbook of Traumatic Stress Syndromes*, New York: Plenum Press.

Weiss, D.S and Marmar, C.R. (eds) (1995) *Assessing Psychological Trauma and PTSD: A Handbook for Practitioners*, London: Taylor & Francis.

Chapter 3

American Heritage Dictionary (1969) Boston: American Heritage Publishing Company International, Houghton Miflin.

Bly, R. (2001) *Iron John*, London: New Edition.

Danieli, Y. (1998) *International Handbook of Multigenerational Legacies of Trauma*, London: Plenum.

Estés, C.P. (1995) *The Faithful Gardener*, San Francisco: Harper & Row.

Estés, C.P. (1998) *Women Who Run With the Wolves*, London: Rider.

Hayward, J. (1996) *Sacred World*, London: Rider.

Herman, J.L. (1992) *Trauma and Recovery*, London: Basic Books.

Johanson, G. and Kurtz, R. (1991) *Grace Unfolding*, New York: Bell Tower.

Johnson, S.M. (1985) *Characterological Transformation – The Hard Work Miracle*, Toronto: Penguin Books.

Kabat-Zin, J. (1996) *Full Catastrophe Living*, London: Pairatkus Books.

Koestler, A. (1976) *Ghost in the Machine*, New York: Random House.

Kurtz, R. (1990) *Hakomi Body-Centred Psychotherapy – The Hakomi Method*, Mendocino: Life Rhythm.,

Levine, P. (1997) *Waking the Tiger*, Berkley, CA: North Atlantic Books.

Oliver, M. (1992) *New and Selected Poems*, Boston: Beacon Press.

Somé, M.P. (1993) *Ritual – Power, Healing and Community*, Bath: Gateway Books.

St. Just, A. (1999) unpublished lecture notes, UK.

Trungpa, Chogyam (1985) *Becoming a Full Human Being* in *Awakening the Heart* edited by J.W. Wellwood, London: Shambhala.

Yeats, W.B. (1983) *The Poems of W.B. Yeats*, ed. Richard J. Finneran, New York: Macmillan.

Chapter 4

Herman, J.L. (1992) *Trauma and Recovery*, London: Basic Books.

Irving, P. (2001) Stress Debriefing: Does it Work? *Counselling & Psychotherapy Journal*, February, pp. 18–21.

Mitchell, J.T. (1983) When Disaster Strikes: The Critical Incident Stress Debriefing Process, *Journal of Emergency Medical Services* (8)1: 36–8.

Moore, R.H. (1993) Traumatic Incident Reduction: A Cognitive-Emotive Treatment of Post-Traumatic Stress Disorder in W. Dryden and L. Hill (eds) *Innovations in Rational Emotive Therapy*, London: Sage.

Parkinson, F. (1997) *Critical Incident Stress Debriefing*, London: Souvenir Press.

Rick, J. and Briner, R. (2000) *Trauma Management vs Stress Debriefing: What Should Responsible Organisations Do?* Available online at: http://www. employment-studies.co.uk/press/0001.html

Rick, J., Perryman, S., Young, K., Guppy, A. and Hillage, J. (1998) *Workplace Trauma and its Management: A Review of the Literature* prepared by the Institute of Employment Studies (Mantell Building, University of Sussex, Brighton, BN1 9RF) for the Health and Safety Executive.

Shapiro, F. (1995) *Eye Movement Desensitisation and Reprocessing: Basic Principles, Protocols and Procedures*, New York: Guilford Press.

Tarrier, N. and Humphreys, L. (2000) Subjective improvement in PTSD patients with treatment by imaginal exposure or cognitive therapy: session by session changes, *British Journal of Psychology* 39: 27–34.

Wesley, S., Bisson, J. and Rose, S. (1998) A Systematic Review of Brief Psychological Interventions for the Treatment of Immediate Trauma Related Symptoms and the Prevention of Post-Traumatic Stress Disorder, *The Cochrane Library* Issue 3.

Chapter 5

Abroms, G.M. (1978) The Place of Value in Psychotherapy, *Journal of Family and Marriage*.

Broadella, D. (1987) *Lifestreams – An Introduction to Biosynthesis*, London and New York: Routledge and Kegan Paul.

Broadella, D. (1988) Biosynthesis in Rowan, J. and Dryden, W. (eds) *Innovative Therapy in Britain*, Milton Keynes: Open University Press.

Broadella, D. (1991) Words, Body and Transference. Article: Lindau Congress. See online at: http://orgone.org/therapy00-biosyn.htm

Broadella, D. and Smith (1986) *Maps of Character*, Abbotsbury.

Bowlby, J, (1969) *Attachment and Loss* Vol. 1, New York: Basic Books.

Boyesen, G. (1982) The Primary Personality, *Journal of Biodynamic Psychology* 3.

Bright, R. (1996) *Grief and Powerlessness*, London: Jessica Kingsley Publishers.

Chessick, R.D. (1993) *The Technique and Practice of Listening in Intensive Psychotherapy*, Northvale, NJ: Jason-Aronson.

Dryden, W. (1988) Editorial Epilogue in *Innovative Therapy in Britain*, J. Rowan and W. Dryden (eds), Milton Keynes: Open University Press.

Dytchwald, K. (1986) *Bodymind*, New York: St Martin's Press.

Figley, C.R. (1985) *Trauma and its Wake Vol 1: The Study and Treatment of Post Traumatic Stress Disorder*, New York: Brunner-Mazel.

Figley, C.R. (1999) *The Traumatology of Grieving, Conceptual, Theoretical and Treatment Foundations*, London: Taylor & Francis Books Ltd.

Gold, J.H. (1992) *Beyond Transference*, Washington: American Psychiatric Press.

Johnson, S.M. (1985) *Characterological Transformation – The Hard Work Miracle*, Toronto: Penguin Books.

Kaufman, G. (1989) *The Psychology of Shame*, London: Routledge.

Kelman, S. (1985a) *Emotional Anatomy*, California: Center Press.

Kelman, S. (1985b) *Somatic Reality*, California: Center Press.

Kepner, J.I. (1987) *Body Process – A Gestalt Approach to Working with the Body in Psychotherapy*, New York/London: Gestalt Institute of Cleveland Press.

Kind, J. (1999) *Suicidal Behaviour – The Search for Psychic Economy*, London: Jessica Kingsley Publishers.

Kirsch, C. (1991) The Role of Affect Expression and Defence, in *In the Wake of Reich* (Second Edition) edited by D. Broadella, London: Coventure.

Kurtz, C. (1991) *The Role of Affect Expression and Defence* in *In the Wake of Reich* (Second Edition) edited by D. Broadella, London: Coventure.

Kurtz, R. and Prestera, H.M.D. (1982) *The Body Reveals*, San Francisco: Harper & Row.

Lee, R.G. and Wheeler, G. (1996) *The Voice of Shame*, San Francisco: Jossey-Bass Inc. A Gestalt Institute of Cleveland Publication.

Liss, J. (1991) Why Touch? in *In the Wake of Reich* (Second Edition) edited by D. Broadella, London: Coventure.

Lowen, A. (1966) *Love and Orgasm*, London: Staples Press.

—— (1971) *The Language of the Body*, New York: Collier Books.

—— (1973) *Depression and the Body*, Baltimore: Penguin Books.

—— (1975a) *Bioenergetics*, New York: Coward, McCann & Geoghengen.

—— (1975b) *Pleasure – A Creative Approach to Life*, Baltimore: Penguin Books.

—— (1977) *The Way to Vibrant Health*, New York: Harper & Row.

—— (1982) *The Betrayal of the Body*, New York: Collier Books.

—— (1991) Reich Sex and Orgasm, in *In the Wake of Reich* (Second Edition) edited by D. Broadella, London: Coventure.

Lowenstein, R.J. (1993) Dissociation, Development and the Psychobiology of Trauma, *Journal of the American Academy of Psychoanalysis* 21(4), 581–603.

Mahrer, A.R. (1985) *Psychotherapeutic Change: An Alternative Approach to Meaning and Measurement*, New York: W.W. Norton & Co.

Mann, D. (1999) *Psychotherapy – An Erotic Relationship: Transference and Countertransference Passions*, London and New York: Routledge.

Masson, J. (1988) *Against Therapy*, London: Fontana, Collins.

Pierrakos, J. (1990) *Core Energetics*, Mendocino, CA: Life Rhythm Publication.

Pierrakos, J. (1991) The Case of the Broken Heart, in *In the Wake of Reich* (Second Edition) edited by D. Broadella, London: Coventure.

Reich, W. (1933) *Character Analysis*, New York: Noonday Press (Farrar, Strauss & Giroux 1972).

Rosenberg, J.L. and Rand, M.I. (1985) *Body, Self and Soul – Sustaining Integration*, Atlanta: Humanics Ltd.

Rothschild, B. (1994) Transference and Countertransference – A Common Sense Perspective, in *Energy and Character* Vol 25, No. 2 September. Online: http://www.nwc.net/personal/babette/arttranster.htm

—— (1995a) Defining Shock and Trauma in Bodypsychotherapy, in *Energy and Character* Vol. 24, No. 1. April.

—— (1995b) *Defence, Resource and Choice*. Paper presented at the 5th European Congress of Body-psychotherapy, April 27–30 1995, Carry-Le Rouet, France. Online: http://www.nwc.net/personal/babette/artdefence.htm

—— (1997a) A Trauma Case History, in *Somatics*, Fall 1996/Spring 1997. Online: http//www.nwc.net/personal/babette/artdiagnosis.htm.

—— (1997b) *Making Trauma Therapy Safe – the body as resource for braking traumatic acceleration.* Online: http://www.nwc.net/personal/babette/artsafe.htm

—— (1998a) *Post Traumatic Stress Disorder: Identification and Diagnosis.* Invited article for *Soziale Arbeit Schweiz (The Swiss Journal for Social Work)* February. Online: http://www.nwc.net/personal/babette/artdiagnosis.htm.

—— (1998b) *A Trauma Glossary.* Online: http://www.nwc.net/personal/babette/artglossary.htm

Rothschild, B. and Jardinaes, E. (1994) Nervous System Imbalances and Posttraumatic Stress: A Psycho-Physical Approach, unpublished manuscript.

Rowan, J. and Dryden, W. (eds) (1988) *Innovative Therapy in Britain*, Milton Keynes: Open University Press.

Rutter, P. (1991) *Sex in the Forbidden Zone*, London: Mandala.

Schaverien, J. (1995) *Desire and the Female Therapist – engendered gazes in psychotherapy and art therapy*, London: Taylor & Francis.

Southwell, C. (1988) The Gerda Boyesen method: Biodynamic Therapy, in J. Rowan and W. Dryden (eds) *Innovative Therapy in Britain*, Milton Keynes: Open University Press.

Thorne, F.C. (1967) *Integrative Psychology*, Brandon, VT: Clinical Psychology Publishing.

Totton, M. and Edmondson, E. (1988) *Reichian Growth Work*, Sturmaster Newton: Prism Press.

Van der Kolk, Bessel A.M.D. (1994) The Body Keeps the Score – Memory and the Evolving Psychobiology of Post Traumatic Stress, *Harvard Psychiatric Review*, 1(5), 253–265. Online: http:www.trauma-pages.com/vanderk4.htm

—— (1996) Dissociation and Information Processing in Post Traumatic Stress Disorder, in Bessel A. Van der Kolk, A.C. McFarlane and L. Weisaeth (eds) *The Effects of Overwhelming Experience on Mind, Body and Society*, Guilford Press.

Van der Kolk, Bessel. A.M.D. and Van der Hart (1995) *Approaches to the Treatment of PTSD.* Online: http://www.trauma-pages.com

Van der Kolk, Bessel A.M.D., McFarlane, A.C. and Weisaeth, L. (eds) (1996) *Traumatic Stress: The Effects of Overwhelming Experience on Mind, Body and Society*, New York: Guilford Press.

Young, C. (1999) *The Process of Scientific Validation and Accreditation.* Online: http://www.cabp.org/scientific-validity-article.htm

Chapter 6

Agger, I. (1992) *The Blue Room: Trauma and Testimony Among Refugee Women – A Psycho-Social Exploration*, London: Zed Press.

Ayer, A. (1936) *Language, Truth and Logic*, London: Penguin Books.

Bateson, G. (1972) Pathologies of Epistemology, in *Steps to an Ecology of Mind*, London: Fontana.

Bettelheim, B. (1986) *The Informed Heart*, London: Penguin Books.

Bonheoffer, D. (1959) *Letters and Papers from Prison*, London: Fontana.

Carli, A. (1987) Psychological Consequences of Political Persecution: The Effects on

Children of the Imprisonment or Disappearance of their Parents, *Tidsskrift for Norsk Psykoloforening* 24: 82–93.

Cooper, H. (1988) Aspects of the Jewish Unconscious, in H. Cooper (ed.) *Soul Searching: Studies in Judaism and Psychotherapy*, London: SCM.

Cox, M. and Theilgard, A. (1981) *Mutative Metaphors in Psychotherapy: The Aeolian Mode*, London: Jessica Kingsley Publishers.

Durkheim, E. (1915) *The Elementary Forms of Religious Life: a Study in Religious Sociology*, London: Allen & Unwin.

Eisenbruch, M. (1991) From Post-Traumatic Stress Disorder to Cultural Bereavement: Diagnosis of South-East Asian Refugees, *Social Science and Medicine* 33(6): 673–80.

Englund, H. (1998) Death, Trauma and Ritual: Mozambican Refugees in Malawi, *Social Science and Medicine* 46: 1165–74.

Foucault, M. (1986) *The Use of Pleasure: The History of Sexuality Volume II*, London: Penguin Books.

Frankl, V. (1963) *Man's Search For Meaning*, New York: Simon & Schuster.

Freud, S. (1927) *The Future of an Illusion*, in The Pelican Freud Library Volume 12, *Civilisation, Society and Religion*, London: Pelican Books.

Gorst-Unsworth, C. and Goldenberg, E. (1998) The Psychological Sequelae of Torture and Organised Violence Suffered by Refugees from Iraq: Trauma Related Factors Compared with Social Factor in Exile, *British Journal of Psychiatry* 172: 90–4.

Gorst-Unsworth, C., Van Velsen, C. and Turner, S. (1993) Prospective Pilot Study of Survivors of Torture and Organised Violence: Examining the Existential Dilemma, *Journal of Nervous and Mental Disease* 181: 263–64.

Guillaume, A. (1956) (second edition) *Islam*, London: Penguin Books.

Heart Sutra (1995) (Maha Prajna Paramita Hrdaya Sutra) Buddhist spiritual text, Moreton-in-Marsh, UK: The Windrush Press.

Heschel, A. (1973) *A Passion for Truth*, New York: Farrar, Strauss & Giroux.

Howard, C. (1988) Aspects of the Jewish Unconcious. In H. Cooper (ed.) *Soul Searching: Studies in Judaism and Psychotherapy*, London: SCM.

Kapleau, P. (1989) *The Three Pillars of Zen: 25th Anniversary Edition*, London: Doubleday.

Kuhn, T. (1970) *The Structure of Scientific Revolutions*, Chicago: University of Chicago Press.

Levi, P. (1988) *The Drowned and the Saved*, London: Michael Joesph.

Liddle, H. (1991) Family Therapy Training and Supervision: A Comprehensive Review and Critique, in A. Gurman and D. Kniskern (eds) *Handbood of Family Therapy* (second edition), New York: Brunner-Mazel.

Main, M. (1991) Metacognitive Knowledge, Metacognitive Monitoring, and Singular (coherent) vs. Multiple (incoherent) Model of Attachment: Findings and Directions for Future Research, in C. Murray Parkes, J. Stevenson-Hinde and P. Marris (eds) *Attachment Across the Life Cycle*, London: Routledge.

Maslow, A. (1972) *The Farther Reaches of Human Nature*, New York: Viking Press.

Merton, T. (1968) *Zen and the Birds of Appetite*, Boston: Shambhala Publications.

Pears, D. (1971) *Wittgenstein*, London: Fontana.

Reynolds, P. (1990) Children of Tribulation: The Need to Heal and the Means to Heal War Trauma, *Africa*, 60: 1–37.

Ruthven, M. (1984) *Islam in the World*, London: Penguin Books.

Sangharakshiva (1987) *A Survey of Buddhism*, London: Therpa Publications.

Schillebeeckx, E. (1979) *Jesus: an Experiment in Christology*, London: Collins.

Shorter, A. (1975) *African Christian Theology*, New York: Orbis Books.

Snelling, J. (1987) *The Buddhist Handbook: A Complete Guide to Buddhist Teaching and Practice*, London: Rider Books.

Steiner, G. (1989) *Real Presences*, London: Faber and Faber.

Straker, G. (1994) Integrating African and Western Healing Practices in South Africa, *American Journal of Psychotherapy*, 48: 453–67.

Suzuki, D.T. (1996) *Zen Buddhism: Selected Writings of D.T. Suzuki*, edited by William Barratt, New York: Doubleday.

Symington, N. (1993) *Narcissism: A New Theory*, London: Karnac.

Unterman, A. (1981) *Jews: Their Religious Beliefs and Practices*, London: Routledge and Kegan Paul.

Vermes, G. (1973) *Jesus the Jew*, London: Collins.

Vulliamy, E. (1994) *Seasons in Hell: Understanding Bosnia's War*, London: Simon & Schuster.

Watts, A. (1957) *The Way of Zen*, London: Penguin Books.

Winch, P. (1958) *The Idea of a Social Science and its Relation to Philosophy*, London: Routledge and Kegan Paul.

Winnicott, D. (1971) *Playing and Reality*, London: Routledge.

Woodcock, J. (1996) Refugees and Western Sensibilities: Whither Reconciliation? *The Way: Review of Contemporary Christian Spirituality* 36: 5–14.

—— (2000) Refugee Children and Families: Theoretical and Clinical Approaches, in K. Dwivedi (ed.) *Post Traumatic Stress Disorder in Children and Adolescents*, London: Whurr.

Chapter 7

Casement, P. (1990) *Further Learning From the Patient*, London: Routledge.

Clarkson, P. (1995) *The Therapeutic Relationship*, London: Whurr.

Danieli, Y. (1985) The Treatment and Prevention of Long-Term Effects of Intergenerational Transmission of Victimisation: A Lesson from the Holocaust Survivors and Their Children, in C.R. Figley (ed.) *Traumas and Its Wake: The Study and Treatment of PTSD*, New York: Brunner-Mazel.

—— (1994) Countertransference in the Treatment of PTSD, in J.P. Wilson and J.D. Lindy (eds) *Countertransference in the Treatment of PTSD*, New York: Guilford Press.

Figley, C.R. (ed.) (1995) *Compassion Fatigue: Coping with Secondary Traumatic Stress Disorder in Those who Treat the Traumatised*, New York: Brunner-Mazel.

Freud, S. (1912) The Dynamics of Transference, in P. Gay (1995) *The Freud Reader*, London: Vintage.

Freud, S. (1915) Observations on Transference Love, in P. Gay (1995) *The Freud Reader*, London: Vintage.

Gomez, L. (1997) *An Introduction to Object Relations*, London: Free Association Books.

Hawkins, P. and Shohet, S. (1989) *Supervision in the Helping Professions*, Buckingham: OUP Press.

Herman, J.L. (1992) *Trauma and Recovery*, London: Basic Books.

Horton, I. (ed.) (1997) *The Needs of Counsellors and Psychotherapists*, London: Sage.

Hycner, R. (1993) *Between Person and Person, Toward a Dialogical Psychotherapy*, New York: The Gestalt Journal Press Inc.

Kornfield, J. (1994) *A Path with Heart*, London: Rider.

Mitchell, J. (1974) *Psychoanalysis and Feminism*, London: Penguin Books.

Munroe, J.F., Shay, J., Fisher, L., Makary, C., Rapperport, K. and Zimering, R. (1995) Preventing Compassion Fatigue: A Team Treatment Model, in C.R. Figley (ed.) *Compassion Fatigue: Coping with Secondary Traumatic Stress Disorder in Those who Treat the Traumatised*, New York: Brunner-Mazel.

Nader, K., Dubrow, N. and Stamm, B. Hudnall (eds) (1999) *Honoring Differences: Cultural Issues in the Treatment of Trauma and Loss*, New York: Brunner-Mazel.

Rainer, T. (1980) *The New Diary*, London: Angus and Robertson.

Ridley, C.R. (1995) *Overcoming Unintentional Racism in Counseling and Therapy*, Thousand Oaks: Sage.

Rowe, D. (1995) *Dorothy Rowe's Guide to Life*, London: HarperCollins.

St Just, A. (1999) Workshop on trauma, Surrey, UK.

Slatker, (1987) *Countertransference*, Northvale, NJ: Jason Aronson.

Stoller, R. (1968) *Sex and Gender*, London: Hogarth Press.

Wilson, J.P. and Lindy J.D. (eds) (1994) *Countertransference in the Treatment of PTSD*, New York: Guilford Press.

Yassen, J. (1995) Preventing Secondary Traumatic Stress Disorder, in C.R. Figley (ed.) *Compassion Fatigue: Coping with Secondary Traumatic Stress Disorder in Those who Treat the Traumatised*, New York: Brunner-Mazel.

Chapter 8

Appel, J.N. and Beebe, G.W. (1946) Preventative Psychiatry: An Epidemiological Approach, *Journal of the American Medical Association* 131: 1468–71.

Daly, R. (1983) Samuel Pepys and Post-traumatic Stress Disorder, *British Journal of Psychiatry* 143: 64–8.

Egendorf, A. et al. (1981) *Legacies of Vietnam*, Vols 1–5, Washington DC: US Government Printing Office.

Freud, S. (1955) *The Aetiology of Hysteria, 1896* in Standard Edition Vol. 3, trans. J. Strachey, London: Hogarth Press.

—— (1959) *An Autobiographical Study 1925* in Standard Edition Vol. 20, trans. J. Strachey, London: Hogarth Press.

Gendlin, E.T. (1996) *Focussing Orientated Psychotherapy: A Manual of Experiential Method*, New York: Guilford Press.

Hall, S. (1996) *Critical Dialogues in Cultural Studies*, London: Routledge, Clarendon Press.

Herman, J.L. (1992) *Trauma and Recovery*, London: Basic Books.

Kardiner, A. and Spiegel, H. (1947) *War Stress & Neurotic Illness* (revised: *The Traumatic Neurosis of War*), New York: Hober.

Leri, A. (1919) *Shell Shock: Commotional and Emotional Aspects*, London: University of London Press.

Mott, F.W. (1919) *War Neurosis and Shell Shock*, London: Oxford Press.

Rick, J., Perryman, S., Young, K., Guppy, A. and Hillage, J. (1998) *Workplace Trauma and Its Management (A Review of the Literature)*, London: HSE Books.

Scott, M.J. and Stradling, S.G. (1998) *Counselling for Post-Traumatic Stress Disorder*, London: Sage Publications.

Shakespeare, W. (1930) *The Complete Works of Shakespeare: Compact Edition*, (eds) Wells and Taylor, Oxford: Clarendon Press.

Showalter, E. (1998) *Guardian*, 23 June.

TACT (2000) *Tact Matters*, No. 16, March.

Wilson, J.P. (1995) The Historical Evolution of PTSD: Diagnostic Criteria from Freud to DSMIV in G.S. Everley and J.M. Lating (eds) (1995) *Psychotraumatology: Key Papers and Core Concepts in Post-Traumatic Stress*. New York: Guilford Press.

Index